AF623240

A Companion to Philip Larkin

Volume - I

Sunil Kumar Sarker

ATLANTIC

PUBLISHERS & DISTRIBUTORS (P) LTD

Published by

ATLANTIC

PUBLISHERS & DISTRIBUTORS (P) LTD

7/22, Ansari Road, Darya Ganj,
New Delhi-110002
Phones : +91-11-23273880, 23275880, 23280451
Fax : +91-11-23285873
Web : www.atlanticbooks.com
E-mail : info@atlanticbooks.com

Branch Office
5, Nallathambi Street, Wallajah Road,
Chennai-600002
Phones : +91-44-64611085, 32413319
E-mail : chennai@atlanticbooks.com

Copyright © Sunil Kumar Sarker, 2009

ISBN 978-81-269-1234-6 (Vol. I)
ISBN 978-81-269-1236-0 (Set)

All rights reserved. No part of this publication may be reproduced, stored in a retrieval system, transmitted or utilized in any form or by any means, electronic, mechanical, photocopying, recording or otherwise, without the prior permission of the copyright owner. Application for such permission should be addressed to the publisher.

Printed in India at Nice Printing Press, A-33/3A, Site-IV, Industrial Area, Sahibabad, Ghaziabad, U.P.

For my dear wife
Manju

Preface

F. Seymour Smith, in his book *An English Library* (E.L.B.S., 1943) speaks a truism: "No modern literature in the world surpasses English poetry and poetic drama, and perhaps none equals it." (p. 249). Now, if we consider this along with Anthony Thwaite's laudation of Larkin that he "is the finest living poet writing in English" (Anthony Thwaite, *Poetry Today*, 1985, Longman, London, p. 40) and Roger Day's objective observation that Larkin is "a best-selling and much loved poet" (Roger Day, *Larkin*, 1987, Open University Press, Philadelphia, England, p. 33), we can instantaneously get a glimpse of the greatness of Larkin as a poet. In the broad galaxy of his contemporary glittering poets—John Betjeman, Seamus Heaney, Douglas Dun, Tony Connor, Elizabeth Jennings, Norman Nicholson, Ted Hughes, Sylvia Plath and many more —Larkin shines distinct and undiminished. Larkin has at least three distinctions: as regards subject matters, he is modern, but as to forms, he is traditional; he is believed by some to be a Movement poet, but he denied wholesale any sharing of the views of the Movement; and he is by far the most pessimistic of modern poets. Like Robert Bridges' poetess daughter Elizabeth Daryush, he staunchly fended modernism in poetry launched by Ezra Pound and T.S. Eliot. For all these and many more things, a study of Larkin's poetry is all the more an investing effort and enjoyment.

In this book, I have diligently endeavoured to present Larkin to the common reader in a way that perhaps would require neither previous orientation nor present additional help to cruise through the multiple essential aspects of the poet. The wide compass of the book will be clear from the 'Contents' of it.

One perhaps uncomely feature of this book that sticks out needs to be justified or, at the least, explained. I have rather too frequently quoted (sometimes at some lengths) from the following sources: Andrew Motion's *Philip Larkin: A Writer's Life*; Andrew Swarbrick's *Out of Reach: The Poetry of Philip Larkin*; *The Whitsun Weddings* and *The Less Deceived* by Philip Larkin; David Timms' *Philip Larkin* and Roger Day's *Larkin*. Honestly, instead of quoting from these works too often, I could, so to say, just paraphrase the quotations to show a "fair front" but that would be a subterfuge. My unflagging aim was to help the common learner, not to pose before the learned.

In the preparation of the manuscript of this book, my two sons, Dr. Suman Sarker and Dr. Sutanu Sarker, immensely helped me by procuring source works from different corners, and my wife Mrs. Manju Sarker extended to me the much-needed yeoman's service by undertaking the tedious and toilsome task of neatly typing the whole manuscript. I thank the three with affection and love. Last but not least, Dr. K.R. Gupta, Honorary Advisor, Atlantic Publishers and Distributors (P) Ltd., New Delhi, also deserves my thanks for promptly publishing this book.

SUNIL KUMAR SARKER

Contents

VOLUME - II

A Brief and Mostly Psychological Biography

1

1

From Birth to End of School Life: 1922-1940

We may begin our account of Philip Arthur Larkin with a biographical sketch of the poet perhaps not unjustly, for, among many other reasons, his official biographer Andrew Motion said that Larkin's poems are 'to a large extent' 'autobiographical', and, much more than that, because Larkin himself confessed that his "poems are nothing if not personal" (Day, 8). And this is not at all unnatural, because generally there is a *fundamentum relationis* between the poet (Latin *poeta*) and the poem (Latin *poema*)—between the 'maker' and the 'made' (the two Latin terms *poeta* and *poema* originate from the Latin verb *poieein*, meaning 'to make'). But, before all that and very briefly at this place, what is the status of Larkin as a poet? Yes, briefly, and so let us be content for the moment with what Barbara Everett, the very discerning critic, wrote in 1980 about Larkin's standing in the galaxy of contemporary English poets: "Larkin has come to be thought of by many as not only the best English poet but one of the best in Europe" (Regan, 55); and what Anthony Thwaite, one of Larkin's literary executors and the editor of his *Collected Poems* (1988), wrote about him in 1985, the year in which he died: "Philip Larkin is the finest living poet writing in English" (Thwaite, 40). Two or three more accolades of Larkin are insuperably tempting here to quote in order to reply to that cardinal question, and so these may be gracefully suffered. Stephen Regan, in the Introduction to *Philip Larkin*, edited by him, writes about the critic Dana Gioia's observation on Larkin:

"Dana Gioia's discerning review in the *Washington Post* acknowledged Larkin as one of the century's [20th century's] 'indisputably great poets', whose writing withstood comparison with those of Thomas Hardy, W.B. Yeats and W.H. Auden. Among critics writing for the British press, Ian Hamilton was bold enough to call Larkin 'the best poet we have since Auden'" (Regan, 6). And P.R. King writes: "Philip Larkin enjoys a high reputation among contemporary poets. As long ago as 1965 one critic [C. Ricks] talked of him as 'the best poet England now has' and ten years later this opinion was reaffirmed by Alan Brownjohn [in his book *Philip Larkin*] when he claimed that "Larkin has produced the most technically brilliant and resonantly beautiful, profoundly disturbing yet appealing and approachable, body of verse of any English poet in the last twenty-five years" (King, 1).

Philip Arthur Larkin—our poet—was born on 9 August 1922 to Sydney Larkin and Eva Larkin (*nee* Day) who were united in wedlock eleven years ago on 5 October 1911. Sydney was the Treasurer of Coventry which was around 20 kilometers in the east of Birmingham. A simplified family-tree of the Larkins may look like the following diagram:

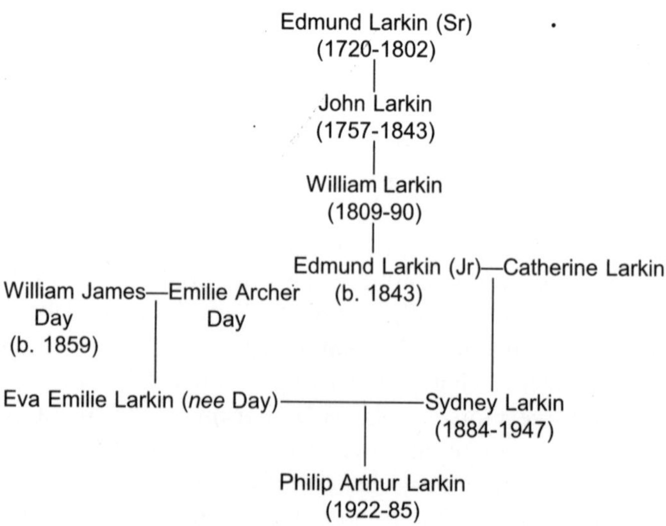

Sydney was the youngest of the seven sons born to Edmund (Jr) and Catherine; Edmund (Jr) was the son of William; William was the son of John, and John was the son of Edmund (Sr)—the great-great-great-grand father of our poet Philip Arthur Larkin. On the other hand, our poet's mother, Eva, was the daughter of William James Day, a first class Excise Officer, and Emilie Archer Day.

The origin of the surname 'Larkin' is utterly confusing, though it is a common surname in Ireland, which fact has puzzled many into falsely assuming that the predecessors of Philip Larkin long ago came from Ireland. Andrew Motion, the official biographer of Philip Larkin writes that the surname 'Larkin' "is equivalent to Lorcain, from Lorc, an old name denoting rough or fierce" (Motion, 3). But immediately afterwards Motion quotes Philip Larkin's father Sydney Larkin as saying that the surname 'Larkin' "is said to be a pet form of the Christian name 'Lawrence'" (*op. cit.*, 4). However, the Larkins, in all probability, came from Kent, and so the surname 'Larkin' has nothing to do with the Irish 'Lorc'.

The earliest history of the Larkins is shrouded in obscurity in spite of all efforts of Sydney Larkin at retrieval, but it is clear that the Larkins lived for many years in the Midlands place doing the same traditional works for generations, all at the same time and gradually internalising the cardinal English traits, such as realism, pragmatism, modesty, etc.—traits that have, in course of time, made our poet Philip Larkin one of the most 'English' poets of all times. Down the ages, in the Midlands place, the Larkins had had variegated experiences in the fields of businesses and professions: for instances, Edmund (Sr) inherited a tailoring business that the Larkins held fast to for quite long down to the times of John and William. Edmund (Jr) added to the traditional tailoring business the sidelines of coach-making and shoe-making. But Ernest, one of the six brothers of Sydney, sold the traditional tailoring business of the Larkins in the Midlands place and moved with all the family branches of the Larkins to London forever in the early years of the 20th century.

Sydney Larkin was born to Edmund Larkin (Jr) and Catherine on 25 April 1884 as their youngest son and as the would be the most successful of their seven issues. Andrew Motion writes about the school life of Sydney: "At Lichfield Grammar School he was a star pupil, and later at King Edward VI High School in Birmingham (to which he travelled daily by train) he passed the Cambridge Junior Local Examination with first class honours. He was a dogmatic, intense and prickly boy, clear in debate, unable to suffer fools, devoutly agnostic, and passionate in his convictions. Although Sydney's greatest gifts were in mathematics he was an avid reader of the classics and contemporary literature. He bought new novels by Wells and Bennett, new plays by Shaw, and new books by Hardy (whom he especially revered) as they were published. He was a stickler for precision and correctness, and seemed bracingly rigorous to some, a disciplinarian to others" (Motion, 6). Sydney was dynamic and prudent as Eva, a voracious reader like him, was mousy and nervous. Born on 10 January 1886, Eva studied in Leigh Grammar School in Lancashire and took up teaching for a stint. "She was bookish but eager, efficient but self-doubting, practical but easily deterred by anxieties. Details of planning and administration rattled her; she was alarmed by newness; she was scared almost into hysterics by thunderstorms" (Motion, 5). "Eva grew into a quietly spoken woman, dark-haired, thin-faced and rather studious-looking, obviously intelligent but nervous" (*loc. cit.*).

The ever first and virtually dramatic meeting between Sydney and Eva and their impetuous falling in love with one another is a romantic story, indeed. Andrew Motion beautifully depicts their first encounter and brisk engagement thus: "Holidaying in Rhyl on the north coast of Wales during the summer of 1906 (when she was twenty), she ran out of the rain on 6 August into a hut overlooking the sea. A young man already standing inside asked, 'Will you shelter here?' She replied, 'I can't think of a reason not to'—and began reading a book. The young man was only a little taller than her, and had a 'serious, rather bad-tempered face, a poisoner's thin lips and a heavy moustache'. He interrupted her reading to introduce himself as Sydney Larkin and was, he explained, on a cycling holiday. He would be staying in Rhyl only for another three days. Before those days were over, Eva had got engaged to him" (*loc. cit.*). And eventually, they entered into wedlock on 5 October 1911.

The union of the two rash lovers first produced a daughter within less than two years, and when this daughter was nearly ten years old, a son—our poet Philip Larkin—was born to them in a full moon night (on 9 August 1922). According to the liking of Sydney, the son was named 'Philip', after the Renaissance poet Sir Philip Sydney, and in course of time the son really became a great poet, like him! The middle name of the child was chosen to be 'Arthur' after the name of Eva's brother Arthur. Within around a month, the child was christened in Coventry Cathedral, though Sydney was quite sceptical about religion. The child, Larkin, was much cossetted and pampered especially by Eva, and only looked over by Sydney, though Sydney was only too glad to have got him, Sydney's father Edmund's (Jr) overmuch sense of the model of a domineering father, like that of a domineering husband may be responsible for all this. However, strange it is that in spite of his mother's over-indulgence with him Larkin in his later life always looked back to his childhood as vacant, boring and full of ennui. In 'Dockery and Son' Larkin expresses the boredom of his childhood when he says that 'Life is first boredom' which feeling of his is echoed in 'Coming' where he writes that 'childhood / Is a forgotten boredom'; and in 'I Remember, I Remember' he gives us an idea of his quite negative attitude towards his own childhood or boyhood when he tells us that it was uniquely uninteresting—'Nothing like something, happens anywhere.' But, in his later years, Larkin used to say that though his childhood or boyhood was quite flat, non-descript, and uninteresting, he was certainly not an unhappy child or boy, because during his early years he "grew up in comfortable material circumstances" (Swarbrick, 2) and because he was the object of great love to his mother.

But though he had, in his childhood and boyhood, enough material comfort and enviable parental love, Larkin, even in so young age, developed some negative traits, which never left him throughout his life—such negative traits as shyness, a sense of 'insulation', a sense of being rejected by the world, etc. Coupled with all these psychological hunches were some of his physical faults: awkwardly 'long back and comparatively short legs'; befuddling and enervating stammering, that might have been due to his being over-conscious of his somewhat ungainly physique; and his weak eye-sight. The constitutionally introverted Larkin, in spite of all these, might actually have seen his future greatness in something like a vision, for he writes in 'I Remember, I Remember': 'There / Before us, had we the gift to see ahead—'. Larkin's vision of his future greatness, of course not necessarily as a poet, at this young age, against the backdrops of so many of his physical and psychological hurdles, may perhaps be interpreted following the individual psychoanalyst Alfred Adler's theory of compensation.

When Larkin was five years old, Sydney moved his family from the suburbs of Coventry to no. 1 Manor Road near the city centre. Here in the house named Penvorn (a three-storey house) the family of Sydney lived from 1927 to 1940, and it was here that Larkin's childhood boredom became all the more intense. While at Manor Road, Larkin was sent to the all-boys grammar school—King Henry VIII School. Here his life was 'completely uneventful' and 'unsuccessful'. He was a studious boy but not brilliant. He was "strongly opinionated—and also proud, confident, and contemptuous of those set in authority over him" (Motion, 15). He was 'remarkably energetic' and 'resourceful with his day-dreams'. Larkin stayed in King Henry VIII School till 1933 when he was eleven. In spite of the pampering love of his mother Eva, Larkin found the junior school (King Henry VIII School) a better place to breathe freely in than the 'stuffily protective atmosphere' of his home. As told earlier, he was not a remarkable student in the junior school though he could pick up some prizes for general knowledge and contributed articles to the school magazine. Andrew Motion writes about him during his years in the junior school, particularly when he was in Form III: "As Larkin's self-confidence grew, his manner and looks began to alter. The mole-like, fuzzy-haired child, peering apprehensively through small round glasses, was now nearly six feet tall, thin, gangling, and openly seeking attention. He grew his long hair, Brylcreaming it, parting it in the middle, and combing it 'very assiduously'. He began to take an interest in painting, and enjoyed his weekly art classes, where he showed a natural ability for drawing" (Motion, 18). And Roger Day writes that during his school years, Larkin "spent a lot of time reading, especially in the Sixth Form when he recalls concentrating 'on English which was the only thing I really had any instinct for'" (Day, 1).

In his school days, in spite of his insuperable stuttering, Larkin could easily make friends, engage with them particularly in snooker and billiard, and invite them home. Andrew Swarbrick writes that "At school, Larkin seems to have won friendship by his power of mockingly mimicking his schoolmasters" (Swarbrick, 1995, 3). His mimicry may be one of his instruments of making friends but in any case certainly not the exclusive one, for he was by nature sociable and society-loving. In fact, though he was to some extent of introverted nature, he was never unsocial; rather we may say that he had a penchant for sociality. Of the friends that Larkin made during his school days, James Sutton (Jim) to whom later on he dedicated his first novel *Jim* was closest. By the bye, it was Sutton who was supplanted Larkin's nickname 'Apey', given by Larkin's sister Kitty, with another nickname 'Snooker', devised by himself. With Sutton, Larkin would enjoy listening to jazz, and thus was especially drawn to American jazz. As we shall see, later on Larkin was a renowned critic of jazz and wrote for some time critical articles in newspapers and magazines on a regular basis. His sense of appreciation and critical acumen as regards jazz is borne by his comprehensive book on jazz, *All What Jazz?* (1970). The lyric and music of jazz much informed the poetry of Larkin as his friend Sutton provided him with enough of encouragement to give vent to his emotion, generated in his 'dream world', through poetry.

As Larkin was growing up, his father's affection for him was getting intenser. In 1936, Sydney took Larkin to Germany on a trip when a curiously facetious incident took place. The father and the son were having a joy ride in a bus, Larkin sitting just beside the driver. After a short while, the driver, not understanding that to Larkin the German language was Greek, asked him how he did like Germany, and the fourteen year old boy, somehow surmising that the driver asked him if he had ever before been to Germany, curtly replied, 'No'. At this, the driver became so offended that he did not utter a single word to Larkin after that. Larkin understood his shameful mistake and felt slapped. This single and triffling incident grew in Larkin a life-long disinclination towards foreign travels, though his 1939 holidaying in Brussels, Antwerp and the Ardennes was 'the jolliest' and he embarked on a second visit to Germany in the 1930s. However, during his later school years, Larkin used to take part in debates and acting in plays, and during the same time his reading habit grew phenomenally, his reading-list especially comprising the works of Hardy, Shaw, Lawrence, Bennett, Wilde, Huxley and Katherine Mansfield. Besides, Sydney persuaded him to be interested in James Joyce, Hardy Christina Rossetti, A.E. Housman, T.S. Eliot, W.H. Auden and Christopher Isherwood—the last six, it may be said here, remained his life-long favourite writers. Alongside his engagements in debates, acting, snooker and billiard, and intense study, Larkin, from the last years of his school life, was 'ceaselessly' turning out poems, short stories, plays and novels (most of all these were exercises, and either were not completed or destroyed, and in any case were not published). His heavy extra-cursal engagement naturally resulted in his poor achievement in the school-leaving examination: he got a 'A' grade in English Language, a 'C' in English Literature and History, a 'D' in Latin, and an 'E' (the lowest grade) in French, Physics and Chemistry. His saving grace was that he could pick up a Senior Prize for his contributions in *Coventrian* and for acting as assistant to its editor.

At this point, we may briefly describe the characters of Larkin's parents, which somewhat shaped his own character. Sydney, with his dense eye-brows, was domineering, though secretly shy; 'somewhat anti-social'; chauvinistic; and agnostic as regards religion. He had an obvious literary taste and kept an appreciable collection of books in his personal library—books especially by Shakespeare, Hardy, Bennett, D.H. Lawrence, and such others. Sydney was much interested in the origin of words, and used to urge Larkin to frequently consult the dictionary, and this may account for Larkin's inordinate command over words. Sydney was a good after-dinner speaker, and from time to time read literary and philosophical papers in the nearby chess-club, of which he was a member. He was a sort of mysogynist and "thought that women were little account, their only functions [being] to be decorative and to wait on men" (Motion, 11). This attitude of Sydney towards women was partially reflected in Larkin's relationship with women, too, for Larkin was undeniably a mysogynist, however many close female friends he might have had. Politically, Sydney was a conservative and an extreme rightist, and Larkin was also politically to some extent influenced by his father, though certainly he had never subscribed to his father's neo-Nazi sentiment. Sydney's neo-Nazi sympathy was not a secret. In the 1930s, he was once falsely held to be a suspect of having connections with the neo-Nazi organisation 'The Link', but, true, he "had a statue of Hitler on the mantlepiece [in the house]" (Motion, 12). But, Larkin, for certain, had no such radical sympathy for neo-Nazism in the least. Larkin's mother Eva, however, was 'too simple' a lady, neither an intellectual nor one interested in literature, but was 'pleasant, unobtrusive', and she preferred to keep within the house. Nevertheless, the highly intellectual Larkin ever preferred his mother to his father. And if anything he got from his mother it was pleasantness of behaviour and love of simplicity.

2

College Life: 1940-1943

In March 1940, Larkin came out of King Henry VIII School successful and got admitted in St John's College, Oxford, at the age of eighteen, and there in the college began to shine as a student, while his poetic genius began tardily to show itself. The poetic themes that he had squared up to during his college life—'isolation, evanescence and choice'—remained with him till the end of his poetic career. In spite of his innate introvertive tendency and defeatist feeling, Larkin showed himself quite a 'flamboyant' undergraduate in the college. Long afterwards, someone recalled that during his college life Larkin "often sported a bow tie and...green cords and a waistcoat'...'With his large glasses, his high forehead and attractive low stutter, he was unmistakable, sort of person who was not only witty in himself, but the cause of wit in other men'" (Motion, 36). And "Others recall his thick black hair flopping forward, the slough-brimmed hat he sometimes wore, the cerise trousers he boasted were the only pair of such colour in Oxford (he wore them on the recommendation—'wear red trousers'—given by Lawrence in *Lady Chatterley's Lover*), and his ostentatious pipesmoking (later he would abandon this in favour of cigarettes, which he continued to smoke in moderation throughout his life)" (*loc. cit.*). He very conspicuously kept himself away from the company of girls, may be due to his snooty attitude toward them, and that he perhaps inherited from his father. His mother Eva, on the other hand, so to say 'banned girls from the house', and so "Larkin's ordinary teenage sexual feelings had struggled vainly for release, turning back on themselves with the shudder of physical disgust which appear in one or two of his early stories, and at moments in his schoolboy poems" (Motion, 37).

In St John's College (Oxford), contrary to his later life, Larkin showed much extravertedness: he buoyantly played squash, eagerly ised to go to the theatre and cinema, and attentively listened to jazz. He also showed some interest in politics and from time to time attended political meetings organised by the Labour Club. Alongside all these diverse activities, though, his principal engagement was in the zone of literature. He developed new interest in such modern writers as Auden, Dylan Thomas, John Betjeman, D.H. Lawrence, Christopher Isherwood, William Empson and Louis MacNiece, Lawrence being his most favourite writer. He was so much bemused by the works of Lawrence that in 1941 he told Sutton: "Lawrence is the only man I can whole-heartedly admire" (*op. cit.*, 43). But, then, "Auden strengthened Larkin's resolve to become a writer; he also swamped his style" (*op. cit.*, 44). It was during his college life, however, that Larkin's interest in jazz deepened. He was attracted to jazz all the more because it creates strong feelings, and also because it was the thing "by which his stammering, shyness could be set aside", and, finally, because "it was the most enjoyable way of feeling part of a community" (*op. cit.*, 47). Andrew Motion writes that during his college life, "Beauty, excitement, intensity, unaffectedness: these were the things Larkin was coming to value most" (*op. cit.*, 44).

When Larkin was in Oxford, the Second World War was raging fiercely. In 1941, he had had one of his very few stunningly unforgetable experiences of his life: on 14 November of that year, at 7 in the morning, German bomber aircrafts dropped 500 tons of explosive on Coventry, killing 554 people and injuring 1,000 others. Soon afterwards, Larkin went to Coventry and witnessed the hellish holocaust, which threw him into utter confusion and bewilderment. The indelible ghostly experience of this unimaginably great human loss and material havoc at a single place he later on partially described or suggested in his novel *Jill* and in his poems 'A Stone Church Damaged by a Bomb', 'Church Going' and 'The Explosion'. The glum of Larkin due to that shattering experience was for a while dispersed when he came to know that in the New Year's Honours list, in the Christmas of the same year, his father Sydney was going to receive the covetous decoration of OBE. However, Larkin continued to be phenomenally influenced by the poetry of Auden, and additionally, by his left-wing political views, though, Sydney's extreme right-wing conviction did never leave him free. Larkin's ever closest literary friendship with Kingsley Amis, his school-fellow as well as college-fellow began at this stage of his life. His doubt about God, that he boastfully maintained throughout his life, was since this time gradually turning into a hard conviction, particularly due to the influence of John Layard, a student of modern languages, and then of psychiatry, at Cambridge. Layard believed that the word 'God' simply denoted our physical desires or the inner laws of our nature, and that the word 'Devil' signified our conscious control of these desires. Layard believed, too, that our only sin was to show obedience to 'God' and disobedience to 'Devil'. Such a blasphemous conviction of Layard at the least reinforced Larkin's earlier disbelief in God that he got especially from his father Sydney. Layard strived to take both Larkin and Amis within the fold of his blatant disbelief, but whereas Amis escaped his net, Larkin could not. Amid this his irreligious indoctrination, Larkin's attitude to women changed, may be due to his preacher Layard's belief that to forestall the outward motion of our instinctis is tantamount to doing evil. So far, Larkin was visibly shy of girls and so kept aloof from them, but now he felt the weight of his aloofness as well as the urge of his instincts, and so since now began to try acquaintances with them.

Afraid of further German bombing on Coventry, Sydney forthwith moved his family to Coten End in Warwick suburb just before Larkin's summer vacation in 1941. Here at Coten End, to drive away his boredom, Larkin constituted a closed coterie of seven friends: Amis, Wilcox, Brown, Russell, Norman Iles, Williams and himself. He named it 'The Seven'. The friends would eat, drink and discuss poetry as a minuscular community. "They had no respect for dons but no wish to challenge them openly. They wished to distance themselves from their parents' generation, but not to abandon traditional forms and beliefs. In these ways, at least, they anticipated the principles which were more coherently described by The Movement in the 1950 (*op. cit.*, 69). In their thoughts and manners, these friends also somewhat resembled the Angry Young Men of the same period. However, meantime Larkin appeared for his compulsory army medical examination, wishing and expecting that he would fail, especially due to his considerably weak eye-sight. Lucky he was, says Andrew Motion, that when, after three months, the result was announced he was found classified as failed—his 'eyes had been graded four'. Andrew Swarbrick of course does not agree with Motion that Larkin wished to fail in the army medical examination, for he writes that Larkin went to St John's College, Oxford, "to study English in the expectation of being called up for war-service after a year" (Swarbrick, 1986, 2). During this time, Larkin changed his style of writing poetry, particularly following the instance of Stephen Spender, and attempted writing a novel, which of course he later abandoned. As he now felt the need of some money, he joined the Fuel Office in City Hall but being disgusted resigned after about only one month. This was Larkin's ever first job.

After Stephen Spender, Larkin was now going to be influenced by W.B. Yeats, initially through the agency of the poet Vernon Watkins who was a close friend of Dylan Thomas and was a Flight Sergeant in the Royal Air Force. Watkins came to the English Club and talked enthusiastically about the poetry of Yeats, and this grew in Larkin an urgent interest in Yeats's poetry, and he was eventually informed by Yeats's poetry, or, to be at all specific, by the music of his poetry, as is evident in Larkin's Introduction to the reissue of his first collection of poems, *The North Ship* (1966). In that Introduction, Larkin wrote that after that talk of Watkins in the English Club he "spent the next three years trying to write like Yeats, not because I liked his personality or understood his ideas but out of infatuation with his music" (*op. cit.*, 84). Besides composing a few poems in imitation of Yeats during his student life in Oxford, Larkin produced some homosexual and lesbian short stories and, withal, two fragmentary novels—all these under his pseudonym Brunette Coleman and all these within just a couple of months. The pseudonym Larkin adopted was originated perhaps from the name of the proprietor of a girls' jazz band of the period—Blanche Coleman. The six poems that he wrote at this time Larkin collected under the rubric *Sugar and Spice*, and one of the two fragmentary novels (of some 143 typed pages) he entitled *Trouble at Willow Gables* and the other (also of about the same length) he called *Michaelmas Term at St Bride's*. His literary output of this period also comprised his queer and fragmentary autobiography that he wrote under his pseudonym Brunette and called *Antemeridian*. All these, none of which did he publish, speak volumes of his ceaseless and indefatigable literary activities during his Oxford days. Amidst this burstling literary activities his final B.A. examination was drawing near. Meanwhile, Larkin had had a boon acquaintance with the novelist, poet and critic John Wain, who was three years his junior and who, too, was greatly interested in jazz and the poetry of Auden and was influenced by his poetry, like himself. At last the final examination was just imminent and Larkin felt crushed under the burden of his preparation for the examination. In a somewhat revolting vein he wrote to Sutton: "I was not meant to study, but to be studied" (*op. cit.*, 103). But study he did and in 1941, at the age of 21, he passed the B.A. examination with a First Class Honours degree in English.

3

From Joining the Public Library at Wellington to Death of Father: 1943-1948

Coming out of Oxford with a B.A. degree, Larkin tried twice for Civil Service, but he was not at all serious in both the attempts either in the written examination or in the interview. In the interview in the second attempt, for instance, he was asked what he wanted to do, and he gave the ludicrous reply that he wanted to 'be a novelist'. Naturally, therefore, he failed to enter Civil Service. But he did not remain jobless: on 13 November 1943, he joined the services of the public library at Wellington. Though librarianship was his mother's first choice as a career, Larkin initially had not much affection for it, though in the course of time he could not think of any service other than that of a librarian. It was during this time that Larkin thought of writing some short stories on various themes or subjects, one such subject being the experience of social dislocation: say, a poor young man becoming a student at Oxford with its elitist atmosphere. Larkin did not actually write the story but told Sutton that the theme could be utilised for a novel. Later on it was this theme that was worked on in Larkin's first published novel *Jill*.

The job of the librarian at Wellington in Shropshire did not suit him and he felt depressed, but his glum was soon blown away as he was attracted at the age of 21 to a 16 year old school girl of the locality—Ruth Bowman—who used to regularly borrow books from the library at Wellington. Bowman was "small, bespectacled, dark-haired, and with a slight adolescent plumpness" (*op. cit.*, 118). In his 1962 poem 'Wild Oats',

Larkin portrayed her as 'A bosomy English rose'. In fact, Larkin was not as much drawn to Ruth as she was to him. She was 'awestruck' by Larkin's enormous erudition, particularly of modern fiction, but she liked the most Larkin's enormous, but disguised, sense of humour. That she was a believer and he was not and that he, all the while, used to put on a gloomy visage did not in any way deter her liking him. So headlong did she fall in love with him! On the other hand, what Larkin had for Ruth was just fascination, nothing more, nothing less, for his opinion about women was not very different from that of his father. He once told Amis: "The whole business of sex annoys me. As far as I can see, all women are stupid beings. What is more, marriage is a revolting institution" (*op. cit.*, 119).

About this time, Larkin was simultaneously working on his novel *Jill* and turning out some poems. Roger Day writes that at Wellington Larkin felt like an alien and unadjusted with his job and so "It is not surprising, then, to learn that during these years [from 1943 to 1946] he wrote 'continuously as never before or since'. He was concentrating on fiction and, according to his own sombrely amusing account of those years, he finished *Jill* and began a second novel" (Day, 2). A bunch of ten poems, composed during this time, Larkin sent to Reginald Ashley Caton of The Fortune Press (among these poems one was 'Next, Please') and all the poems were accepted for publication in the collection *Poetry from Oxford in Wartime*. Soon afterwards, he also sent twenty-one other poems to Caton of the same Press to be published under the title *The North Ship* and, again, this offer was accepted. *The North Ship* first saw the light of day in July 1945. Larkin was mightily boosted up in his ambition to become a writer after *The North Ship* was accepted for publication. He now in 1945 was preparing to write his new novel 'The Kingdom of Winter' which later was entitled *A Girl in Winter*. David Timms writes about materials of this novel: "Larkin spent three years at Wellington, and the experience of working in a provincial public library gave him much of the material for *A Girl in Winter*" (Timms, 8). *Jill*, after some hesitations, on the part of the Fortune Press, was published by the same Press in 1946 but *A Girl in Winter* was forthwith accepted and published by Faber in 1947. *The North Ship*, which was dedicated to Sydney and Eva, was received by the readers "as juvenalia, derivative, faintly ridiculous, a curiosity" (*op. cit.*, 132), but it foreshadowed the mature Larkin features, its recurrent theme of mortality, among other things, being the common theme in his later poetry collections.

Ruth, by now, was accepted by King's College, London, to read English and the affection between herself and Larkin became warm. She took a lodging in Beulah Hill where Larkin would sometimes stop and sometimes Ruth would stay with Larkin in Wellington. Thus it was the beginning of their physical relationship. Meanwhile, Larkin applied for a job at the University College of Southampton and began a correspondence course in Library Classification. Since 1943, when he joined the public library at Wellington, till now, Larkin did never find his job in the library tolerable, let alone entertaining. During the dull years, from 1943 to 1947, when he was slogging in the drudgery of the library, two things gave him unprecedented inspiration and buoyancy: in 1946 *Jill* and in 1947 *A Girl in Winter* were published. Both the novels found a somewhat enthusiastic market, and this encouraged him to write a third novel (his earlier fragmentary novels in manuscript may be ignored).

As we have said, Larkin was not quite happy with his job in the public library at Wellington and so he was on the look out for an escapade from that library. An opportunity soon arrived: the University College of Leicester advertised for the job of a sub-librarian in June 1946. Larkin enthusiastically applied for the job on 3 June and was summoned for an interview in the last week of the month. Eventually, he was offered the job and in September 1946 he joined the library of the University College of Leicester, then affiliated to the University of London. Larkin served the library till 1950, in which year he left England to join the library of the Queen's University in Belfast, North Ireland.

In the early spring of 1947, the second woman came to Larkin's life—Monica Jones. She was fair and small, and used to dress peculiarly, but was considerably impressive to look at.

Her hair was black and she would wear black sweater and brilliantly patterned dirndl-like skirts and black-rimmed glasses. She was one of the most talked about women of the region both for her uncommon physical attractiveness and for her academic attainments and not-to-be-ignored poetic faculty. Born on 8 May 1922, she was three months older than he, was very interested in English literature, and wrote poetry from time to time. Larkin was drawn to her—and at one time violently—for her unique "mixture of formality and family intimacy" (*op. cit.*, 167). Ruth and Monica so much unhinged Larkin that he could not even think of loving any other woman. But the amorous pulls could not divert his attention and effort away from his literary ambitions: in the end part of 1947, he selected twenty-four of his poems and sent them to Alan Pringle at Faber and Faber for publication under the title *In the Grip of Light.*

The beginning of 1948 was disappointing for Larkin. For one thing, *In the Grip of Light* was refused by Faber and Faber for publication; and secondly, his father fell terminally ill. The frustration caused by the refusal of Faber and Faber Larkin tried to overcome by engaging in his third novel (which was never written to the end), but the omen arising out of his father Sydney's hopeless condition drowned him in deep despair. For, in spite of his preference for his mother and in spite of anything and everything, "Sydney had been the dominating figure of his life—a model of intellectual rigour, an audience of his writing, and an example, too, of how an independent mind might be snared in a domestic trap. The son had often been alarmed by his father's severities but had always looked up to him, and over the years they had steadily grown closer to each other. To lose him, Larkin thought, will be to lose part of himself" (*op. cit.*, 174).

But the inevitable could not be averted: Sydney Larkin died of cancer and his body was cremated on 31 March 1948 "following his instructions to adapt the service so that it made no reference to the resurrection" (*loc. cit.*). Sydney's death was a heavy blow to Larkin, as foreknown, but one positive thing Larkin realised after the demise of his father—his unstinted independence. Many of Sydney's personality traits, both appealing and repelling, Larkin internalised from his father, such as a slant to be conservative, an awareness to be 'clear-cut, consistent, disconcertingly logical' in thought and to express in a 'language of crystalline clarity', and a confirmedly negative attitude towards women. Larkin, before long, paid his respect to Sydney's memory by writing an elegy.

4

From His Engagement to Ruth to the End of His Life in Ireland: 1948-1954

His bereavement for the demise of his father having subsided, Larkin began to gradually get him engaged in normal activities and soon came back to his former moderately vibrant self. About five months after the death of his father, Larkin broke the stunning news to Sutton through a letter that he had recently got engaged to Ruth. When the news reached Eva, she saw omen for Larkin and sobbed, and when it reached Ruth's family everyone there felt depressed while Ruth's grandfather warned her about the engagement: "This young man [Larkin] is having the best years of your life" (Motion, 180). The engagement of course did not last long, let alone end in marriage, and the two rash lovers began to lead 'semi-separate lives'.

After the publication of *A Girl in Winter*, Larkin embarked on writing not one, as he in later life recalled, but two novels, none of which, though, did he complete. One of the two projected but abandoned novels was going to be written on the relationship between the two principal characters of it, Dr Butterfield and Augusta Bax, Butterfield having parallels with Larkin and Augusta having similarities with Monica. But Larkin could not finish either of the two projected novels, because since his father's death (in 1948) he remained constantly overcast with gloom. Not only that he could not finish the projected novels, he left writing novels forever, and, further, for one year since his father's death he also could not turn out even a single poem. But, strangely enough, in the year 1950 and about it he produced 13 poems, including some of his famous ones, such as 'Coming', 'Deceptions', 'Dry-Point', 'Spring', 'If, My Darling' and 'Wants'—all of which were eventually published in *The Less Deceived* (1955). Larkin's gloom did not at all lift up in spite of his poetic productions until he had come by the poet and critic Charles Madge's compliment to him for his poems in *The North Ship* which Madge had only recently read, but then the gloom not long afterwards once again settled on him.

So far, Larkin could not find any job in London and so applied for a post of sub-librarian at the Queen's University, Belfast, North Ireland, on a relatively handsome salary. Soon he was offered the job, but he dithered for a time to join, primarily because of his mother and secondarily because of Ruth, with whom he had spent seven happy years,—both of whom he would have to leave behind in case he joined. But ultimately on 16 September 1950, he left England on board the *Ulster Duke* for North Ireland to join the Queen's University, Belfast. He was delighted to see the city of Belfast, and the University library that was established in 1865. There in Belfast, Larkin had a regular busy schedule in the library, but yet he could produce, in his first nine weeks there, seven poems, of which 'No Road', 'Wires' and 'Absences' found place in *The Less Deceived*. Interestingly, in most of the seven poems Larkin "explores what it means to arrive in a new and strange place" (*op. cit.*, 203).

Besides composing these poems, Larkin was haltingly progressing with the writing of his third (unfinished) novel. By this time, his friendship with the painter Sutton and the poet Amis began to cool for various reasons, but particularly because Sutton was coming away from his earlier devotion to art and Amis was husbanding a 'sluttish' family and also because of his existence in a distant land (Ireland). To spend the Christmas of 1950 with his mother, Larkin came back to England and after the Christmas returned to Belfast in January 1951 and began to write his second play *Round Another Point*, a sequel to his first play *Round the Point*, written earlier in 1950. The first play was not so much 'a drama as a Shavian dialogue' concerning the essential lowliness of the female character. In the spring and summer of the same year (1951), Larkin also wrote eight poems, including 'Next, Please' and 'Latest Face' (expressing his feeling for Monica)—the best of the eight. Larkin's fascination for Monica's beauty and his flirting attitude to her is aptly described in 'Latest Face': 'will / The statue of your beauty walk?' 'Latest Face' was published by Larkin as have been written keeping in mind Monica's face, but "In fact the impetus came from a 'later' face than Monica's; it was written about Winifred Arnott, the young graduate working in Queen's library [the library of the Queen's University] whose name appears over and over again on the final page of the poem's manuscript" (*op. cit.*, 208). Arnott was the third woman that came to Larkin's life to sway it for some time, or, may be, for ever.

Larkin's fascination for his third woman now began and it was gradually but surely being reinforced more and more, though Winifred was quite hesitant to respond to him: "The more Larkin saw Winifred the more he liked her. She was open, confident and fun. To Winifred, Larkin seemed amiable but shy, and a good deal too old for her" (*op. cit.*, 209). Larkin liked her and perhaps loved her but stopped short of being intimate to her, may be considering his own age. But, contrary to expectation, Winifred ultimately "was likely to get engaged to her English admirer [Larkin] at any moment" (*op. cit.*, 212). Occasionally, Larkin and Winifred would push their talks towards marriage but just at the suggestion of marriage from her end the talks would veer towards other more worldly subjects. There were some uncompromisable differences between them, particularly that as regards the point of marriage; while it was a priority to Winifred, to Larkin it was the most disgusting institution. It was for this reason that any chance of engagement between them did not fructify. Nevertheless, Winifred or her association with him could, curiously, influence Larkin's conception of poetry. How? Earlier, when some serious differences arose between himself and his beloved, Larkin would backtrack, but in the case of Winifred the differences worked rather as a magnetic pull. He could not, in reality, possess her but he still continued to love her, to feel for her, to think of her, and to imagine about her, in spite of the differences or contradictions between himself and herself—his love for her was latitudinarian, lax. This realisation of his Larkin grafted with his earlier theory or notion of poetry and made it more flexible. Since now, he began to hold that poetry was not that logical, that it could harbour contradictions, and that it was, therefore, flexible. He wrote to Sutton: "For me, a poem is a crossroads of my thoughts, my feelings, my imaginings, my wishes and my critical sense" (*op. cit.*, 213).

Larkin was very hurt and depressed when *In the Grip of Light* (which comprised 23 poems and which was prepared as long back as in 1947) was not accepted for publication by as many as six publishers—Faber, Allen Lane, Methuen, Macmillan, John Lehmann, and Dent. (The poems of *In the Grip of Light* were published by Faber and Faber in *Philip Larkin: Collected Poems* as lately as in 1988.) Soon afterwards, Larkin took courage to select 20 poems from among all the poems he had written during the last few years and sent them to Carswells, the printer, for publication. Carswells published them in 1951 in a pamphlet with the title *XX Poems*. The pamphlet Larkin had dedicated to Kingsley Amis. The response to *XX Poems* once again forced Larkin to pull a long face, abashedly: to promote the sale of the pamphlet, he himself sent a number of copies to some persons belonging to the clerisy but they simply ignored it, though the pamphlet 'contained Larkin's best work to date [1950]'.

In the beginning of the year 1952, when he was 29, Larkin was full of steam, full of ideas, and hopeful of his future, his glum temporarily having been blown away. During this time, Monica, who did not forget Larkin though he was far away from her, suspected that he was in an affair with a married woman—Patsy Strang, the fourth woman who for a time unhinged him romantically—and her suspicion was not unfounded. At the very outset of her relationship with Larkin, Patsy could introduce a change in his perception of life and in some of his convictions. "She easily persuaded Larkin to break his vow never to get involved with a married woman; she dissolved his worries about sex; she even made him waive his rule that woman shouldn't swear as freely as men" (*op. cit.*, 221). Larkin's relationship with Patsy was for the best part plainly erotic and Larkin, though he had the qualm of conscience and the will not to cheat her husband, somehow fell into her trap. But, of course, he cannot be wholly absolved of his improbity. Being unmarried, wanking was his only outlet of releasing his libido or sexual drive. But that was only a weak substitute, and so when Patsy showed openness to him, he only plunged into the pool of her desire, blindly and the sooner. To enhance their eroticism, Larkin insisted on pornographic pictures 'to play a part in their love-making'. In spite of his carnal relationship with Patsy, though, Larkin continued to visit Winifred, of course with some hesitation and with 'opposing wills'.

Meanwhile, Larkin completed three drafts of his third and never published novel *A New World Symphony*—the first draft consisting of 41, the second 46 and the third 95 pages. All the three drafts show the same story and the same cast of characters, the hero and the heroine being Sam and Stella. The story centres on the hesitating, dithering, uncertain attitude of Sam towards taking Stella as his life partner. It quite reflects its author's attitude to women: sex, of course, but never marriage. This novel, stuffed with glum, scenes of sexual, disgust, and violence to women failed to stand by *Jill* and *A Girl in Winter*. The failure of *A New World Symphony* landed Larkin in the centre of sorrow. This artistic failure censured him so decisively and crushingly that, enraged against himself, he said good-bye to novel-writing, and henceforth spearheaded his energy towards poetry.

To drive away his gloomy mood due to the shock of the failure of his third novel, Larkin, along with Monica, went on a brief holidaying to the island of Skye off the west coast of Scotland. Flirtation with Patsy continued till she got a legal divorce from her husband Colin Strang and married Richard Murphy and with him sailed for Greece. But despite his flirtation with Patsy, Larkin was always being haunted by the memory of Winifred. Winifred appears in the first poem of the pamphlet *The Fantasy Poets No. 21* (1954) which is also the beginning poem of *The Less Deceived* (1955), i.e. in the poem 'Lines on a Young Lady's Photograph Album'. Winifred exerted a great influence on Larkin's literary works: "she helped him reaffirm his devotion to 'Art' rather than 'Life'" (*op. cit.*, 235). "She also made him realise that while he continued to avoid marriage [Winifred once pressed him to marry her in order to love her, but he always shirked her mentioning of marriage for fear], he couldn't give his other and even greater fear the slip so easily" (*loc. cit.*). This 'greater fear' of Larkin was his fear of death, and the intelligent Winifred could very rightly read Larkin's mind.

Meantime, Larkin broke his engagement with Ruth. In Easter vacation of 1954 (April), he hurried back to England and stayed with the Amises in Swansea for two nights, and with Monica (whose full name was Monica Margaret Beale Jones) in Malvern for a brief holiday, besides staying with his mother Eva and then returned to Ireland. Before this in the early spring of 1953, George Macbeth and Oscar Mellor, editors of the Fantasy Press, requested Larkin to send a few poems to be published in a pamphlet. The Fantasy Press was established in 1952 at Swinford near Oxford and since then was publishing 'small gatherings' of works by principally graduates and undergraduates of Oxford, such as Elizabeth Jennings, Geoffrey Hill and Kingsley Amis. Larkin sent five poems which were published in a pamphlet in March 1954 under the title *The Fantasy Poets No. 21*. It was during this time that Larkin came closer to The Movement, a term or name coined by J.D. Scott in an article in his *Spectator*. The Movement was a new poetic line or direction that demanded poetry to be anti-phoney, anti-wet, sceptical, robust, ironic and anti-modern, of course among other things. Andrew Motion writes about Larkin that "...The Movement marks one of the most important moments in his career as a poet" (Motion, 244).

5

From Joining the Library of the University of Hull and the Publication of *The Less Deceived* to the Publication of *The Whitsun Weddings*: 1955-1964

Larkin always wanted to come back to England though he enjoyed his stay in the library of the University of Belfast,

Ireland, and an opportunity soon came to him. In September, 1954, he came to know of an advertisement for the post of librarian at the University of Hull, England, and he applied for the post. It should be mentioned here that while he was serving as an assistant librarian at the University College in Leicester, a city not very far from Wellington, Larkin's boss (the head librarian) was Miss Rhode Bennett, who was very sympathetic to him. It was under her persuasion that he ultimately passed the Library Association examinations and became an associate member in 1949. However, he was called for interview by the University of Hull. Hull is a big port on the estuary of the river Humber in north-east England and is the birthplace of Andrew Marvell and is also the place where Larkin wrote *The Whitsun Weddings* and *High Windows*. The Chairman of the interview panel was 'very impressed' by Larkin, and he was offered the job, and in course of time Larkin joined the library of the University of Hull, which is today known as Brynmor Jones Library, in March, 1955, his salary being 1,550 Pounds (per annum), nearly double what it had been in Ireland (when he died his salary at the same University was 22,000 Pounds). Now he could afford modest luxury, but he did not, or rather could not, because he was too busy in the library. When away from his busyness, he would get the company of his mother Eva and Monica. Eva's affectionate influence on Larkin would have been much more than what it actually had been had not Monica been there with him as well. Monica was his most desired companion and intellectual support, and she had been his "confident and companion for nearly forty years" (*op. cit.*, ix). Her friendship with him was never tarnished.

Not long after his joining the library of the University of Hull, Larkin got acquainted with George Hartley and his wife Jean Hartley of Marvell Press (Jean was its founder)—the press that first published a collection of his 29 poems under the title *Various Poems* in November 1955, and made him famous as a poet. "Larkin was lastingly grateful to the Hartleys for making his name after many other publishers had failed him" (*op. cit.*, 261). The title of the collection was changed from *Various Poems* to *The Less Deceived* when it was reprinted in 1956, due to the persuasion of George Hartley. The publication of *The Less Deceived* made the nearly unknown Larkin a front-ranking poet almost overnight, and since then he began to grow incessantly in popularity. Invitations for giving public readings of his poems continued to come to him in shoals till the 1960s, most of which he was obliged to decline due to preoccupations. It was perhaps because of his almost blanket refusal to those dozens of warm and respectful invitations that he then acquired for ever the epithet 'hermit', which he certainly did not entirely deserve, for he of course preferred to give the public glimpses of his inner being and, withal, he was never desirous of completely withdrawing from the world like a hermit. After the success of *The Less Deceived*, he, however, resolved to keep alone, in solitude, principally for keeping engaged in poetic creations, though, in fact, his poetic production during this time was scant: in 1956, for instance, he wrote just two poems. In the same year, Larkin took up a new flat at Pearson Park, where he stayed for long eighteen years.

Meanwhile, Robert Conquest, poet, historian, critic, and for a time literary editor of *The Spectator*, requested Larkin's permission to include some of Larkin's poems in his anthology *New Lines*, which was the pioneer of The Movement, and Larkin delightfully sent him the following poems: 'Maiden Name', 'Church Going', 'I Remember, I Remember', 'Skin', 'Born Yesterday', 'Triple Time', 'Toads', and 'Lines on a Young Lady's Photograph Album'. The anthology was published on 14 January 1956. It was these poems, printed in *New Lines* that ushered in The Movement, for which Larkin is generally grouped with the other poets of The Movement—Amis, Donald Davie, D.J. Enright, Thom Gun, Elizabeth Jennings, John Wain and Conquest himself—though Larkin did never like to be thought to belong to The Movement or to any other movement. Since then Conquest came closer to Larkin and it was he who encouraged him to be interested in pornography. And Larkin's interest in pornography may to a great extent be responsible for his use of some four letter and vulgar words in his poetry.

The Less Deceived assuredly established Larkin as "one of the best poets of his generation" (*op. cit.*, 278). In December

1957, *The Times* appreciated the collection as one of the outstanding books of the year. The demand of the collection rose so high that a paperback edition of it had to soon be published. In 1957, the Queen paid an official visit to the University of Hull, but Larkin was not asked to meet her. He expressed his grumbling at this in a letter to his mother with wounded pride: "'Ah well,' he told his mother, 'one day I shall meet her as Philip Larkin and not as the paltry librarian'" (*op. cit.*, 283). As we will see, his boasting proved true: one day in his advanced age he was in fact invited by the Queen to meet her. In 1958, the B.B.C. broadcasted a selection of his poems. Anthony Thwaite, who was an admirer of Larkin since he read his poems in the early 1950s, met him. Thwaite, who was then about twenty-eight and was a trainee radio producer with the B.B.C., since his meeting with Larkin was steadily growing up as a fast friend of his. Later, Thwaite became the literary editor of *New Statesman* and co-editor of *Encounter*, and helped Larkin publish many of his poems and reviews in these two journals. Thwaite also collected and edited *Larkin at Sixty*, and assisted Larkin in editing *Oxford Book of Twentieth Century English Verse* and in selecting pieces for his *Required Writing* (which Larkin dedicated to him). As Larkin's reputation as a poet and literary critic began to rise up steadily, the London-based PEN (Poets, Essayists and Novelists; an international association) Committee requested him to edit, along with Bonamy Dobree and Louis MacNeice, the seventh anthology of *PEN New Poems* against a fee of just twenty-five guineas, and he accepted the offer readily. One of the most important events of Larkin's in the year 1958 was composition of one of his most representative poems, 'The Whitsun Weddings'. The poem was soon followed by 'Self's the Man', which may be called a companion poem to the former.

The next year, i.e. 1959, Larkin said was his busiest. In this year he continued to produce a series of poems: 'Far Out', 'The Building', 'Afternoons', 'Talking in Bed', etc. So long, since 1943, he would not have felt accustomedly comfortable if identified as a librarian (besides, of course, introduced as a poet), but from around 1959 he felt sort of proud publishing himself as a librarian. For instance, in the *Who's Who* of 1959, Larkin gave his occupation "as 'librarian' rather than 'novelist and poet'" (*op. cit.*, 294). And this is confirmed by what Larkin told John Haffenden in an interview that took place sometime between January 1979 and April 1980: "I tried twice for Civil Service, during the war of course, but even in those days they had some standards. I'm glad now they didn't take me, though I was a bit surprised then. I've been much happier as a librarian" (Haffenden, 115).

Larkin's nagging fear of death suddenly began to increase since the same year, 1959, especially after he heard of the deaths of Monica's mother and then of her father. The mortality of man now to him became a truth displayed in the glaring light of the sun in hot summer. His awareness of this truth was accentuated by his own gradually failing health. "As his hearing grew weaker in the years ahead he felt more and more isolated, trapped in an incompetent body, foolish and pathetic. Work in the library became awkward, talking in public places (bars, for instance) a trial, even listening to jazz at home—one of his greatest pleasures—was a strain by the mid-1970s" (Motion, 292). Sexually, too, he was deteriorating, though during this time Monica aspired after possessing him both spiritually and physically.

Though the Monica episode was till then continuing, the fifth woman, who undulated Larkin's soul for some time, entered to his life—Maeve Brennan. "Small, with a good figure, short brown wavy hair, an eager face and unusually hairy forearms and legs (which Larkin found 'very exciting'), Maeve was unsophisticated, conservative, cautious and capable of behaving coquettishly. She was more trim than glamorous, more emotionally canny than intellectually able. It was for her intense enthusiasm that Larkin began to love her—and for not frightening him, for being cozy, for recognizing he was special, and for being—he thought—someone he could easily control and pamper. Monica, who was his 'Bun', admired him but was never in awe of him. Maeve, who became his 'Mouse' and would in due course be inundated with gifts of little furry creatures (a mouse in a chorister's costume, for instance), always looked up to him.

If Larkin thought this meant she would do his every bidding, he was soon proved wrong. Maeve was quick-witted and highly principled. She was also devoutly Catholic" (*op. cit.*, 298). At one time Larkin was so enamoured of Maeve that she reminded him of Maud Gonne (of W.B. Yeats).

If Larkin was busy in 1959 he was more so in 1960 producing a flow of lyrics. In 1960, he applied for the post of librarian of the University of Reading, was called for interview, went to Reading to attend the interview, but astonishingly returned without facing the interview board. He explained this his queer behaviour to his mother telling her that he had made a record by not attending the interview. In the beginning of 1961, Larkin became a regular jazz critic for *Daily Telegraph*. Since that year Maeve's attitude towards Larkin and her relation with him was gradually changing for the better and better. Andrew Motion writes: "As the year [1961] went by, Maeve says that she started to feel 'exquisitely happy' with her new life in Hull, '—and so did Philip. Temperamentally we complemented each other. I was outgoing, lively, and made him more sociable. He deepened my spiritual side, taught me to enjoy music more deeply, to read poetry out loud; he increased my sensual pleasure in things'" (*op. cit.*, 310). Larkin's relation with Maeve, as she confessed, was "extremely sensual". She of course desired his advancement but she believed "he could not ask her to sleep with him" (*op. cit.*, 305) because of her Catholicism, for he was either a non-believer or an agnostic. Thus "By combining charity with excitement, Maeve linked her role in Larkin's ordinary daily life to her function as a 'fantasy figure'" (*op. cit.*, 307).

On 10 January 1961, Larkin wrote 'Ambulances' and on 5 March of the same year, mysteriously, he collapsed during a Library Committee meeting quite unconscious and was carried in an ambulance to Kingston General Hospital. The cause of his collapse could not be ascertained; it could only be suspected that his break-down might have been caused by his tension between two forces pulling him with equal strength from two opposite directions, once force belonging to Maeve and the other to Monica. Like Maeve, Monica, too, behaved with

Larkin very coquettishly with a view to draw his amorous attention, his gloating, towards herself, and she was successful, for he certainly responded to her very readily and with all enthusiasm. Sometimes their relationship would go far beyond the bound of civility. For instance, they played porno with Iris Murdoch's novel *The Flight from the Encounter*: they playfully changed the sentence of the book 'Her lips were parted and he had never seen her eyes so wide open' into 'Her legs were parted and he had never seen her cunt so wide open' (*op. cit.*, 319).

Signs of psychological senescence were showing in Larkin since as early as 1961 when he was only near forty. He was falling into depression intermittently, taking stock of his life's work frustratingly, and counting his career as a failure. In 1961, for instance, he told Judy Egerton: "The sense of approaching forty is strong upon me, and [of] having completely wasted the time of twenty to forty, when power should be greatest and relish keenest. Anything I do now will be a compromise with second or third best. I suddenly see myself as a freak and a failure, and my way of life as a farce" (*op. cit.*, 315). His fear of death also perhaps got stronger during this time, for it was at this time that he wrote 'Ambulances': 'the solving emptiness / That lies just under all we do'. But, in spite of all this, he was turning out poems, some of them famous ones, such as 'Here' (originally called 'Withdrawing Room'), 'Nothing To Be Said', etc.

On his fortieth birthday in 1962, Larkin realised, as he wrote in 'Send No Money', composed in the same year, that 'Half life is over now'. Yet, in this year he wrote at least two poems where two of his favourite women are present: 'Wild Oats' (which was written keeping Ruth in mind) and 'Toads Revisited' (in which a reference is made to his secretary Betty: 'My loaf-haired secretary'). The reputation of *The Less Deceived* (1955) reached America two years previously, and St Martin's Press of that country published one thousand copies of an edition of the collection, which was warmly received by the poetry-loving public as well as by other poets and critics. "Robert Lowell, for example, declared, 'No post-war poetry has so caught the moment, and caught it without straining after its ephemera. It's a hesitant groping mumble, resolutely experienced, resolutely perfect in its artistic methods'" (*op. cit.*, 328). Larkin must have been highly encouraged by this appreciation made by a famous American poet. But, at home, in the spring of 1962, "the then much-respected literary critic A. Alvarez, compiling *The New Poetry* for Penguin, had attacked Larkin in his Introduction, charging him with 'gentility', neo-Georgian pastoralism, and a failure to deal with the violent extremes of contemporary life" (*loc. cit.*). When Alvarez made such a harsh comment about Larkin, he profusely praised Larkin's coeval poet Ted Hughes in the same *The New Poetry*. And this must have mortally hurt Larkin.

Nevertheless, by now Larkin completed the manuscript of *The Whitsun Weddings* and sent it to Charles Monteith of the Faber and Faber publishing firm. The firm offered Larkin 75 Pounds instead of the usual 50 Pounds (and thus showed our poet a gesture of honour). They also gave him a royalty which was much higher than usual. *The Whitsun Weddings* came out of the press on 28 February 1964, and its reception was exceptionally warm: for instance, the 4,000 copies sold within only two months. Seven months after the publication of the collection, the Random House in New York brought out their edition of the book, which did not sell so well in America: only 2,000 copies of it were sold in two years.

6

From the Publication of *The Whitsun Weddings* to the Publication of *High Windows*: 1964-1974

While serving in the library of the University of Hull, Larkin occasionally used to travel to London by train to see his mother there. On such a train journey he had a happy experience of some marriage parties travelling with him, which experience he indited in one of his best poems, 'The Whitsun Weddings' which in turn lent itself to the title of his collection of poems published nine years after *The Less Deceived*—*The Whitsun Weddings*. In between the publications of the two collections, *The Whitsun Weddings* (1964) and *High Windows* (1974), Larkin was variously busy: besides his services in the library, he continued to compose poems, though tardily, write articles, do the job of the president of some associations, and even make love, or rather, play love-making. In 1966, he felt much honoured when he was invited by the Oxford University Press to revise and update the *Oxford Book of Modern Verse* which was thirty years ago edited by W.B. Yeats. With Anthony Thwaite's yeoman-like help, Larkin commandably accomplished the colossal task at an early date, though he was then involved in some other important concerns: the Arts Council, the Poetry Book Society, the Manuscript Committee, and the Gregory awards.

In the poetic zone, Larkin was preparing "for an assault on the pastoral narratives of the Georgians" and so was turning out "an urban narrative of his own" (*op. cit.*, 363). He continued to flirt with Monica and Maeve. During the summer of 1966, he 'continued to play his double game', comforting Monica, who demanded his assurance that he loved none else but herself, and at the same time declaring to Maeve that he loved only Maeve Brennan. Nevertheless, he was depressed and hankered after solitude. The highly sexually charged poem 'Annus Mirabilis' Larkin wrote during this period, to be exact, on 16 June 1967. The poem may superficially suggest his regret for not enjoying sexual freedom in young years, but, in fact, in the poem he only raised the point whether such a freedom could contribute to better life. The poem is ironic in the sense that though in it he pleaded for sexual freedom, he opposed such a freedom, tongue in cheek. This is evident from the fact that immediately after finishing 'Annus Mirabilis', he began 'This Be The Verse' (which, of course, he finished four years afterwards in 1971) in which he aggressively censored sexuality: 'Man hands on misery to man. / It deeps like a coastal shelf. / Get out as early as you can, / And don't have any kids yourself.'

Larkin was never interested in politics, though he always kept himself very minimally or cursorily abreast of the current political waves and turmoils around him, but now he developed some 'strong reactionary political prejudices'. He, however, continued to produce his monthly instalments of critical contributions for the jazz column of *Daily Telegraph*. Two famous poems he wrote in 1968: 'Sad Steps' (24 April) and 'Posterity' (17 June). The two may be taken as companion poems, and they express Larkin's drive for sarcastic self-degradation or self-denigration. In the same year, the Compton Fund Committee of the University of Hull was established with the money left by the literature-loving philanthropist Joseph Compton to the Arts Council of Great Britain for purposes 'to do with poetry'—the money that earned 25,000 Pounds a year. The Committee was headed by Charles Osborne, who chose Larkin as one of the small coterie of members of the Committee. Larkin gladly accepted the offer.

Larkin had been elected to the Poetry Book Society and had worked there from 1960 to 1963. In 1968, he was re-elected to the Society. The same year he decided to collect the critical articles he wrote about jazz and publish them in book form. The result was his book *All What Jazz: A Record Diary 1961-68* published by Faber in 1970. As we have said, Larkin was never interested in politics but had some political prejudices or unconsidered beliefs or convictions, which of course he guardedly kept to himself. But since Harold Wilson's Labour Party came to power in 1964 and especially since 1968, he began to voice his political prejudices more and more openly. "To colleagues on campus like John Kenyon, or in letters to friends like Monica, Amis, Conquest and Pym, he regularly complained about socialist policies and proposals, repudiating anything that challenged his 'true blue' beliefs. Immigrants and the trade unions had been his original bugbears;...and many aspects of government policy—particularly defence" (*op. cit.*, 388). Larkin violently opposed the Russian aggressive policy and the British policy of shrinking from external overlordships. For instance, in 'Homage to a Government' he bitterly criticised the British policy of closing the British base in Aden (now part of the Republic of Yemen).

In the spring of 1970, Larkin underwent a surgical operation to get a polyp in his right nostril removed. In the same year, he composed two more of his finest poems: 'The Explosion' and 'Dublinesque', which is, as Larkin told Maeve, a transcription of one of his dreams: "a dream—I just woke up and described it" (*op. cit.*, 395). The most important work that Larkin published in 1970 (on 9 February) was *All What Jazz*, but that we have already said. What remains to be said is that it was the Introduction to *All What Jazz* in which Larkin first gave vent to his objection to modernism. Andrew Motion writes: "Attacking 'the two principal themes of modernism, mystification and outrage', he [Larkin] tells us: 'I dislike such things not because they are new, but because they are irresponsible exploitations of technique in contradistinction of human life as we know it. This is my essential criticism of modernism, whether perpetrated by Parker, Pound or Picasso: it helps us neither to enjoy nor endure. It will divert us as long as we are prepared to be mystified or outraged, but maintains its hold only by being more mystifying and more outrageous: it has no lasting power. Hence the compulsion on every modernist to wade deeper into violence and obscenity: hence the succession of Parker by Rollins and Coltrane, and Rollins and Coltrane by Coleman, Ayler and Shepp'" (*op. cit.*, 397-98).

Larkin now got a visiting Fellowship from All Souls College for the winter term of 1970 and the spring term of 1971, and he gladly accepted it. His behaviour—he was now 48—showed some visible changes. He became jealous some of his contemporary writers, for instance, of Kingsley Amis, and sometimes irrational and fastuous, for instance, in a letter to Conquest he wrote: "Fuck the non-working classes", and again "fuck the students (fuck your students everywhere), fuck the Common Market e'en. Hurry for Ian Smith, Ian Paisley (fuck all branches of the IRA)" (*op. cit.*, 409). During 1971-72, Larkin was suffering from heavy mental stresses as a result of which his neck began to ache. Earlier, he had been suffering from eye and nose troubles and now he had pain in the neck—he was really undergoing a distressing condition. Medical examination of his neck revealed narrowing of the joints in the neck, indicative of arthritis. Larkin believed his disease to be incurable and so was worrying much. To add to his mental stress, in January 1972 his mother Eva broke a bone of her leg by falling in the kitchen in her advanced age. Even in such a distressing circumstance Larkin composed some beautiful poems, such as 'The Building' and 'Going, Going,' (this poem he wrote at the request of the Countess of Dartmouth for writing a poem on environment). In the following six months after these poems he wrote 'Heads in the Women's Ward' and 'The View'—two poems that may be treated as codas to 'The Building'.

1972 was the year of his fiftieth birthday and this birthday reminded Larkin of his approaching death and made him somewhat funky, more so when he was also noticing the rapid decline of Eva's health. The same year (in May), his friend, the Poet Laureate Cecil Day-Lewis, died of cancer. Larkin's gloom thickened and he temporarily lost the urge to write poetry. The jazz-reviewing, which he enjoyed for long, also interested him no more. 'The Old Fools', which he wrote on 12 January 1973, gives us an impression of the state of his mind at this period, particularly an impression of his ever increasing fear of death: 'At death, you break up: the bits that were you / Start speeding away from each other for ever / With no one to see.' But even in this period of nagging gloom he had reasons to feel for a while that life was not all that dark. For one thing, Faber published a paperback edition of *The North Ship*. Secondly, he sent to the press the manuscript of *High Windows*. Thirdly, he was awarded the Cholmondeley Award, worth 500 Pounds, by the Society of Authors. Fourthly, his own college, St John's, invited him to become an Honorary Fellow and he was installed as an honorary Doctor of Letters at the University of Warwick. Fifthly, David Timms for the first time published a full-length study of his work done uptill then—*Philip Larkin*. And lastly, to cap all these, *The Oxford Book of Twentieth Century Verse*, which was meantime published, contained six of his poems.

In March 1974, Larkin was delighted to know that he was selected for the Russell Loines Award by the National Institute of Arts and Letters in America. He himself could not collect the Award for unavoidable reasons; Robert Giroux collected the Award for him. Two months afterwards, Larkin had reason to be much more delighted than he was to receive the American Award. In May 1974, *High Windows*, about which he had higher opinion than about all his other poetry collections, was published. The sale of the book was very encouraging. The first impression of 6,000 copies of the book sold in just three months. This must have been a matter of great joy to Larkin. In November of that year, he willingly gave a reading of his poems—an event rarely to be expected of a self-effacing and reclusive poet like him. During this time, Maeve suddenly and unexpectedly surfaced in his life, overshadowing Monica, and came rather too close to him—they now behaved not unlike that of a married couple, not even excluding the point of sex. Andrew Motion writes: "Their feelings for each other were rekindled immediately, and in the course of the following weeks and months [after their first meeting this time] their affair blossomed as never before. Maeve explains, 'We resumed a companionable pattern, meeting several times a week, doing the things we had always enjoyed. I was aware that Philip felt more committed to Monica now, so marriage was not mentioned. This did not trouble me: I was just content that we had drawn so close again.' Eventually, Maeve admits, she 'yielded to temptation, but only on very rare and isolated occasions, and at a cost of grave violation to my conscience, since I never, in principle, abandoned my stand on premarital sex'" (*op. cit.*, 447).

7

From the Publication of *High Windows* to the Signs of Death: 1974-1984

Larkin was inordinately sensitive by nature and so he would have been affected the more and the sooner at the slightest suggestion of 'slings and arrows of outrageous fortune' and become overcast with gloom, and to drive away his gloom he would frequently resort to boozing. After the publication of *High Windows* in 1974 and his receiving of some new honours, he seemed for a time an extravertedly happy soul, but not very long afterwards his free-floating gloom returned and he took to smoking 'menthol cigarette' besides his habitual overdozes of drinks. His constant unhappiness and his nagging half-awareness and fear of his approaching death pushed him into a grim despair to drive away which he would desperately consume wine and menthol cigarette. His condition in 1975 he described in 'Aubade' which he had begun in the previous year: 'I work all day, and get half-drunk at night. / ...I see what's really always there: / Unresting death'. But even so, in the same year (1975) he became sexually involved with his secretary at the library of the University of Hull—with Betty Mackereth. The incident of one day (1975) Betty herself narrated to Andrew Motion on 12 February 1992, which we may here cite so that one can have a glimpse of the sexuality of Larkin. Betty told Motion: "Philip took Pauline and me in his car, and drove us home, dropping Pauline off first, which vaguely crossed my mind as not being the right order, as she lived nearer to Hull. When we arrived at [my home] he asked me if I was going to invite him in for coffee. I was surprised, but said yes, and he later told me that he had arranged the whole thing in his mind. Nothing much occurred that evening, though Philip did break a saucer! But once on the slippery slope, there seemed nothing I could do to stop (nor did I want to)" (*op. cit.*, 451). Betty was then in her fifties and Larkin was about the same age. Larkin liked her particularly because she used to feel sympathetic to Larkin with his mental afflictions. Betty later admitted that she was a sort of wife to him, and that he would sometimes remind her that T.S. Eliot married his secretary.

In the spring of 1975, Larkin came to know that he was going to be offered the CBE (Companion of the British Empire) award. In the same year the Royal Society of Scotland honoured him with the Benson Medal and the FVS Foundation of Hamburg awarded him the Shakespeare Prize. In 1976, Alan Brownjohn 'sent him a copy of his appreciative short study of his poems, published by the British Council'. In the same year Larkin was invited to record some of his poems for broadcasting. In 1977, he was appointed one of two judges for a poetry competition launched by the *Hull Daily Mail.* Also in that year he was photographed 'for the sleeve of the recording of *The Less Deceived* ' and was 'filmed with Betjeman for the Monitor programme'. On 10 February 1977, Larkin received the Coventry Award of Merit, and in the spring of that year he became the Chairman of the Book Prize Committee. It was in a meeting of this Book Prize Committee to select a book for awarding prize that Larkin expressed his considered opinion that there is no appreciable difference between a good prose and a good poetry, and also said, "I think it is harder to write a good novel than a good poem" (*op. cit.*, 464). In the same year bad news also came to him: Patsy and then Robert Lowell, an American poet and an admirer of Larkin, died, and then came the most crushing news for him—Eva died in her sleep at 91 on 17 November in the Barrystead Nursing Home, outside Leicester where she had been staying for about five years. Larkin, in his great sorrow, recalled that Hardy's mother also died at 91 (and this points to the fact that Hardy was his favourite writer and always subsisted in his consciousness). Perhaps Larkin had been contemplating her death since at least three years ago, and maybe her on-coming death prompted him to write 'Aubade': 'Death is no different whined at than withstood.'

Next year, i.e. in 1978, more honours were showered on Larkin and more invitations came to him. For instance, this year, in July, he was made a Companion of Literature by the Royal Society of Literature. He was also requested to act as a literary advisor for revision of the *New English Bible*. But he ceased to act as such after sending a couple of suggestions because he noticed that all these non-poetic activities baulked his poetic productions. The cessation of his non-poetic activities, though, did not improve the quantity of his poetic productions: he wrote only eleven short lyrics between Eva's death (1977) and his own (1985). The cause of the fall in the quantity of his productions lied elsewhere: his increasing free-floating glum, ever growing fear of death and fast aggravating physical condition. Maeve now could realise that Monica was nearer to him than herself, and so she was inchingly deviating from Larkin's nearness, adding to his mounting sadness due to the loss of his mother. As Maeve was gradually drifting away from him, Monica was slowly coming closer and closer to him, and he was, on his part, gingerly accepting as his Palladium.

As we have said, Larkin had little interest in politics, and yet he had a slant for Conservatism. This is why when in 1979 the Conservatives formed the government with Mrs Margaret Thatcher as the Prime Minister, he was happy. He had a special fascination for Mrs Thatcher (Prime Minister from 1979 to 1990), particularly for her good looks, and especially for her 'pretty face', and for her tough stands. Larkin was first introduced to Mrs Margaret Thatcher in 1980, when she was the Prime Minister of England. Later, he used to tell the story that on the occasion of their first meeting Mrs Thatcher welcomed him thus: "Oh, Dr Larkin, I am a great admirer of your poems." He then instantaneously asked her to quote a line from his poems, whereupon she recited: "All afternoon her mind lay open like a drawer of knives" (*op. cit.*, 497). At this Larkin must have been beside himself in delight! However, since 1980, Larkin was slowly but irreversively descending into darker and darker gloom and more and more solitude, isolation and deprivation. His despair doubled when he heard of the death of the novelist Barbara Pym in January 1980. Pym was introduced to him by his sister Kitty way back in 1961, and since then he was an admirer of her and her books. In 1981, Larkin included an entry on Barbara Pym in *Dictionary of National Biography*. On 7 May 1980, Larkin opened an exhibition organized by the University of Nottingham on the occasion of the fiftieth death anniversary of D.H. Lawrence.

From the very beginning Larkin was a confirmed agnostic, and yet in 1983, when he was on the wrong side of sixty, he showed for a time some interest in the matter of religion, i.e. in Christianity. This change of his attitude towards religion was due to his close friendship with A.N. Wilson, whom he first met in 1981 or earlier. Wilson, a devout Christian, tried to infuse into Larkin a sense of religion, so much so that in July 1983 he [Larkin] bought for 120 Pounds a large Oxford University Press Bible and began to read a few pages of it each day, and thus read the whole of it. After this, or while he was reading the Bible, he was even toying with the idea of going to church, which idea of course did never materialise, except for once when he attended, in 1983, the "Evensong at St Stephen's with Monica" (*op. cit.*, 485). Larkin's advanced age may be responsible for his rare fancy of going to the church, for once though. Larkin of course did not believe in God, and yet he believed in the tradition of rituals: he "continued to hope that religious rituals, like the secular ones he had celebrated in 'Show Saturday', would 'always be there', embodying formal values and enshrining time-honoured traditions" (*op. cit.*, 486). In the beginning of 1981, Larkin was shocked to hear that Lesley Dunn, the young wife of his colleague in the library and poet Douglas Eaglesham Dunn, had died of cancer. In the same year, Larkin's cantata *Bridge for the Living*, which was commissioned by the composer Anthony Hedges in 1975 and Larkin wrote it that year, was performed in Hull's City Hall on 11th April to mark the opening of the Humber Bridge that connects the north and the south banks of Humber at Hessle. And in the May again of the same year (1981), Larkin was elected Chairman of the Poetry Book Society.

In 1982, when Larkin became 60, well-wishings came to him in shoals, and Anthony Thwaite started collecting and editing Larkin's biographical and critical essays to be published by Faber under the title *Larkin at Sixty*. On Larkin's attaing the age of sixty, his 'name filled the pages of papers in the spring and summer of 1982'. In the same year, the American critic and admirer of Larkin, and, amusing enough, an amateur magician, Dale Salwak, came to Hull and met him, and after dining with him showed some magical legerdemains that amused him. This Dale Salwak edited and published in 1989 some critical essays on Larkin under the title *Philip Larkin: The Man and His Work*. In the summer of that year, Larkin wrote an Introduction to *A Rumoured City*, an anthology of works by local poets. In 1982, Hugh Thomas, the head of the Conservative government's Centre for Policy Studies, invited Larkin to a dinner in his house along with Mrs Thatcher, the Prime Minister. In the dinner, Larkin was surrounded by a number of intellectuals including Stephen Spender, Anthony Powell and Isaiah Berlin. Monica, who like Larkin also became sixty that year, suddenly fell and cut her head and was admitted to Hexham General Hospital, in October. Larkin saw her writhing in pain and felt himself in distress. However, in 1982, the New University of Ulster conferred upon Larkin an honorary D. Litt. degree. It was in this year that he was preparing the manuscript of *Required*

Writing: Miscellaneous Pieces 1955-1982—a collection of writings, mostly commissioned or requested—which was published in 1983 by Faber and was highly appreciated.

In January 1983, Larkin received the W.H. Smith Award worth 4,000 Pounds. He was now a much talked about poet and personality, and was being frequently photographed. But Larkin was not as happy for all these as we might expect him to be because he was then frustrated with his scant literary productions, and because poetry-writing no more inspired him. Monica became weighed down by her advanced age and associated ailments, and this added to Larkin's already increasing worry and weariness. In spite of all these, Larkin could compose his last poem 'Party Politics' that bears suggestions of his weariness and brokenness: 'Some people say, best show an empty glass: / Someone will fill it. Well I've tried that too. / You may get drunk, or dry half-hours may pass. / It seems to turn on where you are. Or who.' Larkin now became more and more critical and censorious and became fastuous with others and disgusted with himself—and all these for no reasons known even to himself. He was also inordinately depressed; and yet for a while he was buoyed up, before once again sinking down in despair, when the Oxford University conferred upon him the honorary D. Litt. degree on 27 June 1984. He felt this honour was 'the big one'. In the same year, i.e. in 1984, Humphrey Ocean, the famous portrait-painter, began to draw a portrait of Larkin in several sessions, in some of which—later on Larkin would jocularly say—he would fall asleep. Anyway, Ocean finished the portraiture within a month. Larkin was then, so to say, being 'harassed' by photographers and TV people. On the death of Betjeman in December 1983, the Laureateship of poetry was offered to Larkin but he candidly declined to receive it.

8

From the Intimations of Death to Death: 1984-1985

Signs of death's 'unresting' advancement began to show themselves more and more obviously in the body and mind of Larkin since the beginning of the year 1984, when he was sixty-two. He was then overweight and 'terribly deaf'. Psychologically, he was winding up himself within himself, fully aware his days were numbered. To overcome his physical infirmities and drive away his worries and anxieties, he was increasing the dozes of wine and port. National politics, trade union matters, even gaily noisy children irritated him too much. Only his solitary existence in the library of the University of Hull gave him a little peace of mind. His health began to deteriorate fast: he was showing cardiac spasms, syndromes of hypochondria and mental depression, besides phobia of cancer and fear of death. A barium meal revealed a polypoid tumour in his oesophagus, and suspecting cancer the doctors decided to remove it. When in the Hull Royal Infirmary Dr Christopher Royston removed the polypoid tumour from the oesophagus on 11 June (1985), it was found that the suspicion of the doctors was not unfounded. It was, moreover, found that there was a well-developed carcinogenous tumour in his throat, which was beyond surgical intervention. Monica, who was suffering from Parkinson's disease, did not want to tell Larkin about his cancer, but when he was soon removed to the ICU (Intensive Care Unit) of the Nuffield Hospital, he must have understood that his condition was alarming.

After a stay for a couple of days in the Nuffield Hospital, Larkin showed signs of some improvement, due to the removal of the polypoid tumour. He even made some telephone calls. But on 19 June 1985, immediately after drinking a large quantity of whisky, Larkin profusely vomitted and then fell unconscious. Dr Hovell, who was by, drained off the consumed whisky from his stomach but yet consciousness did not come back to him. For fear of death, Larkin was rushed to the ICU and there after some time he regained consciousness, and the doctors said he was abundantly lucky to remain alive. On 28 June 1985, Maeve came to see him when he was not really out of danger, and yet he affectionately reprimanded her for being over-anxious for him and for phoning Monica about his condition. Larkin was then not in the Nuffield Hospital but at home. But his relatively stable condition soon left him and so he was rushed back to the Nuffield Hospital, and there his condition improved a little. Letters bearing enquiries about his health and good wishes for him were thickly arriving by post. "Pitifully thin, forcing himself to walk round the apple-tree dotted lawn outside his room once a day, leaning on his stick and the arm of whosoever was visiting, he insisted that he had nothing to live for. He gazed at the small television in the corner of his room, and for hour after hour watched the Test Match and the Wimbledon tennis tournament. The Men's Singles pleased him: he thought that the winner, Boris Becker, looked 'just like the young Auden'" (*op. cit.*, 516). On 17 July 1985, Larkin asked his solicitor, Terence Wheldon, to amend his will that he made ten years ago: a bequest to Maeve was deleted, and now Monica, the Society of Authors, and the Royal Society for Prevention of Cruelty to Animals (he was very sympathetic to animals; at the sight of any cruelty dealt to animals he would fly into a rage, though he would swallow it silently) were now the only beneficiaries of his bequest of 2,86,360 Pounds that he would leave behind after his death.

After he had come out of the Nuffield Hospital, Larkin's condition slightly improved, so much so that once he ventured to drive his car a short distance, and when he was driving he scraped the vehicle at the time of negotiating 'the entrance to the station car-park'. But soon his condition worsened. On 10 August 1985 fell his sixty-third birth-day. Himself pathetically weak, both in body and mind, Larkin became anxious for Monica who was 'slowly degenerating physically'. As the days were slipping out, one after another, he was becoming more and more about the imminency of his death. After forcing himself to somehow discharge his duties in the library of the University of Hull for a few days, each day just half a day's work, he found even this impossible for him. During this time, he wrote a few letters, occasionally spoke to Maeve, and read Anthony Powell's *A Dance to the Music of Time*, a sequence of 12 novels, with pleasure. He also wrote a short obituary of his former colleague, Eric Walter White, and then thought of reviewing Dylan Thomas's *Collected Letters* but abandoned it.

Knowing of Larkin's pathetic state of health and fearing his days are numbered, Maeve was very sad for him and believing that she 'had played a special part in his life' wished, in the confinement of her bed, she could greet him 'with silence and tears'. Ultimately Larkin's final days arrived. Mrs Thatcher, the Prime Minister, and an admirer of him, wanted to honour him 'in some other way' because previously he declined to be the Poet Laureate: Mrs Thatcher made him a Companion of Honour. As Larkin was too ill, the investiture was sent to him through the post. This was Larkin's second accolade: about twenty years ago he was awarded the covetous Queen's Gold Medal for Poetry. Larkin was immensely delighted to receive the second honour, too.

But his delight was a sort of irony, for now his absolute extinction or death was just at the door step, and all the more pathetic a fact it was that he himself knew it. He told Monica that he was 'spiralling down towards extinction'. On 28 November 1985, Larkin's voice became 'very slurred'. On the next day, he collapsed (for the second time) in the downstairs lavatory after he had shut the door, his face lying on the heating pipes, and in extreme agony he whispered, 'Hot! Hot!' A neighbour broke open the door and rescued him. On 30 November 1985 (it was a Saturday), Michael Bowen and Monica, who were his unrelenting companions till his end, were frightened at his grave condition. Next day, i.e. the first day of December (1985) was Larkin's ever last earthly day. Bowen and Monica silently sat by his bed, and when the visiting hour of the hospital was over even they left Larkin to the hopeless care of the nurse. Away from the hospital, Monica was eagerly waiting, sleeplessly and silently, by the telephone for any news of Larkin. Sunday passed by and Monday, the unfortunate Monday, the 2nd December, 1985, arrived and at 1.24 a.m. on that Monday Larkin slowly turned to the attending nurse and holding her hand, as if the hand was that of a saviour, faintly told her, "I am going to the inevitable" (*op. cit.*, 521)—and breathed his last.

The memorial service of Larkin was hold on Friday, the 6th of December, 1985, at noon, in the Westminster Abbey, which was attended, among many others, by Roger Day (Day, 4). Larkin's funeral service took place on 9 December (1985) in the church of St Mary the Virgin in Cottingham, where his sister Kitty, and Kingsley Amis and his first wife Hilly, among many others, were present. Rev. Terence Grigg, who conducted the funeral service, and Father Brown, who gave the address, "tried to reconcile Larkin's 'Anglican Agnosticism' to the Christian faith" (Motion, 523). "Bouquets of flowers were laid out in the shape of a ragged 'S' on the grass in front of the grave—there was one from Anthony and Ann Thwaite" (*loc. cit.*). This Anthony Thwaite first published all Larkin poems in 1988 in his *Philip Larkin: Collected Poems*, and in his Introduction to the book very justly dubbed Larkin as "one of the best-known poets in the English-speaking world, and one of the best loved" (Thwaite, 1988, xv). Roger Day writes: "The nation's tribute came in the form of a 'Service In Memory of Philip Larkin, CH, CBE' on Friday 14 February at noon in Westminster Abbey which I had the fortune to attend...and the Abbey was crowded not just with figures from the worlds of literature and librarianship but also with people who simply had loved his work (Charles Monteith, his publisher, was later to comment that the house of Faber had never had so many letters from 'ordinary' people on the death of one of their authors, expressing their gratitude.)" (Day, 4-5).

More than one year after Larkin's death, in March 1986, a memorial meeting of his was held at Riverside Studios, where Harold Pinter, the British dramatist who got the Nobel Prize in 2005, read 'Aubade' (Regan, 246). Before this, on 14th February (the Valentine Day), 1986, another memorial service had been arranged at Westminster Abbey, where jazz and religious music were played. Glorifications and extolments of Larkin were found in the obituaries of a spat of newspapers and journals. Even the Communist daily unexpectedly wrote about Larkin: "Best-Selling Poet Dies in Private Hospital" (Motion, 523). But the epithet that the *Evening Standard*, in its obituary, used for Larkin remains even today: the "Hermit of Hull" (*loc. cit.*). After some months, in the same year, a gravestone was erected, in which was inscribed, as ordered by Monica, the following:

Philip Larkin
1922-1985
Writer

Why 'writer' and not 'poet'? Because, as Monica insisted, Larkin was not just a poet: he "lived a *writer's* life" (Motion, 524), too.

Larkin died of cancer (in the oesophagus)—the disease that he mentioned 31 years before his death in 'Church Going' ('Pick samples for a cancer') and 23 years before his death in 'Sunny Prestatyn' ('Now *Fight Cancer* is there'). He well knew that smoking drastically cuts down longevity—perhaps also knew that smoking does this by implanting cancer in the body—as is obvious in 'Essential Beauty' ('dying smokers'), and yet he was a hard smoker. Further, he was certainly not oblivious of the fact that his father Sydney Larkin died of cancer, the disease that is promoted by smoking, and yet he was a persistent smoker as much as he was a hard drinker. Though he was always funky about death, could it be that a life-negating force was very much predominant in him, so that, all unawares, he himself was gingerly consuming himself, to reach the 'unfenced existence' ('Here') which is 'out of reach' ('Here') to the inhabitants of this earth?

Some Distinctive Aspects of the Person and Personality 2

1

Looks, Manners and Health

Larkin's physique was unsymmetrical: even while he was a child, he had a "long back and comparatively short legs" (Motion, 9), and this ungainly physical feature did not change, or did change very little, in his mature years, though his overall looks certainly altered. Andrew Motion, his official biographer, writes of his physical features and behaviour when he was reading in the third Form: "As Larkin's self-confidence grew, his manner and looks began to alter. The mole-like, fuzzy-haired child, peering apprehensively through small round glasses, was now nearly six feet tall, thin, gangling, and openly seeking attention. He grew his hair long, Brylcreeming it, parting it in the middle, combing it 'very assiduously'. He began to take an interest in painting, and enjoyed his weekly art classes, where he showed a natural ability for drawing" (*op. cit.*, 18). In his young days, Larkin "began wearing boldly patterned sports coats and grey flannel trousers and—at the weekends—flashy bow ties. His friends thought it merely turned him from looking like a swot into a natty swot" (*op. cit.*, 19). While in the school, Larkin had, as his friend said, "thick specks, Brylcreemed hair, long body, short legs" (*op. cit.*, 20). Sutton also said about Larkin that "Something about him compelled respect. He was no softy, and he had presence" (*loc. cit.*).

At St John's (College, Oxford), Larkin was "an opinionated and even flamboyant personality.... His contemporaries only had to look at him to see that he was apparently brimming with self-confidence. 'Philip [Larkin] often sported a bow tie and...green cords and a waistcoat' one remembers. 'With his large glasses, his high forehead and attractive low stutter, he was unmistakable, the sort of person who was not only witty in himself, but the cause of wit in other men.' Others recall his thick black hair flopping forward, the slouch-brimmed hat he sometimes wore, the cerise trousers he boasted were the only pair of such a colour in Oxford..., and his ostentatious pipe-smoking (later he would abandon this in favour of cigarettes, which he continued to smoke in moderation throughout his life)" (Motion, 36). "At Oxford, too, he had dressed from his first term onwards in away which most people in his college acknowledged to be 'camp'.... 'Somehow he looked more like an old man reaching back for his youth than a young blade breaking out'" (*op. cit.*, 62). His vision was weak enough, and this was the reason of his being rejected by the army. Larkin's landlady, when he was in the library of Leicester University, recalled that in 1957 when Larkin was 35, he looked "older than his years. I recall his quiet unassuming manner and slight stammer; his wit and turns of phrase; his bow ties (unusual then) and his very very slight preoccupation with thinning hair" (*op. cit.*, 149).

Impressions of some of Larkin's friends of him, while he was at Oxford, were as follows: "'a very private, rather remote and often inscrutable person' who on acquaintance turned out to have 'a good fund of mischief'" (Henry Mackle); "'Flamboyant bow ties', Piggott remembers, 'patterned sports jackets, coloured shirts, the sort of things which weren't stock in trade at the time'". Another friend recalls "pink shirts, strong white bow ties, 'reverse image' shirts and coats and equally sharp eye (no doubt encouraged by Monica) for the way others dressed too"; and "He was excellent pub company, full of anecdote and malicious gossip, and a good mimic: he did the Belfast accent to perfection" (Colin Strang) (*op. cit.*, 199). When Larkin joined the library of the University of Hull in 1955, he put up in a rented house of George and Jean Hartley's. Hartley described Larkin thus: "...repeatedly giving 'white rabbit' glances at his pocket-watch, he seemed 'a dignified gent, slim, with dark hair (receding), very formally-suited, serious and quite smiling...with his chin tucked well in he paced up and down our small living room, his tall body bowed to avoid a head-on collision with the light bulb'" (*op. cit.*, 260). Before this, when Larkin appeared before the interview board for the selection of a librarian at the University of Hull, the Chairman of the board was 'very impressed' and Ray Brett, another interviewer of Larkin, wrote this about him: "a tall, shy, serious-looking young man with thick-lensed glasses and a slight stammer" (*op. cit.*, 245). In 1976, Andrew Motion, the official biographer of Larkin, went to the University of Hull to teach English there, and there he was introduced to Larkin. Motion writes about his first impression Larkin: "he was disarmingly courteous. Taller than I had expected, heavier, dark-suited, he seemed stern but at the time amiable, withdrawn but forthright, rigorous but sometimes extravagantly funny" (*op. cit.*, xv).

Larkin was a confirmed hypochondriac—he frequently complained of mostly fictitious ailments: of the stomac, of the chest, of the throat, etc. Once being influenced by his description of pain in the stomach a doctor even suspected an ulcer in his stomach. Larkin sometimes felt giddiness, but neck ache in advanced years was real—the ache which was possibly due to narrowing of the joints in the neck and was also possibly 'indicative of pre-arthritic state'. In the 1970s, Larkin had a trouble in the nose and he had to undergo a surgical operation to remove a polyp that was the cause of that trouble. He had also trouble with his legs, which gave him much pain from time to time. Larkin was suffering from agoraphobia, a sort of mental abnormality in which one has dread of open spaces. He would also become panicked at the thought of being x-rayed. The physical handicap that gave him much trouble and a feeling of inferiority and shame was his weakness of hearing, which was aggravating with age. In 1961, Larkin suddenly "collapsed during a Library Committee meeting and was carried 'unconscious and incontinent'—by ambulance—to Kingston General Hospital. He regained consciousness as he arrived, but was detained for 'neurological investigation'" (*op. cit.*, 311). Depression was a perennial symptom of Larkin, as was his fear of dying and fear of growing cancer (perhaps because his father died of carcinoma). The last fear of his was not at all unfounded, for he died of cancer.

2

Stammer and Shyness

Whether the individual psychoanalyst Alfred Adler's theory of overcompensation, i.e. a mental patient's tendency to overcompensate his inferiority complex due to his physical or mental drawbacks is tenable in the field of literary creation we do not know for certain, but there certainly are instances of such overcompensations. To take only a few instances: Homer and Ossian were blind but they are celebrated poets; Sir Walter Scott was lame, Alphonse Daudet was almost stone deaf, James Joyce had a very poor eye-sight, and Somerset Maugham was a puzzling stutter, and yet they are great novelists; Charles Dickens had an unhappy childhood and E.M. Forster had an inferiority complex due to homosexuality, but they are popular as well as adroit novelists. Larkin, like Maugham, was a stammerer, and like Dickens had an unhappy childhood, and, as Alfred Adler would say, he overcompensated his drawbacks by becoming a celebrated poet.

Larkin was not born a stammerer, but by the "age of four he had started to stammer badly. 'It was', he said, 'on words beginning with vowels rather than consonants....' There was no obvious reason for it: no left-handedness or physical accidents. If I had some deep traumatic experience I've forgotten it. This went up to the age of thirty-five or so, after which the impediment slowly faded away, only to return when I am tired or confronted with a 'stammering situation'—post offices, for instance'" (*op. cit.*, 9). Larkin's stammer was not just a little shaming difficulty but a great handicap in communicating with others. "'Up to the age of 21', he confessed, 'I was still asking for railway tickets by pushing written notes across counter'" (Timms, 45). Larkin himself saw the aetiology of his stammer in his almost inherent and inalienable shyness and in his inordinate self-consciousness. He may have inherited his shyness from his father through imitation. "'I remember', Larkin said, 'when I was quite young, telling my father I was shy', and he said very crushingly, 'You don't know what shyness is', implying that he'd been more shy'" (*loc. cit.*). According to psychoanalysts, stammering may be caused by shyness, and inordinate self-consciousness may lead to shyness, which is but a manifestation of inferiority complex. We know of Larkin's Gasconade, particularly during his Oxford days, and his Gasconade may be the sign of his inferiority complex and shyness as well as of his unconscious or subconscious working towards over-compensating these his faults. Some of his behaviour patterns may reinforce this view of ours: he would, in his early life daydream of becoming a great novelist, and, as Andrew Motion tells us, "he was opinionated—and also proud, confident, and contemptuous of those set in authority over him" (Motion, 15).

When Larkin was above 20 years of age, his stammer began to abate. He then stammered only in public but not privately. He also to a great extent got over his unfounded shyness. Earlier, he felt uneasy in the company of girls but now he overcame it. Larkin very slyly and curiously ensconced his unmanageable shyness in the title of his poem 'Next, Please'. On the authority of Larkin's sister Kitty, Andrew Motion tells us that Larkin always felt nervous and frightened while nearing the head of a queue, because soon he would have to talk with some one stammeringly and with shyness to the satiric amusement of others about him. In the poem 'Next, Please', he says that as death approaches us we become funky, panicky, like he felt as he reached the head of a queue.

3

Pornography, Homosexuality, and Flirtation with Girls

Larkin's libido was robust and articulated even in his relatively younger age, as is evident from his diaries of those periods. He would release his pent up accumulated libidinal drive by masturbating in his young days, and filled his early diaries with masturbatory fantasies. Andrew Motion claims that many of his particularly early poems are but artistic sublimation of his sexual desires. In the poems of his maturity also we find allusions to sublimation of his sexual drive—in such poems as 'Lines on a Young Lady's Photograph Album', 'Sunny Prestatyn', 'Wild Oats', 'The Large Cool Store', etc. Andrew Motion writes about the sexuality infused in all these poems: "In all these [poems], working unseen, Larkin transforms a masturbatory impulse and an addiction to solitude into poems of great beauty and sociable truthfulness" (*op. cit.*, 234).

Larkin had much sexually driven interest in pornography, right from the onset of his adolescence. During the period of his love affairs with Patsy Strang, he used to employ the aid of pornography to heighten their sexual desires. Andrew Motion writes about Larkin's great interest in pornography (let us quote at some length): "Larkin had been keen on pornography since Oxford, when he had began to collect whatever (modest) magazines he could get his hands on. It had been the same in Washington and Leicester, where he continued to be quite open with his friends about his predilections. By the end of his life he had accumulated several large boxfuls of magazines, ranging from the innocuous-seeming items of his youth (girls standing around in their underwear) to the cruder pictures he collected later. He didn't go for 'hard core' material, and neither did he show an idiosyncratic sexual taste. What he liked was straightforward—pictures of women with no clothes on, and none of them taken too close up, so that he could see clearly what was what. Other women friends apart from Patsy realized how much he liked it. In letters to Monica, for instance, he reports on visits to pornographic films, sometimes complaining that bad dialogue is made 'only slightly better by the speakers having no clothes on'. In due course his secretary at Hull would become aware that he kept magazines in his office. Also in Hull he once showed a woman friend 'a large cupboard full of both literary and photographic pornography' and when she asked him what it was *for*, he replied (somewhat embarassed), 'to wank to, or with, or at'" (*op. cit.*, 222). Larkin's interest in pornography was accentuated and whetted when he was co-operated in this regard by Conquest who was also very interested in pornography. Conquest used to send Larkin pornographic magazines from time to time, even while he travelled abroad. Larkin's interest in pornography was quite innocuous, just sort of 'spanking', Conquest observed.

According to Andrew Motion, Larkin perhaps had a homosexual tendency, too, as may be inferred from some of his scriblings in his diaries of his school-going days—scriblings, such as "Pretty bloody actually. ANUS" and "Balls. Shit all. Cunt. Arsehole" (*op. cit.*, 30). But evidences of his gay tendency may have been borne more explicitly by his unfinished juvenile novel, 'Present Laughter', which is "the story of 'a boy who went to public school just for one summer term, but *on account of his extraordinary beauty completely and farcically wrecked the place*'" (emphasis added) (*op. cit.*, 30). That the boy was used as a catamite is sufficiently insinuated in the quote. Larkin "pursued it for 25,000 words, then immediately burnt it" (*loc. cit.*). Larkin, of course, had no clear syndromes of being gay, and yet in some of his letters to his intimate friends as well as in a few of his short stories, written in his adolescence, he had shown a little inclination towards homosexuality. Just a couple of suggestions in this direction. Andrew Motion writes: "If Larkin found girls so difficult, was it partly because he was really attracted to men? At school, by his own admission, he had 'fallen in love, with a number of his contemporaries, and at Oxford he broadcast his admiration for Julian Hall's novel *The Senior Commoner*, which deals directly as well as obliquely with its Elonian hero's 'not very romantic' feelings for a junior boy called Murray Gawthorne ('there was something altogether immodest in [his] figure'). At Oxford, too, he [Larkin] had dressed from his first term onwards in a way which most people in his college acknowledged to be 'camp', even if it didn't always have quite the authority he intended" (Motion, 62). In his short story, written in 1941, we find homosexual inclination of Patrick towards David: "After a visit from David, Patrick 'walked over to the fire and noticed the other had left nearly half of a cup of coffee on the arm of the sofa. He picked it up and drank it, putting his mouth where the other's had been'" (*op. cit.*, 63). And next we find that "David and Christopher have been snoring in each other's arms" (*loc. cit.*). There are some other homosexual scenes in that short story. However, before we try to reach any conclusion about Larkin's homosexuality, we should keep in mind the fact that in those days homosexuality was more despicable than today, and so the potential homosexuals kept their unnatural sexual tendencies strongly guarded.

Not that in his adolescence Larkin was never drawn to girls. He was, and in fact he even tried to have their company, but in spite of all his genuine efforts he failed, principally due to his insurmountable bashfulness. Even at the very immature age of five Larkin "'conceived a violent passion for a little girl named Mary'...and 'tried to make advances to her'—only to be 'violently repelled'. The embarassment lasted for years, festering in solitude" (*op. cit.*, 19). While at King's College, Oxford, Larkin frequented the English Club where most of the officers were women. There in the Club, Larkin wanted to mix with the female members but there also he failed due to his shyness and resilience. Andrew Motion writes about some of Larkin's ludicrously flopped encounters with girls at that time: "Margaret Flannery, for instance, 'edged towards him but made him gigle'. Hilary Allen of St Hilda's upset him by beating him at table tennis. Another girl, when he took her a bunch of flowers, alarmed him so much merely by opening the door to his knock that he was literally unable to speak to her; he thrust his flowers into her arms and fled. A fourth, when he tried to kiss her in a punt, told him, "I'd sooner not, thanks" (*op. cit.*, 61-62). A concatenation of such failed attempts made him aggressive and hostile towards the women folk in general, and that as well might have temporarily shown him the alternative route of homosexuality, but we are never sure.

However, one reason why Larkin failed to come close enough to girls, as we have already said, was his insurmountable bashfulness. The other obvious reason was his mother Eva's sternly keeping all girls away from the periphery of the house, and shutting the door to the outside world and keeping Larkin within the four walls, thus making him somewhat unsocial. And yet, driven by instincts, Larkin aspired after the company of girls though he would the sooner resile at the first positive response from them. Besides, in at least one known case his political sympathy or antipathy stood in his way to the closeness of girls: in the final year of his study at Oxford, Larkin found a girl, Chitra Rudingerova, a Czech member of the Labour Club, 'decidedly attractive', but he could not muster all his will round liking her because she was a communist. On the other hand, girls, too, though they found him 'proper', rejected him for mysterious causes. And this accentuated his inherent depression and doubled his natural hatred towards women as this, too, pushed him for a time towards homosexuality.

Larkin's approach-avoidance syndrome towards girls and his rudimentary homosexual tendency may be understood, perhaps even without the technical skill of the psychoanalyst, from the 95 dreams of his that he recorded in the last three terms at Oxford, when he was around 21 years of age. A few dreams from among those 95, though very briefly narrated, may give us a glimpse of the problems of Larkin with girls and of his nascent homosexual tendency. All the dreams occurred in 1942 and were recorded by Larkin the same year. On 26 October (1942), he dreamt that he entered a lavatory near the Covered Market in central Oxford. Larkin recorded this dream as follows: "I started to piss, and simultaneously a man on my left started to piss across my legitimate seclion and with a long malformed penis. This annoyed me. After a time a woman came up on my right and also started pissing, also with a penis, but normally shaped. This surprised me" (*op. cit.*, 81). Andrew Motion writes about two other dreams of Larkin (of those 95 dreams): "...dream number fourteen: 'I was trying to toss off a boy with a penis like a Turkish cigarette. I had dreamt about him before that night and thought he was a Russian.' Or a dream shortly before term ended [Larkin's last term at Oxford]: 'I seemed in the custody of four girls.... It seemed that I was going to bed with [one of them, a girl he knew slightly at Oxford]. We two went back to the first room and she lay on the floor. She was wearing a flame coloured skirt and brilliant yellow knickers. I began fucking her and she talked dreamily about copulation. After a while I stopped fucking, not feeling I was getting anywhere, and we both stood up. She maintained her indifference'" (*loc. cit.*). Larkin stopped recording his dreams in January 1943. His recording was not a matter of silliness but was due to his belief that dreams are a pylon to understanding the self (astonishing it is that he was not acquainted with Freud at that time). He said: "I can read the history of my soul in my dreams" (*loc. cit.*).

4

Sex, Love and Marriage

After he came out of Oxford, Larkin's rudimentary homosexual tendency drastically abated and he now noticeably overcame his nervousness and shyness in the ambience of women and was being titillated by heterosexual drive. At that time he readily got two women to release his heterosexual drive: Diana Gollancz (part model of Brunette Coleman) and Ruth Bowman. With the first he merely flirted but with the other he even went to bed. Andrew Motion writes about Diana and her relation with Larkin: "A year older than Larkin, and the second of the publisher Victor Gollancz's five daughters, she was 'beautiful, bright, outgoing and socially good', and relaxed enough with men to let Larkin forget his shyness. Her stories of school life amused him...as did her 'complete lack of social conscience'. She was quick but 'not academically bright', committed to her work but not pretentious, flirtatious but not threatening. In effect, she appealed to him because he could treat her as an honorary man. Yet even with her, as with all other women he knew [at that time], 'nothing happened'" (Motion, 79-80). Ruth Bowman was a school girl of sixteen when Larkin came to be acquainted with her. She was 'a prim little small town girl' and it was especially her tender age that made her all the more attractive to Larkin, so much so that he really 'fell in love' with her. Ruth happened to be a frequent borrower in the library of Wellington where Larkin served, and it was this library where their two souls were first drawn to each other. Though Ruth was a Methodist, holding high up belief in God and moral rectitude, and Larkin was an agnostic with no great sense of moral probity, they fell in a semblance of love with each other—semblance of love, because their love was more prompted by libido than by spirituality or by their hearts. Ruth was drawn to Larkin also because she felt he 'starved for company'. The two, in course of time, became physically too close to each other.

The other women with whom Larkin had sexual relationship were, approximately in the order of their entering into the life of Larkin, Monica Jones, Winifred Arnott, Patsy Strang, Maeve Brennan and Betty Mackereth. The fact that Larkin dedicated *The Less Deceived* to Monica Jones (full name: Monica Margaret Beale Jones) may speak volumes about the depth of Larkin's affection for her. The only child of her father, Monica was about three months older than he. She was a young lecturer in the English department. She was small, had fair hair, used to wear horned spectacles and dressed 'rather specially'. In the early spring of 1947, Monica first spotted Larkin in the library, and she was informed by some one that Larkin was the author of *The North Ship* (1945). This first meeting made her lean towards Larkin who found in her 'a clever, slightly flirtatious career girl', and was already drawn to her. On the other hand, what in Larkin most attracted Monica was that, as she confessed, 'he was intellectually self-assured: amusing, ironical and ambitious, and that he was 'a great novelist'. Larkin happily found Monica intellectually stimulating and light-hearted and full of jollity. Consequently, they were complementary to each other, so that mutual attraction soon grew stronger between them and remained so for seven years till 1954 when Monica suspected Larkin's affection for his old friend Ruth Bowman and for another new woman who had already made a ripple in his life—Winifred Arnott (about whom he wrote 'Latest Face' in 1951 and 'Lines on a Young Lady's Photograph Album' in 1953). But, in fact, by this time Larkin had freed his inclinations towards both Ruth and Winifred and anchored them on Monica, though, of course, his affection for Maeve Brennan, the recent plume in his love-making cap, till then lingered. Soon, Monica also came to know of Larkin's affairs with Maeve and got exasperated and demanded of him to tell her if he till then did cling to Maeve. Larkin dishonestly denied his feelings for Maeve, but, in truth, he was playing a double game.

Larkin's relationship with Winifred Arnott was the most spiritual among all his affairs with around half a dozen women, for no other reasons but for his being 'a good deal too old for her', as she thought. Winifred was born in London and studied English in Queen's College in Belfast. She was brown-haired, round-faced, and she had good looks. Winifred Arnott (later

Bradshaw) knew of Larkin's for her, and she thought that he was attracted to her particularly because she was very cheerful, and, contrarily, she found him to be gloomy and too old for her. This was why their relationship did never cross the bound of civility, though she certainly could produce a ripple in the life of Larkin, as is evinced by the two above-mentioned poems.

Maeve Brennan, like Ruth and Patsy Strang, was for a time Larkin's sexual partner, Maeve being that for the longest period and the most satisfying. Maeve was a member of the staff of library of the University of Hull, where Larkin was the librarian. The daughter of an Irish dental surgeon, she was born in 1929, which means that she was younger than Larkin by seven years. In 1960, Larkin had been coaching her for examination, and after about seven months of coaching her he became infatuated by her, so much so that he once told her that she 'reminded him of Maud Gonne [of W.B. Yeats]'. During the period in which Larkin was coaching her and was occasionally and cautiously expressing his warm affection for her in her presence, she was seeking a legal divorce from her second husband, Philip Brennan. She now got herself legally free and began to respond positively to Larkin's affection; and so much now she became a dear object to Larkin that he began privately to call her his 'Mouse' as earlier he called Ruth his 'Bun'. Maeve's Catholic morality could not contain her hunger for sexual satisfaction because she was naturally romantic and because Larkin's extreme sensuality always titillated her sexual desire—she ultimately gave in to him, mentally and physically. Afterwards, Maeve wrote about her relationship with Larkin: "Temperamentally we complemented each other. I was outgoing, lively, and made him more sociable. He deepened my spiritual side, taught me to enjoy music more deeply, to read poetry out loud; he increased my sensual pleasure in things" (*op. cit.*, 310).

Like with Maeve, Larkin also had warm and uninhibited sexual relationship with Patsy Strang (her actual name was Patricia but her friends used to call her Patsy, and her maiden name was Avis), the wife of Colin Strang (her second husband was the Irish poet Richard Murphy). Colin was the son of the distinguished diplomat Sir William (later Lord) Strang, and Patsy was the daughter of a Catholic South African diamond mining magnet. Born in 1928 (and so she was six years younger than Larkin), she read medicine at Somerville College, Oxford. She was easy-going, easily bored, glamorous, uninhibited in conversation, entertaining, generous, assertive and promiscuous. She used to spend weekends with Larkin drinking and flattering him, and this raised her up to his admiration day by day, after which she became the most intimate with him, both mentally and physically. Her husband Colin was intelligent but dry, and this was the principal reason of her relationship with her husband becoming sour. Larkin liked her husband and so did not want to disrupt the relationship between Colin and Patsy, but the inevitable led both Larkin and Patsy to its whim's way. As she was coming closer to Larkin, Patsy was gingerly divulging to him her strained relationship with her husband and her intention of divorcing him. This confession of Patsy whetted Larkin's interest in her. On the other hand, Patsy was gradually showing her interest in doing everything for Larkin so that he could concentrate on only one thing—writing. "She easily persuaded Larkin to break his vow never to get involved with a married woman; she dissolved his worries about sex" (*op. cit.*, 221). Larkin's relationship with Patsy, frankly, was dominated by sex, and their relationship was 'happily erotic', and yet to accentuate their eroticism Larkin, along with Patsy, took the aid of pornography.

Like his relationship with Ruth, Monica, Maeve and Patsy, Larkin's relationship with his secretary in the library of Hull, Betty Mackereth, was also tarnished with sexuality. Betty was tall and handsome. She had the rare quality of having in herself the 'combination of tact and directness, tolerance and strictness', and this rare quality of hers attracted Larkin's attention. In 1975, their relationship began to take the physical path, Larkin, one day, first showing her the way, as we have earlier narrated that one day's incident—Larkin's cozening of Betty while taking her and Pauline to their respective residences by car. Since that day, Betty was also leaning towards him, and though, later on, she came to know of his affairs with Monica and Maeve, she could not, or rather did not want to, rein herself in from the erotic grip of Larkin. Larkin, too, was helplessly attached to her and once even was inclined to marry her. He told her on some very intimate occasion that T.S. Eliot had married his secretary, and long afterwards she confessed that she had been "really a sort of wife to him" (*op. cit.*, 452).

But, if so much of sex with or withal a little love for various women, why did not Larkin marry? One reason of his shirking the idea of marriage he somewhat inherited from his father: his father Sydney detested women in general, having very low opinion of them, which was reflected in his not so warm relationship with his wife Eva. This is also evident in a letter of Larkin: "'I contain [within myself] both [my mother and father],' he wrote to Sutton, 'and that...is the cause of my inertia [against the idea of marriage], for in me they are constantly opposed'" (*op. cit.*, 82). Larkin's own view of the fair sex, or simply sex, was not positive, too. In a letter of 1943 to Amis, he frankly said that he did not think it prudent to waste a great amount of time and energy to get sexual pleasure with a girl for a little while, though in the same letter he quoted the following four verses of his:

> I would give all I possess
> (Money Keys wallet personal effects and articles of dress),
> To stick my tool
> Up the prettiest girl in Warwick King's High School.
>
> (*op. cit.*, 118)

Andrew Motion writes about Larkin's further frank admission to Amis about his fear of undue and huge trouble, and his feeling of non-challance, about sexual pleasure: "'The thought of going to bed with a woman', he told Amis (elsewhere), was 'so much trouble, almost as much trouble as standing for parliament'. And elsewhere again: 'The whole business of sex annoys me. As far as I can see, all women are stupid beings. What is more, marriage is a revolting institution.' In his serving pocket diaries, he twice made the same point even more bluntly. 'Sex is too good to share with anyone else', he jotted down in one, and in another: 'Re sexual intercourse: always disappointing and often repulsive, like asking someone else to blow your nose for you'" (*op. cit.*, 119). But in spite of all these, we cannot count Larkin as a misogynist or misogamist, for he showed at least twice his intention of getting married: once to Ruth and again to Maeve. In the case of Maeve, he even bought a copy of Catholic marriage service—for Maeve was a Catholic—to know of the customs and tradition of Catholic marriage service. However, perhaps throughout his life Larkin vascillated between getting married, to enjoy its bliss, and lead a life of celebacy, for fear of being incapable of adjusting himself with the quite new life—the life of a married person. But then why was he so much wary of women, of being trapped by them into marriage, even though he frequently flirted with as many as five or six women? What motive did lurk behind his chariness? The answer to this question may be found in what he wrote to his close friend (James Ballard) Sutton in January 1950: "'My relations with women are governed by a shrinking sensitivity, a morbid sense of sin, a furtive lechery', he wrote in January. 'Women don't just sit still and back you up. They want children: they like scenes: they want a chance of parading all the emotional haberdashery they are stocked with. Above all they like feeling they "own" you—or that you "own" them—a thing I hate'" (*op. cit.*, 190).

5

View of Religion

Larkin was never a believer and never did he show an interest in matters religious. His non-belief or agnosticism Larkin perhaps mostly inherited from his father, which he later on reinforced with his experiences and judgements. In this regard, Andrew Motion writes: "Ever since childhood Larkin had followed his father's advice—'Never believe in God!'—without the slightest hesitation or guilt, while at the same time retaining an interest in the value of ritual. 'I'm an agnostic I suppose', he [Larkin] habitually said to anyone who asked, 'but an Anglican agnostic of course'" (*op. cit.*, 485). Larkin's agnosticism was no hindrance to his relationship with others, or to his friendship with women. For instance, the mutual attraction between Ruth and Larkin did never sag though they nursed quite contradictory attitudes towards religion—she was a confirmed believer and he could not stand even a reference to God. Ruth said that Larkin would at times become so much as infuriated at her 'sense of the luminous'. Larkin's agnosticism, or scepticism about religion, might have been influenced or reinforced by John Layard, who had been 'a student of modern languages and then of psychiatry at Cambridge'. During his Oxford years, Larkin once attended a lecture by Layard and perhaps was moderately influenced by him. Layard declared that "the term 'God' really means our physical desires, the inner law of our own nature, and that 'the Devil' is in fact the conscious control of these desires. The only real sin, he believed, was obedience to 'God' and disobedience to 'the Devil'" (*op. cit.*, 60).

But, as generally happens, in his advanced age Larkin changed his position, or sometimes thought of changing his position, as regards his attitude towards religion. Even before that he was not always squeamish or fastidious about religion. For instance, as we have said, when for a time he decided to marry Maeve, giving in to her repeated persuasions, he bought a copy of Catholic marriage service, for Maeve was a hardened Catholic, contravening his own agnosticism. It was perhaps a fact that though he dangled and publicised his agnosticism with all pride, inwardly he nursed a doubt about just that. Andrew Motion has suggested that subconsciously Larkin might have harboured the concept of the numinous. Motion writes about Larkin: "he couldn't altogether deny the appeal to the subconscious, which he felt when listening to jazz. And since it existed in music, why not elsewhere too?" (*loc. cit.*). Howbeit, in his old age a religious sentiment took roots in him, especially being influenced by his friend A.N. Wilson, the literary editor of the *Spectator*. In 1983, under the influence of Wilson's unflinching religious conviction, Larkin, when he was 61, bought a large Oxford University Press Bible with 120 Pounds and, as he himself wrote, "set [it] up in my bedroom on a hideous office lecture to remind me of matters spiritual"

(Motion, 485). Andrew Motion writes that Larkin then "read a few pages [of the Bible] every day while shaving, beginning at the beginning and working steadily through. He also began to toy with the idea of going to church—or at least of going to the nearby St Stephen's in Hull, where the extreme Anglo-Catholic priest, Father Bown, was a friend of Wilson's" (*loc. cit.*). At last, after enough of hesitation, Larkin "attended Evensong at St Stephen's with Monica" (*loc. cit.*). But this does not mean that he became a believer, for he did never became, and yet, as he confessed, he was "much impressed" by the Congregation at St Stephen's on that occasion and "really quite enjoyed it" (*loc. cit.*).

Whether Larkin had any time believed in religion or no is a different question, but it is a fact that, like his father, and as his father advised him, he believed in the importance of the rituals and he has expressed this belief of his in his poem 'Church Going'. In 'Church Going', he predicts that the traditional functions and rituals, even if they be superstitious must never die out, because these are the cementing forces of society and so they 'never can be obsolete'. Further, in his poem 'Solar', as Roger Day suggests, religious adumbration is obvious. Here the sun is described as a pagan anthropomorphic god, Roger Day means to say. He refers us to the three expressions in the poem—'You pour *unrecompensed*', 'like *angels*' and 'You give *for ever*' (emphases mine)—and writes: "These connotations raise, for me, the question whether Larkin is in any sense (intentionally or otherwise) 'religious'. It was a notion he always resisted; but could one not describe 'Solar' as religious in the sense of acknowledging dependence on something external to the self?" (Day, 77).

6

Political Views

Like his attitude towards religion, Larkin's political views were also mostly informed by his father's sympathy towards right-wing politics, though Larkin was not interested in politics as his father had been. His father Sydney had been a radical right-winger, showing respect even to such political radicals as

Herr Hilter. Sydney's political views bordered on fascism. Sydney was an ardent admirer of anything German and nursed a hidden sympathy for the Nazi. Larkin did not blindly and completely subscribe to his father's political views, but, of course, his father's political views greatly informed his right-wing political position. Even while in school, Larkin showed his antipathy towards left-wing political thoughts, particularly towards Marxism: "he had affected an interest in politics—briefly forming with Sutton and Antrobus a facetious anti-Marxist trinity, supporting Franco's cause in the Spanish Civil War" (Motion, 27). Though he had never a well-considered political view he somehow maintained a right-wing political view. Once he confessed: "I've always been right-wing. It's difficult to say why, but not being a political thinker I suppose I identify the Right with certain virtues and the Left with certain vices" (Swarbrick, 1995, 141). Nevertheless, Larkin had once in his young age a transitory interest in left-wing politics. Being attracted to Auden's style of poetry, he was also indirectly influenced by Auden's left-wing political sympathy.

Barring that short left-wing spell, we may say that Larkin was an unwavering right-winger in politics. His national feeling was of the highest order. He openly supported British policy of colonialism, as is, for instance, obvious in his ironical poem 'Homage to a Government', where he bitterly criticised the Harold Wilson government's effeminate policy of withdrawing its troops from its base in Aden on economic reasons, thereby losing its authority over the Suez Canal:

> Next year we shall be living in a country
> That brought its soldiers home for lack of money.

Andrew Swarbrick writes about the intended import of the poem: "I lament the closure of a British colonial base in Aden (now in the Republic of Yemen) for economic reasons and condemns the decision as an index of Britain's imperial decline and moral corruption" (Swarbrick, 1995, 140).

Though his political views were cloudy, and though he tried to keep himself miles away from the national political mud-slingings, Larkin sometimes dabbled in politicking, in spite of himself and in spite of his only avowed vocation of poetry. For instance, for some years beginning with 1968, he persistently criticised the left-wing Labour Party when its member Harold Wilson became the Prime Minister. Andrew Motion writes: "Larkin...admitted, 'I don't know anything at all about anything [political] and it's no use pretending I do.' Yet ever since Harold Wilson's Labour government had been elected in 1964, the same year as *The Whitsun Weddings* came out, and especially since 1968, he had aired his political prejudices more and more freely. To colleagues on campus like John Kenyon, or in letters to friends like Monica, Amis, Conquest and Pym, he regularly complained about socialist policies and proposals, repudiating anything that challenged his 'true blue' beliefs" (Motion, 388). But, as he was growing old, Larkin was gradually coming away from even whatever little politicking he used to sometimes dabble in, and yet his prejudiced but strong reactionery political inclination he continued to privately harbour. His political views were never well-considered—they were mostly just his fads.

7

Some Other Minor Aspects of Larkin's Personality

In his young age, Larkin was, so to say, a fanatical cinema-goer and an eager listener of jazz. He would sometimes enjoy cycling into the country and looking at the churches ('Church Going') and playing 'spin-cricket, crossword puzzles and marbles'. In the school, he looked extrovert: he joined the school debating society and the play-reading group, wrote regular letters to the school magazine, and participated in the annual school plays (backstage). He was a voracious reader just from his school days. Xenophobia was an especial trait of his personality, that he acquired from his first visit to Germany. As we have already narrated, in Germany he was riding a bus when the driver asked him how he felt there in Germany. Failing to understand the driver's question in German, the embarrassed boy simply said 'No'. From that moment the miffed driver kept his silence till the end, and this made Larkin feel humiliated.

This was perhaps the origin of his xenophobia. Larkin was a misogynist, like his father, and was never at all fond of children.

Though he was resilient, Larkin was always ambitious. At the time of their coming closer to each other, Monica clearly noticed this: "'He wanted to be a great man', she realized, 'and most of all a great novelist; he would sit around thinking about it'" (Motion, 169). But his ambition would have sometimes been toned down by his philosophical conclusion about life—that life is subject to the tyranny of chance. This realization of his came particularly from the fact that he came by the post of librarian at Wellington as "a matter of chance rather than decision" (Swarbrick, 1986, 2) and that he could never change his profession of librarian ever since he joined the library of Wellington in over forty years. So, he thought, chance guided our lives and nothing else. Not only did he think but, as Andrew Swarbrick writes, "in his poems Larkin frequently comments on the tyranny of chance in our lives" (*loc. cit.*). This sounds philosophical, and so we may legitimately ask: did Larkin have a philosophy? The answer must be in the negative, for he was intolerant of ideas. He was a snobbish man. We have no certain knowledge about Larkin's love of animals but we definitely know that he could not stand cruelty done to animals, so much so that if the cruelty happened to be unbearable to animals, he would fly into a rage and sometimes would even develop paroxysm. Larkin was 'tremendously sensitive', highly opinionated and impressionable. He was naturally withdrawn and gloomy, inwardly, but outwardly he would put up a shiny face, a jacose manner with all modesty, and a sharp appearance. He would sometimes entertain friends or make a heavy situation light by his rare quality of ventriloquy and mimicry. He 'could mimic almost any accent'.

In his advanced age, say in the later part of 1970s and in the early part of 1980s (before his death in 1985), Larkin naturally changed a great deal both physically and mentally, though the quintessence of the person Larkin remained in him all the same, vibrant and charming. Andrew Motion draws a picture of the Larkin of that period when his physique was deteriorating noticeably: "Anyone meeting Larkin day by day in the University [of Hull] might easily not have noticed this deterioration. The tall heavy figure, slightly stooped, sometimes cupping an ear with one hand, was invariably courteous even if he seemed withdrawn. He would make sad or savage asides, but deliver them with such pleasure that it was hard to take them wholly seriously. There would be sighs and shrugs and despairing flaps of the hand, but these could reasonably be seen as the gestures of a man playing a part. Besides, the conversations they decorated were often extremely funny—loaded with vulgar deprecations, attacks on other writers, flights of ironical fancy. Occasionally he would lash out at the incompetence of colleagues.... More usually he was austere but accommodating—a popular boss in the library" (Motion, 448).

Larkin's Works

3

Larkin's writing career began, in a sense, with his making entries in diaries. Since his senior years in the school—which means around 1936-37—he developed the habit of keeping diaries, a habit very rarely to be found in boys of that tender age. From the diaries he wrote in during the period in which he was in King Henry VIII School it is clear that even at that young age he habitually "wrote ceaselessly" (Motion, 29). Andrew Motion, in his *Philip Larkin: A Writer's Life*, gives us an account of Larkin's childlike literary exercises of those days: "The 'earliest pieces' were 'little sketches and short stories written around real people' (his dentist, for instance). Then came an abstract for a play about revolutionary schoolboys called 'With Shining Morning Face'. Then came several diatribes against various things, such as education and Christianity (though his agnosticism did not prevent him from also writing a verse drama for Holy Week in 1939, called 'Behind the Facade'). Then came 'the most important rigmarole called *Death Underwater*, complete with a Chinese detective who solved the mystery in the last chapter'. This was Larkin's ever first attempt at novel writing. The outcome was just a prolix and incoherent discourse without any well-organised story let alone appreciably developed characters, and yet let us call *Death Underwater* his first novel. This was soon followed by *Death in Swingham* which was 'nearly a full-length novel, and was about a great saxophonist who is poisoned'" (*loc. cit.*), and let us call it Larkin's second novel.

Roger Day says that Larkin's first writing was a required writing and from that began his writing career. Day writes about Larkin: "He began to write at about the age of sixteen and recalls that 'the first poem I ever wrote was set for homework [while at school]. We had to write one, about anything. We were all absolutely baffled and consternation reigned. What started as a task soon became a form of hobby for he began to write 'ceaselessly...new verse, which I sewed up into little books, now prose, a thousand words a night after homework'" (Day, 1). In the summer of 1938, he was spewing series of poems which were about the sky, trees, seasons, etc., and most of them were full of erotic impulses and strong feelings. The poems of this period were influenced by Keats and Aldous Huxley. In the December of the same year, Larkin wrote the poem 'Winter Nocturne' which was published in *The Coventrian* in the same month, and is now to be found in his *Collected Poems*, edited by Anthony Thwaite and published by Faber and Faber in 1988. This poem is now generally taken to be Larkin's ever first published poem. Andrew Motion claims that Larkin had many unpublished (even today unpublished) poems, amongst which 'Butterflies', which was written in 1939, is one. In any sense, the poem is not ordinary or unenjoyable, and it certainly contained a promise for Larkin, like his some other unpublished early poems.

Soon after finishing his first nearly full-length novel *Death in Swingham*, Larkin began writing another novel, while he was still in the school, on the story of "a boy who went to public school just for the one summer term, but on account of his extraordinary beauty completely and farcically wrecked the place" (Motion, 30). Larkin wanted to entitle the novel as *Present Laughter*, "pursued it for 25,000 words, then immediately burnt it" (*loc. cit.*), perhaps shamefacedly, because the novel was going to be blatantly homosexual. This was his third novel. Not long after burning the draft of his third novel, Larkin began to turn out poems after poems, as if with a vengeance.

In 1940, Larkin got admitted at St John's College, Oxford, and while he was studying English there, he was also producing a spat of poems and writing his fourth novel (unentitled). Andrew Motion writes about the fourth novel of the puerile writer that Larkin was while at St John's: "The boy who had been merely 'good at English' was on his way to being exceptional.... The fantasist who 'got to work upon...dreary school life' was turning into a fastidious craftsman, drafting yet another novel. 'It is planned for 100,000 words to be cut down considerably and is very advanced and modern', he [Larkin] announced to Sutton. 'I shall try to have it published by the Hogarth Press but probably I shall outgrow it quickly. Broadly speaking it is my fourth novel.' He was eighteen" (Motion, 32). Larkin also began a free-verse drama, called 'The Ships at Mylae', that was just two pages long. By 1942, he made seven collections of poems, some of the poems being Eliotic and some Audenesque. Two of the collections were called simply *Poems* (each one) and the five others were called *Seven Poems*, *The Village of the Heart*, *Further Poems*, *Nine O'Clock Jump* and *The Seventh Collection*. Larkin then collocated his other writings—poems, fragmentary plays, short stories and essays—and made a bonfire of them all. Later on Larkin made very derogatory remarks about the poems of these collections, but nevertheless the persistent themes of these poems continued to be the major themes of the poems of his maturity as well. For instance, the ideas and images of 'Ultimatum' that he wrote in 1940 were repeated in his important later poems. The 'ship' in the third line of 'Ultimatum' appears, e.g. in 'The North Ship', 'Next, Please' and 'Poetry of Departures'. Further, Larkin's themes of his mature period well appeared long before in his early poems—the themes of isolation, escape, evanescence and choice.

We have said that Larkin burnt his short stories, but a short story that he wrote between January and July 1941 somehow survived. The story is obviously homosexual—it hinges around three gay youths, Patrick, David and Christopher Warner (the last name is also employed in Larkin's novel *Jill*). The story is somewhat like this. The three Oxford college friends chatter in the college about homosexual matters. One day, "After a visit from David, Patrick 'walked over to the fire and noticed the other had left nearly half a cup of coffee on the arm of the sofa. He picked it up and drank it, putting his mouth where the other's had been. It was almost cold.' "The following evening, attention switches from Patrick to David. It turns out that he is keen on a girl called Elizabeth (another name re-used in *Jill*), whom he takes to a rowdy party given by Jack Tranter. There's a 'forest of bottles and glasses; on the floor beneath these were several crates of beer, and next to it was a large barrel'. Not surprisingly, everyone gets drunk; the party ends with some of the undergraduates throwing darts at photographs of naked girls, then brawling with each other. When David comes to his senses he discovers that he's in bed with Christopher. He can't remember how he got there, hastily climbs out, is sick in the grate, accidentally sets fire to a cushion and a book, then leaves his rooms in pursuit of more drink. He immediately bumps into Patrick, who becomes the focus of Larkin's interest for the final pages of the story. Incoherent, bleary, haggard with guilt, Patrick (we are left to assume, but are not told) has been with another man—presumably 'Vivian', who has been sometimes mentioned but never seen—while David and Christopher have been snoring in each other's arms" (*op. cit.*, 63). Not long after finishing this story Larkin wrote yet another homosexual story. This fragmentary story is woven around seven Oxford undergraduates who call themselves 'The Seven'. These two short stories, by the bye, clearly point to Larkin's homosexual leaning, though for a short period during his Oxford years.

Till 1941 or 1942, Larkin as a young writer was moving along the influences of Keats, Aldous Huxley and Auden, leaving the influence of one behind and taking up that of the other, but after that the style of W.B. Yeats fascinated him the most. During this time, he wrote a lesbian story 'I Would Do Anything For You' about two beautiful women. In 1942 Larkin's rate of literary production was greatly accelerated. "Within a matter of months he had produced two novels (one of 143 typed pages called *Trouble at Willow Gables* and one of exactly the same number of handwritten pages called *Michaelmas Term at St Bride's*), a 'sheaf' of six poems (*Sugar and Spice*), and a fragment of autobiography. All were finished by the following October, all were written under the pseudonym Brunette Coleman (The name seems to have been adapted from a jazz band of the period—Blanche Coleman and her Girls' Band.)" (*op. cit.*, 86). When these were completed, Larkin began the queer thing: Brunette Coleman's autobiography, *Antemeridian.* In *Antemeridian* "Brunette reveals herself to be the daughter of an eccentric Cornish priest, who during her childhood on the coast had acquired a large number of seaside memories. (Some of these weirdly anticipate Larkin's later poems 'Absences' and 'Livings II': 'the spray flies twenty feet into the air and the rocks are submerged by a swell of white foam'.) After a mere nine pages, the account stumbles to a halt, closing with a would-be comic set piece describing drunken lifeboatmen, wrecks, and people skidding on fish-heads. Evidently the failure of this scene was reason enough for Larkin to want to abandon the autobiography. Evidently, too, the idea of starting Brunette's first novel [*Trouble at Willow Gables*] was proving irresistible" (*op. cit.*, 87).

Larkin's first assay in dramatic writing may be said to begin with his free-verse drama, 'The Ships at Mylae', which we have already mentioned. It was followed by a Shavian dialogue, 'The Unfinished Marriage: A Dramatic Situation', which he wrote about 1943. In it "Dick and Sally are marooned on their honeymoon in a remote house after a motoring accident. (The dialogue is unpublished but preserved among Larkin's papers.) In their isolation, the couple experience a rapid time acceleration, during which they glimpse the practical demands of their married life to come. We watch Dick trying to get money off his father, applying to his old school for a teaching job, and eventually (with Sally pregnant) settling in an office. Dick's death swiftly follows" (*op. cit.*, 82). 'The Unfinished Marriage: A Dramatic Situation' may be called Larkin's second dramatic production. After a silence for seven years about dramatic writing, in 1950, after he published one collection of poems and two novels—*The North Ship* (1945), *Jill* (1946) and *A Girl in Winter* (1947)—, Larkin wrote his third dramatic venture, a twelve-page play called *Round the Point.* "It is not so much a drama as a Shavian dialogue—between Geraint (whom we first meet teering up a novel he has written) and Miller (a poet who enters singing his latest poem: a version of 'Fiction and the

Reading Public'). In the conversation which follows, Geraint reproduces Larkin's own difficulties as a novelist: 'My energies are...free to devote to whatever I want. But NOTHING HAPPENS. Why not? I've done it once. Why can't I do it again? Five years: the difference between 23 and 28, between success and failure, creation and stagnation, sanity and despair.' Miller, seeking to counter this, argues that 'the race is not for the swift, nor the battle for the strong'. This precipitates the main argument of the play, which concerns the relationship between the man who suffers and the man who creates. Geraint reckons they're one and the same. Miller disagrees" (*op. cit.*, 190-91).

Round the Point was followed by its sequel, again the Shavian dialogue—*Round Another Point*. Unlike its predecessor *Round the Point*, whose theme was literary creation, *Round Another Point* is about sex. The key characters of the two dramatic pieces are the same duo—Geraint and Miller. Quashing aside love and marriage as troublesome avenues for sex, Geraint proposes free sex clubs for willing and uninhibited partners of opposite sexes. Miller cannot squarely retort. He only tells Geraint that his sex is selfish, vulgar, subhuman, mechanical pleasure. Geraint agrees with him, and adds that "so long as sex is geared to the conventions of the pre-contraception age I can have no part of it, lacking both the deceitful insensitivity necessary for promiscuous fornication and the brutish insensitivity necessary for marriage" (*op. cit.*, 207-08).

For three years after coming out of Oxford and unsuccessfully trying for Civil Service, Larkin was writing full steam. "'As far as my writing was concerned', he said later, 'leaving Oxford was like taking a cork out of a bottle. Writing flooded out of me'" (*op. cit.*, 106). It was during this time that Larkin wrote his first completed, published and successful novel *Jill* (Fortune Press, 1946). Next year, another completed and successful novel of his was published (Faber): *A Girl in Winter*. We shall discuss about these two novels in the next chapter. We may recall that before *Jill* Larkin had written as many as six fragmentary novels, beginning with *Death Underwater*, and so *Jill* was his seventh novel and *A Girl in Winter* his eighth. Of the eight novels, as we have said, *Jill* and *A Girl in Winter* are Larkin's only two completed and published novels, the others being fragmentary and unpublished. In August 1947, Larkin began yet another novel (he counted it his third novel, but we may take it to be his ninth)—*A New World Symphony*. He began writing it twice and twice he put it aside; then he took it up for writing for the third time but before long abandoned it for ever fragmentary. The story of this novel revolves round its hero Sam's dilemma about his getting married. We shall also briefly discuss this novel in the next chapter. Roger Day writes that "There were plans, too, for a fourth [according to us his tenth] novel which was to be a saga involving many people's lives" (Day, 2).

We have already said that by 1942, Larkin made seven 'collections' of poems but did not publish any one of them. The seven collections were: *Poems*, *Poems* (again), *Seven Poems*, *The Village of the Heart*, *Further Poems*, *Nine O'Clock Jump* and *The Seventh Collection*. These seven collections were soon followed by another unpublished collection, *Sugar and Spice*, the eighth collection. In 1945, came out of Fortune Press Larkin's first published collection of poems entitled *The North Ship* (it contained 31 poems). When in 1966, the second edition of *The North Ship* was published by Faber, the collection included one further poem from *XX Poems*: 'Waiting for Breakfast'. The 32 poems of *The North Ship* are the following (in the order in which the poems were published):

All catches alight
This was your place of birth
Dawn
Conscript
Kick up the fire
The horns of the morning
Winter
Climbing the hill within the deafening wind
Within the dream you said
Night Music
Like the train's beat
I put my mouth

Nursery Tale
The Dancer
The bottle is drunk out by one
To write one song, I said
If grief could burn out
Ugly Sister
I see a girl dragged by the wrists
I dreamed of an out-thrust arm of land
One man walking a deserted platform
If hands could free you, heart
Love, we must part now: do not let it be
Morning has spread again
This is the first thing
Heaviest of flowers, the head
Is it for now or for always
Pour away that youth
So through that unripe day you bore your head
The North Ship
Waiting for breakfast (*added to the first Faber edition, September 1966*)

In *The North Ship*, W.B. Yeats's and Vernon Watkins's (1906-67) influences are obvious: Yeats's manner, attitude and lyricism and Watkins's transcendentalism. The title poem 'The North Ship' presents us with a signature of the general emotion and import of the collection. The 'north ship' proceeds towards north negotiating a perilous and cold sea under 'a fire-spilling star' and ultimately reaches 80 degree north, when the 'drunken boatswain' sings: 'A woman has ten claws'. This myth narrated through the sequence of five poems is that 'The North Ship' symbolises Larkin's sexual dilemma. Andrew Swarbrick writes: "The poem's dreamy evocation of remote coldness merging with sexual fear suggests how Larkin used the Yeatsian model as a way of externalising and mythologising his own psychology" (Swarbrick, 1995, 25). Besides the influences of Yeats and Watkins, one can find in *The North Ship* the influences of Auden and Dylan Thomas as well, though these influences are marginal. However, evaluating *The North Ship*, David Timms writes: "The poems in *The North Ship* are juvenalia, and will not bear the very close critical reading that is appropriate to Larkin's mature work; but as one reviewer remarked on the publication of the second edition [of *The North Ship* in 1966], 'the juvenalia of the best poets are always worth reading'. Besides, set against *The North Ship*, the virtues of *The Less Deceived* and *The Whitsun Weddings* may be seen more closely" (Timms, 22). Andrew Motion agrees with Timms in saying that *The North Ship* "could safely be regarded as juvenalia" (Motion, 172).

Larkin's project of publishing another collection of poems, to be entitled *In the Grip of Light*, aborted—it could not get published. Larkin had sent the typescript of *The North Ship* to the press in 1944 (it was published in the next year) and since then was contemplating publishing another collection of poems. "By the end of 1947 he was ready: he selected twenty-four poems written since *The North Ship* and began typing them out to send to Alan Pingle at Faber under the title *In the Grip of Light*" (Motion, 172). Unfortunately for Larkin, "On 3 February [1948] he heard from Alan Pringle (via his agent Peter Watt) that Faber had decided against publishing *In the Grip of Light*" (*op. cit.*, 174). The twenty-four poems of the collection were as follows (in the order as arranged by Larkin):

> 'The wind blew all my wedding-day'
> 'Heaviest of flowers, the head'
> Plymouth: 'A box of teak, a box of sandalwood'
> 'At the chiming of light upon sleep'
> 'Who whistled for the wind, that it should break'
> 'Come then to prayers'
> 'Coming at last to night's most thankful springs'
> 'Lift through the breaking day'
> 'Past days of gales'
> 'I put my mouth'
> The quiet one: 'Her hands intend no harm'
> Getaway: 'One man walking a deserted platform'
> 'Many famous feet have trod'
> Night-Music: 'At one the wind rose'
> To a Very Slow Air: 'The golden sheep are feeding, and'
> Traumerei: 'In this dream that dogs me I am part'

'Within the dream, you said'
'Some must employ the scythe'
Winter: 'In the field, two horses'
Deep Analysis: 'I am a woman lying on a leaf'
Thaw: 'Tiny mortal streams are on the move'
Dying day: 'There is an evening coming in'
Two Guitar Pieces: I 'The tin-roofed shack by the railroad'
II 'I roll a cigarette, and light'
'And the wave sings because it is moving'

Why *In the Grip of Light* was rejected by Faber we do not know, but it should not be presumed that its low poetic quality was responsible for the rejection, for nine poems of the collection were later on published in *XX Poems* and *The Less Deceived* or were earlier published in *The North Ship*, as shown below:

XX Poems: 'The wind blew all my wedding-day'
'Some must employ the scythe'
Dying day: 'There is an evening coming in'

The Less Deceived: 'The wind blew all my wedding-day'
Dying day: 'There is an evening coming in'

The North Ship: 'Heaviest of flowers, the head'
'I put my mouth'
Getaway: 'One man walking a deserted platform'
Night-Music: 'At one the wind rose'
'Within the dream, you said'
Winter: 'In the field, two horses'

In April 1951—and by this time his only two completed and published novels, *Jill* (1946) and *A Girl in Winter* (1947) established him as a novelist—Larkin privately published a collection of 20 poems under the title *XX Poems*, while he was in Northern Ireland. He "sent copies off to leading critics but it was mostly ignored, possibly because, as he admits, he had failed to put stamps of the right value on the envelopes but, more probably, because the predominant style of the poems was not yet then acceptable" (Day, 3). *XX Poems* contains the following poems, thirteen of which—which are asterisked—were later on included in *The Less Deceived* with the titles shown in the brackets.

* Wedding-wind: 'The wind blew all my wedding-day' (Wedding-Wind)
Modesties: 'Words as plain as hen-birds' wings'
* 'Always too eager for the future, we' (Next, Please)
* 'Even so distant, I can taste the grief' (Deceptions)
* 'Latest face, so effortless' (Latest Face)
Arrival: 'Morning, a glass door, flashes'
'Since the majority of me'
* Spring: 'Green-shadowed people sit, or walk in rings' (Spring)
'Waiting for breakfast, while she brushed her hair'
Two portraits of sex. I Oils: 'Sun. Tree. Beginning. God in a thicket.' (Crown)
* II Etching: 'Endless, time-honoured irritant' (Dry-Point)
* 'On longer evenings' (Coming)
* 'Since we agreed to let the road between us' (No Road)
* 'If my darling were once to decide' (If, My Darling)
'Who called love conquering'
* 'The widest prairies have electric fences' (Wires)
The dedicated: 'Some must employ the scythe'
* Wants: 'Beyond all this, the wish to be alone' (Wants)
* 'There is an evening coming in' (Going)
* At grass: 'The eye can hardly pick them out' (At Grass)

Larkin's next poetic venture was *The Fantasy Poets No. 21* published in March 1954. The Fantasy Press was issuing pamphlets containing poems by undergraduates or recent graduates of Oxford since 1952. Responding to the invitation of George MacBeth and Oscar Mellor, editors of the Fantasy Press, Larkin sent five poems, which were published as a pamphlet (no. 21) in March 1954. This is *The Fantasy Poets No. 21*. It contains the following five poems, all of which reappeared next year in *The Less Deceived* (the two, asterisked, earlier appeared in *XX Poems*).

Lines on a Young Lady's Photograph Album: 'A last yielded up the album, which'

Whatever Happened?: 'At once whatever happened starts receding'
* If, My Darling: 'If my darling were once to decide'
Arrivals, Departures: 'This town has docks where channel boats Come sliding'
* At Grass: 'The eye can hardly pick them out'

However, the 85 poems for which Larkin is now so famous were published in three collections of poems after *The Fantasy Poets No. 21*: *The Less Deceived*, published by the Marvell Press in November 1955, containing 29 poems; *The Whitsun Weddings*, published by Faber in February 1964, containing 32 poems; and *High Windows*, published by Faber in June 1974, containing 24 poems. We shall discuss about these three collections in three later chapters wholly devoted to them.

After 1974, when he was merely 52, Larkin published no collection of poems—as also did he neither write nor, so, publish any novel or dramatic piece—but he continued to turn out poems, gingerly though, and publish them in different journals or magazines, such as *Poetry Book Society Supplement*, *Times Literary Supplement*, *Humberside*, *Observer*, *Poetry Review*, etc. Some of the famous poems he wrote after *High Windows* i.e. after 1974 are: 'The Life with a Hole in it' (1974), 'Aubade' (1977), 'The Winter Palace' (1978), 'Love Again' (1979), 'Long Lion Days' (1982) and his supposedly last poem 'Party Politics' (1984). In 1988, the Marvell Press published all the 250 collected poems (or 242, if we do not count the relatively independent 'Parts' of some of the poems, but only their titles—'Two Guitar Pieces' has 2 'Parts', 'Two Portraits of Sex' has 2 'Parts', 'Livings' has 3 'Parts', and 'The North Ship' has 5 'Parts') of Larkin, edited by Anthony Thwaite, with the title *Philip Larkin: Collected Poems*.

We have said that since his Oxford days, Larkin was enormously drawn to jazz and wrote a regular column on jazz records from 1961 to 1971 for *The Daily Telegraph*. Jazz is a form of music that began in the United States about 1900. It was originally played by Negroes of New Orleans, the leading centre of the music. Jazz has much in common with African music, especially rhythm. Much of jazz is improvised, i.e. much of it is not written but a musician goes on inventing tunes and rhythms as he continues playing on his instrument. "Jazz developed from *work songs*, *spirituals* (religious folk songs), and *blues* (songs about everyday life, often sad), as well as European popular music. The instruments are often played with a tone and expression that imitate the human voice. A traditional jazz band usually includes a trumpet, a clarinet, and a trombone, that play the melody and improvise together, and a banjo, a double bass and drums—the *rhythm section*, which provides the beat. A typical *modern* jazz group may use trumpet, saxophone, piano, double bass, and drums. The musicians take *soles* when each in turn is the main improviser. Jazz has influenced dance music, popular songs, and some modern classical music. The leading centre of jazz in the early 1900s was New Orleans where Louis Armstrong, and other well-known jazz musicians were born" (Goode, 819-20).

Jazz "was first played on battered, secondhand instruments discarded by marching and military bands. The musicians were self-taught, though some were trained in traditional methods. Jazz was orig. [originally] played for the entertainment of and to express the feelings of the musicians and their friends, at parties and dances...the music began to absorb more elements of white American music.... In Chicago,...many young white musicians heard and imitated the Negro players, and the first important school of white jazz emerged.... With the attraction of radio, recordings, and more cities to play in, more and bigger bands were formed.... Styles changed, the small New Orleans group (...) gave way to the larger group playing written arrangements, and in the 1930s the style known as 'swing' became predominant.... The latest developments, perh. [perhaps] most appealing to the modern ear, are bop and cool jazz, or progressive jazz.... Bop is known for its long, breathless series of notes often in high registers and for quick changes in key and tempo; unusual rhythms, ..., are used. Cool jazz orig. [originated] on the West Coast c1950 and took much of its impetus from the work of modern classical composers. The music is known for its close, intricate harmonies, its improvisations..., etc." (Goode, 185-86).

In 1970, Faber published a collection of Larkin's critical articles on jazz entitled *All What Jazz: A Record Diary 1961-68*. What Larkin wrote in the Introduction to this book tells us much about his great interest in jazz: "Larkin begins the Introduction by sketching his jazz education. He tells us we should only believe what we can prove on our pulses, then illustrates the point by telling us how he listened to the 'hot' numbers on the wireless in the 1930s, went to performances of dance music at the Hippodrome in Coventry, cherished an ambition to be a drummer, made jazz at Oxford 'part of the private joke of existence', suffered a painful separation from his records in Wellington, then was united with them in Dixon Drive, and confirmed his attention to jazz at the Plaza in Belfast before reaching Pearson Park. As Larkin recounts these things he affirms one priceless fact: jazz have given him 'more pleasure in life' than anything else because it has offered him a 'unique private excitement'" (Motion, 396-97). It was in this Introduction that Larkin first articulated his 'teasingly polemical anti-modernist' literary and aesthetic stance, and in it also perhaps he obliquely affirmed his pleasure-principle of poetry.

Larkin wrote, being commissioned, only one cantata, 'Bridge for the Living' (the title was not chosen by him but by those who commissioned him), for the occasion of the opening of the Humber Bridge (on the river Humber near Hull). The forty-line poem (ten stanzas of four lines each) was dated December 1975, was composed for cantata by Anthony Hedges, and was first performed at the City Hall in Hull on 11 April 1981. In the Christmas of 1981, the poem was printed in *Poetry Book Society Supplement*. Cantata was "originally the name applied to a sort of musical narrative by one person, accompanied by a single instrument; subsequently an air was introduced—the modern concert-aria: now also a choral work, a short oratorio or opera intended for concert performance only" (*Chambers Twentieth Century Dictionary*, 1981, entry: 'cantata'). After setting Larkin's poem 'A Bridge for the Living' to music, the composer Hedges entitled the cantata as 'A Humberside Cantata'.

In 1978, the Sycamore Press, Oxford, issued a broadsheet (a sheet of paper printed on one side only) containing a single poem of Larkin—'Femmes Damnees'—under the rubric: 'Femmes Damnees. Sycamore Broadsheet No. 27'. The poem was written in 1943 and thirty-five years after it was first published in the broadsheet. The poem may suggest Larkin's debt to the French Symbolist writers, but he consistently denied any such debt. In 1983, i.e. two years before his death, Faber published Larkin's *Required Writing: Miscellaneous Pieces 1955-1982*. The idea of such a book was first mooted by Anthony Thwaite in 1974, and then by Blake Morrison in the 1980. When Charles Monteith of the Faber agreed to publish such a book, Larkin, with the help of his secretary Betty Mackereth's constant help, began orderly arranging a selection of his prose writings from 'press cuttings' and thus emerged the manuscript of *Required Writing*. *Required Writing* includes many very important articles, Introductions, essays, reviews, other prose pieces and interviews of Larkin, such as the Introduction to *Jill*, 'The Pleasure Principle', Introduction to *All What Jazz*, his interviews with *Observer* and the *Paris Review*, etc. In 1988, The Marvell Press published Larkin's *Collected Poems*, edited by Anthony Thwaite and in 1992, Faber and Faber published *Selected Letters of Philip Larkin 1940-85*, edited by Anthony Thwaite. Andrew Swarbrick writes about the *Selected Letters*: "The publication of Larkin's *Selected Letters* in 1992 met with widespread consternation. The volume was accused of revealing an intemperate, foul-mouthed misogynist and racist bigot whose 'gouts of bile' (as Larkin himself admitted) passed for political opinion" (Swarbrick, 1995, 7). However, this account of Larkin's works is certainly not complete, some of his prose works are of course remaining outside this inventory though the important ones are perhaps not left out, but none can at all at any time guarantee exhaustivity.

Larkin: The Novelist

4

To only a very small minority of readers of Larkin is he now known as a novelist as well as a poet, because his fame as a poet has almost fully overshadowed his early and inchoate renown as a novelist. In his young days—to be precise, while he was at Oxford—he had two fond wishes: to be a great writer and, when he was irreversibly attracted to jazz, to be a drummer. Since his school days, Larkin was trying his hand at all the various genres of literature—poetry, novel, drama, essay and autobiography, but, curiously, never in his early years did he so much want to be a poet as a novelist. Monica could well have an insight into the secret corner of his mind during his early manhood. She once wrote to Andrew Motion about Larkin's wish to be a novelist: "'He wanted to be a great man,' she realized, 'and most of all a great novelist; he would sit around thinking about it'" (Motion, 169). Long afterwards, to provide a booster to the publicity for the sale of his second published novel *A Girl in Winter*, Larkin wrote to Alan Pringle of Faber on 4 March 1947: "The writing of novels has always been my ultimate ambition, and, if I can say so without pomposity, few days pass when I don't realize afresh how much it is my chief pleasure, task and—almost—debt. I only wish I had done more and done it better" (*op. cit.*, 160). Not only that but Larkin had done a long exercise at writing fictions before his first finished, published and successful novel *Jill* was produced. Before *Jill*, he was writing as many as six novels but all of them he left on the way. These six fragmentary novels, as we have cited in chapter 3, are *Death Underwater*, *Death in Swingham*, *Present Laughter*, an untitled novel, *Troubles at Willow Gables* and *Michaelmas Term at St Brides*. So much of desire to be a great novelist and so much of exercise, and yet Larkin has only two finished and published novels—*Jill* and *A Girl in Winter*! Why? We shall answer the question later on, and for the present let us briefly discuss these two novels.

The autobiographical novel *Jill* Larkin began to write just after coming out of Oxford, when he was 21. The story of the novel was developed from one of many 'ideas' for short stories that swarmed his mind during this time. He told James Sutton, to whom he dedicated *Jill*, that the story of the novel concerned a poor, young, feminine, shy boy who went to Oxford and there shared a room with another guy who was quite his antithesis: an extract of an affluent family, and so having social pretensions, and a crassly extroverted mountebank. When this poor chap entered and shared a room with his antithetical hero he began to acquire the distinguishing traits of his model, of his hero. As so far as he internalised those upper-class traits, he was distancing himself from the ethos of his own lower class, thus making himself socially dislocated. In course of time, the poor boy imitated not only the manners of his model, his room-mate, but those of other very well off boys. He was now a sort of social maverick—he was an outcast in his own community, but he is not accepted by the higher crust of the society. He was, consequently, rejected by his original class as well as by the upper class, the class to which he pretended to belong. Disillusion therefore dawned on him, and he felt desolate, and so he began self-examination. He was dreaming fulfilment of his fantastic wishes of belonging to the higher class and of making his life blessed with perfection. But in real life he was utterly confused: he realised that we have really no choice in life, no control over it, and that we are like trees that are swayed this way and that according as wind changes its direction. Larkin told Sutton: "It's a jolly good story...and interests me greatly—BUT I CAN'T WRITE IT!" (*op. cit.*, 107).

But write the novel he did and that he did quite well. Soon after telling Sutton that he could not write the novel, in September 1943, he began writing it (*Jill*) at a fast pace and told Sutton: "I have been hacking at a novel" (*op. cit.*, 108). In March 1944, Larkin was about the end of the novel of around

250 pages. In the early summer of the same year he sent the typescript of the novel to Gollancz (publishers) who rejected it. However, ultimately the Fortune Press accepted the typescript of the novel (*Jill*) and published it in 1946. Larkin was extremely delighted as well as miffed at. Miffed at, because the press had deleted 'a few mild obscenities' from the typescript of the novel without his prior permission.

The sentiment and perception of the novel *Jill* is very much in accord with those of some contemporary novels of the so-called Angry Young Men novelists: *Lucky Jim* by Kingsley Amis, *Hurry on Down* by John Wain, and *Room on the Top* by John Braine. The story of *Jill* is the story of John Kemp (the hero), a "young man disoriented from his social class by his education" (Timms, 37). For a resume of the story of *Jill* we cannot do better than quote at some length from David Timms's book *Philip Larkin*: "John Kemp is a working-class boy, the son of a retired policeman. He comes from a northern town, Huddlesford. At his grammar school, a young and rather cold English master, Higgins-like, cultivates John as an experiment. The result is that John, intelligent and hard-working, though quite passive, wins a scholarship to Oxford at the age of eighteen, in 1940. His passivity stems from an almost total lack of self-confidence and nearneurotic shyness. Travelling to Oxford on the train, he feels so embarrassed about eating in front of the other occupants of his carriage that he goes to the lavatory to eat his food, and then stuffs it out of the window when someone rattles the door.

It seems that John needs someone to imitate: his great fear is of being alone, of having nowhere to fit and no pattern to fit into. Having left his home, he is confronted at Oxford with two contrasting societies. One is Christopher Warner's. Christopher is a brash, over-confident young man with whom John shares rooms. He is John's opposite in every way, radically different in character and in social class. He has little intelligence and less industry, but all the traditional characteristics of the 'hearty': he is a sportsman, a drinker and a womaniser. His over-plus of social confidence makes him selfish: he does not worry about borrowing other people's possessions, or about eating their sparse, rationed food. Where John's deference to the wishes of others is painfully self-effacing, Christopher is always ready to manipulate his friends to his own advantage. Christopher's circle of friends is quite unlike the stolidly working-class society John comes from, where father is a patriarch and mother is maternal, where the front room is preserved for use only on special occasions, where father speaks a dialect.

The alternative is the society of the other working-class scholars in the college. The Christopher of this society is Whitbread. He is determined to 'get on': he works like a machine, in much the same way as John worked before Oxford. Whitbread, in John's mother's phrase, is 'of his own standing'; but he is also repulsive. Whenever we meet Whitbread, he is cramming food into his mouth, whether forking in whole potatoes, or scraping up custard with his spoon. He is physically ugly, mean, and always concerned to 'make an impression' on those who may be of use to him. In fact, Whitbread and Christopher are alike in being totally mercenary about their human contacts; Christopher is more attractive only in that his surface glitters more. John is sensitive enough to detest Whitbread, but gullible enough to be taken in by Christopher. Emulating Crouch, John's former English master, had got him to Oxford; copying Christopher, John thinks, will enable him to survive there.

John's going to Oxford destroys the continuity of his life, in disrupting the pattern established by his upbringing. This fact is emphasised in one of the most effective parts of the novel, when John hears that his home town has been blitzed. He travels home, having no news of whether his parents have survived the raid or not, and finds Huddlesford in ruins, an image of the 'waste land' he had felt would open before him at Oxford if he failed to win the friendship of Christopher. He is relieved to find his parents' house undamaged, and a note pinned to the door, saying they are in Preston, staying with a relative. John still has parents, but his scouting round the parental home, staring through the windows to see all more or less unchanged, symbolises just how far he is now excluded from his native place. There it is perfect; but he can only stare in from a landscape that has lost all its landmarks. He is surrounded by wreckage, with—literally—only question marks looming above it here and there:

> Dozens of places he knew well had been wrecked: the local dingy cinema, fish shop; great gouts of clay had been flung against posters. As he walked he looked at the ruins, tracing the effects of single explosions on groups of buildings, great tearing blows that left iron twisted into semi-interrogative shapes.

But Christopher's society will not accept John, though he had thought he had secured his idol's friendship. John finds out the true state of Christopher's feelings towards him by accident. Christopher gets rid of his room-mate for an afternoon, wanting the place to himself in order to facilitate the carefully-planned seduction of his girl friend, Elizabeth. John leaves the room soon after Elizabeth's arrival, and as he shuts the door he overhears her comment on how well he has been 'trained', and Christopher's guffaws about the fact that they are drinking from John's china and eating his butter.

> He heard Elizabeth explode with laughter.
> 'Well, of all the—! It's too bad. He *must* be a
> feeble sort of worm.'
> 'Mother said he looked stuffed.'
> 'Stuffed! That's *just* the word!'

Again, John is completely disorientated, realising that their openly expressed attitudes had been hypocritical. He no longer knows how to behave. Just as the patterns of behaviour he had established at home were inappropriate for Oxford, he sees now that his attitudes towards Christopher and his society will no longer do. Significantly, his new desolation is expressed in metaphors of wrecked masonry. The pattern established by his upbringing has been disrupted; his home town is to be literally ruined; his attempt to build a new edifice in Oxford is metaphorically ruined.

> How should he face Christopher now? And at this thought the last remnants of his illusion collapsed like the last wall of a demolished house. After all, then, he

> was on his own; he had failed, utterly and ignominiously failed to weave himself into the lives of these people. And as he had feared, the door had swung open again and he was alone again, doubly alone. The days would be scrappy, bits and pieces of action. No objects, no continuity.

On the collapse of one illusion, John invents another Christopher seems to regret only one thing in his life, and that in his tenuous family connections, especially his estrangement from his sister. In order to strike back at Christopher, John invents a younger sister, Jill, with whom he is supposed to have a very close relationship. However, in his lack of 'objects' and 'continuity', 'Jill' becomes the only fixed point in his life, and the fantasy soon takes over for its own sake. He writes to Jill, and expresses to her his real feelings about Christopher and his friends—although he writes in much the same way as those friends might write to each other. The letters are a way of achieving Christopher's status, and by their means he is able to place himself—writing establishes the continuity he misses by fixing him in a relationship with another person.

In comparison with the life he invents for Jill, John sees how colourless his own life is. Jill comes to the forefront of his consciousness:

> Suddenly it was she who was important, she who was interesting, she whom he longed to write about; beside her, he and his life seemed dusty and tedious.

He finds that he is able to build up a much fuller and richer image of Jill by erasing himself from the picture. He begins to compile a continuous narrative about a young girl who has his own sensibilities and sensitivity, but Christopher Warner's advantages. She is of the middle classes, and attends 'Willow Gables', a minor public school, an Angela Brazil version of Christopher Warner's Lamprey. But like John, she is unhappy in her social situation—her best friend leaves the school, and her father dies. John had lost his father too, though in a different way. Finding herself alone, she conceives a 'crush' on an older girl—much as John had had a 'crush' on Christopher.

The great difference is that the older girl behaves towards Jill in the way that John would have had Christopher behave towards him. Having fleshed out Jill with a solid situation and background, he goes on to write a more or less daily diary for her.

John is really attempting the impossible: he wants a relationship with someone else but as Jill is his creation, she can never be independent of him. But just as he concedes the impossibility of his task, he sees a young girl who fits almost exactly the description of his imaginary Jill. He devotes all his time to getting to meet her, and finally does, ironically enough through the agency of Christopher. The real Jill is Elizabeth's cousin.

Through Christopher John meets Jill formally, but when he tries to get to know her, he finds that she is not as eager for his friendship as he is for hers. John is delighted to find that 'Jill's' name is in fact almost that: Gillian. But when he calls her Jill, she insists that he use the full form of her name. In doing this, she symbolically refuses her part in John's fantasies, though he does not realise this at the time.

> 'It seemed I knew you—I knew your name was Jill—' 'It's not Jill!' During a lull in the traffic her voice rang out perhaps more sharply than she had intended, and she turned, for the first time a laugh broke over her face, drawing back her mouth, heightening her savage cheekbones. 'I'm sorry, that's just a thing with me. I told you yesterday—oh, no, you weren't there. No, I won't be called anything but Gillian, please....'

At this point, their conversation is interrupted, and John arranges to see her for tea the following afternoon; but in the end, their meeting is prevented by Elizabeth.

Soon afterwards, Huddlesford is bombed. One after another, all his defences have crumbled—family, hopes of friendship with Christopher, the illusion of Jill, the Gillian whom he hoped might play 'Jill's' part. Now his inner state is externalised—the ruined city is an analogue of his attempts to orientate himself. Returning to Oxford, he evaluates his life; the wrecked town has taught him something.

> And then again, it was like being told: see how little anything matters. All that anyone has is the life that keeps him going, and see how easily that can be patted out. See how appallingly little life is.

John reorientates himself according to this lesson. It is not that he has found some landmarks, but that he has recognised that there are no landmarks, and seen the futility either of expecting others to provide them, or of inventing illusory ones. When he is next together with Christopher and his friends, he has lost the over-solicitousness that marked his behaviour before: he helps himself to beer, the nervous 'Er...' with which previously he had prefixed everything he said has disappeared, he refuses to lend Christopher money, and even asks his former idol to give him a cigarette. In fact, he has gained Christopher's assurance through his own new indifference. When he meets Elizabeth again, he reacts much as Christopher might:

> 'Good-bye', he said, yawning. 'Bitch', he added to himself, stirring his coffee.

When he meets Jill for the last time, it is again as Christopher might. He has spent the evening drinking, alone, and finally he staggers to a party he knows her to be attending. As she leaves with Elizabeth and Christopher, John steps before her, takes her in his arms, and kisses her. Christopher knocks him down, and then, with the help of others, throws him into the college fountain.

"After his drenching, John contracts bronchial pneumonia. In his fevered state, he dreams out his relationship with Jill, and comes to the realisation that their fantasy relationship has worn thin—the love he bore her has died. Reflecting that this death seems inevitable whether the relationship is illusory or no, whether love is fulfilled or no, his conviction of 'how little anything matters' is reinforced:

> Let him take this course, or this course, but still behind the mind, on some other level, the way he had rejected was being simultaneously worked out and the same conclusion was being reached. What did it matter which road he took if they both led to the same place?

The trees outside his bedroom window are an appropriate image of his view of life. Bent randomly here and there by a furious wind over which they have no control, they none the less return again and again to the vertical. John's conclusion is something like the conclusion Larkin himself reaches in a mature poem, 'Dockery and Son' where he says of life:

> Whether or not we use it, it goes,
> And leaves what something hidden from us chose,

John's outlook on life is bleak at the end of *Jill*; but at least he has lost his passivity, at least made an autonomous gesture. The book ends with John's parents coming to collect him, and Christopher leaving the college with Elizabeth for the Christmas vacations. As they say good-bye to the porter, a small white dog sniffs his way from the street into the college. At first he cowers as the porter threatens him; but he becomes bolder, and when Elizabeth tries to coax him towards her he growls. The dog has repeated John's gesture" (Timms, 37-43).

Andrew Swarbrick's abstract of the story of the novel is very brief: "*Jill* tells the story of John Kemp, a provincial grammar-school boy at Oxford who, overwhelmed by feelings of social inferiority, constructs a fantasy sister, 'Jill', to whom he writes letters and whose diary he invents. Then he meets the living embodiment of 'Jill', Gillian, to whom he feels a proprietorial attraction. After his clumsy advances, he ends the novel humiliated. Disgraced and ill, he muses:

> Somewhere, in dreams, perhaps, on some other level, they had interlocked and he had had his own way as completely as in life had had been denied it. And this dream showed that love died, whether fulfilled or unfulfilled. He grew confused whether she had accepted him or not, since the result was the same: and as this confusion increased, it spread to fulfilment or unfulfilment, which merged and became inseparable. The difference between them vanished.

This is followed by a passage describing the trees thrashing in the wind outside before we return to John's thoughts. If there was no difference between any opposites, 'Was he not freed, for the rest of his life, from choice?' He watches the trees outside. 'What control could he hope to have over the maddened surface of things?'" (Swarbrick, 1995, 29).

Jill echoes in some respects Larkin's two earlier novels known as Brunette Coleman's (Larkin's pseudonym) novels—*Trouble at Willow Gables* and *Michaelmas Term at St Bride's*. But there is a great difference between these two novels on one hand and *Jill* on the other, for while these two novels are silly in treatment and exude eroticism all over, *Jill* deals with a serious subject and never allows either lightness of treatment or mindless intrusion of eroticism. On the surface of it, *Jill* appears to be a novel of 'conflicting social situations' in so far as we encounter its hero, John Kemp, as torn in the conflicts between two contradictory social levels or classes—Kemp's original lower class and the class of most of the Oxonians to which he leans at Oxford but which refuses him any harbour. But Timms says that the novel is more than that and that it is about the fact that in life we cannot have any choice because life is so much in a flux, and also that we cannot get anything from life according to our choice. Timms writes: "*Jill* is not so much about conflicting social situations, and the stresses attendant on crossing class boundaries, as about our reactions to life and our expectations of it. John [Kemp] is unable to cope with life when he has no fixed context within which to live.... The lesson he learns is that life's landscape really has no such fixed points, no constant pattern. We cannot expect anything from life because in the end we have no control over it, no more than the trees have control over the way they bend" (Timms, 43). "Howbeit, David Timms has found that in the novel there are many of the real trappings of war-time—black-outs, rations, and so on" (*op. cit.*, 44).

Andrew Swarbrick has found a most identifying quality of Larkin's works, ventriloquism, in both *Jill* and *A Girl in Winter*. We have said that in the school and at Oxford, Larkin used to amuse friends with his skill of ventriloquism imitating some of his teachers and others. This skill and habit of his pervade many of his poems as well as in his two published novels, *Jill* and *A Girl in Winter* (in the case of the novels, the ventriloquism is not pronounced or sounded but written). Andrew Swarbrick writes: "Both novels are constructed from ventriloquisms. In *Jill*, John Kemp begins by writing letters to his 'sister', but then *construct her identity by writing 'her' diary*.... The process refines itself into perfect ventriloquism. Katherine (of *A Girl in Winter*), 'the girl in winter', begins where John Kemp's creation ended. Although Larkin casts the novel as third-person narrative, *it is written from Katherine's centre of consciousness* (emphases added) (Swarbrick, 1995, 30). In *Jill*, John Kemp is ventriloquising his 'sister' while writing 'her' diary and in *A Girl in Winter* Larkin is ventriloquising Katherine.

Jill is a peculiar thing, besides being an appreciable novel: it works as model for writing fictions or it tells us how to fictionalise reality. To defeat Christopher's overbearing superiority, Kemp creates a 'sister' of his, i.e. fictionalise a character like novelists do in their works, and Kemp does it superbly and thus sets a model for writers of fictions. And by creating the character of his 'sister' writing letters to her and also writing 'her' diary, Kemp neutralises his inferiority complex in the presence of Christopher and thus gets some sort of vicarious solace. Here Larkin instantiates the truth that the act of creating art provides us with a sort of vicarious solace. Roger Day writes of *Jill*: "It is, in its own peculiar fashion, the act of an artist, for Kemp creates and modifies a world, and one which is outside his own experience. In a different way, this is what Larkin is doing too. Perhaps, then, *Jill* is in part a model about the writing of fiction and the function of art. Kemp's 'art' provides him with solace and, in the absence of happiness, a form of consolation—a theme which recurs later in the poetry ['Reasons for Attendence']" (Day, 19). Roger Day says that "*Jill* is indeed rich in conscious artistry" (*ibid.*) and this is attested by Larkin's confession in an interview with Ian Hamilton that he was even careful in employment of words—"if he used a word on page 15, not to use it again on page 115" (Timms, 44). His alert care is evident also in the perfectly symmetrical structure of the novel that moves "from narrative to fiction within fiction, to dramatised 'flashback'..., and back to reported narrative" (Day, 19). While writing the novel, he had also an eager eye for details—he painted a scene or described a character or incident citing all possible details.

Interestingly, in *Jill*, food has much to do, as, for instance, in E.M. Forster's novels and short stories, tea or parties and picnics have conjured up occasions for defining moments or at least for crucial turns in the course of them. Andrew Motion writes of *Jill*: "In a book so concerned with the embarrassment of appetite, so conscious of wartime rationing, and quickly brought to a crisis by a kiss (a mouth), food has to do a good deal more than simply be eaten. The first time we meet Kemp, on the train to Oxford, he is too ashamed to eat in front of strangers and gobbles his sandwiches in the lavatory. When he reaches his college...it is his crockery which has been appropriated by warner, and the meal being eaten off it violates Kemp's sense of himself. Later, other characters also define themselves by reference to food—Warner by vomiting, and the Yorkshire scholar Whitbread by behaving 'like a man scouring his plate with a piece of bread'" (Motion, 157).

David Timms has criticised *Jill* on three counts. Firstly, he says that the minutest details of the descriptions in the novel are uncalled for, unnecessary, and superabundant as well as 'over-precise' in most cases, while some few cases inadequate and so 'less precise'. Secondly, Larkin "is often carried away into drawing comparisons through similes that in no way advance the story or illuminate the theme" (Timms, 44). And thirdly, says Timms, "...John's character is not consistent. Larkin wanted to present us with a naïve young man, quite out of things in the company of a group of young sophisticates.... And yet when he becomes involved with the fantasy Jill, he has a perfect command of the idiom appropriate to a girls' boarding school" (*op. cit.*, 45). Andrew Swarbrick has found the gravest drawback of the novel in Larkin's hazy and undefined objective in writing it, the undefined objective that is reflected in the novel. Swarbrick writes about *Jill*: "The novel is ultimately unsatisfactory because Larkin cannot decide whether he is writing a psychological portrait in the manner of Katherine Mansfield or a documentary social comedy in the manner of Kingley Amis" (Swarbrick, 29).

David Timms has come across some faults in *Jill*, but he says that these are 'niggling' defects, particularly when they are considered beside 'the many good qualities' of it. Timms highly appreciates the novel's dramatics or '*coup de theatre*'. Besides, he says that the novel's dialogues are excellent and its fantasies are convincing (Timms, 45). *Jill* is full of poetical flights and this has not been overlooked by Timms. Larkin himself has admitted that both *Jill* and *A Girl in Winter* 'are really extended poems'. In his interview with John Haffenden, held in 1979 or 1980, Larkin also said the same thing about the two novels: "I don't think my books were novels, they were more kinds of prose poems" (Haffenden, 116). But Timms says that "Certainly, we may criticise *Jill* for being too poetical" (*op. cit.*, 44).

We have said that *Jill* is an autobiographical novel. But how far is it so? In the same interview referred to just now, John Haffenden put the same question before Larkin and Larkin answered it both in the negative and in the positive. He said that he certainly shared rooms with one of his school friends while at Oxford but, like Kemp, he was not ostracised—he had plenty of good time with friends. Also, unlike Kemp, he 'didn't have any fantasies about a schoolgirl sister'. But Larkin admitted that the feeling that is there in the novel he did experience: "The incidental details are mostly imaginary, but the feeling is absolutely true" (Haffenden, 115). Again, the hero of the novel, John Kemp, is both similar to, as well as different from, Larkin. In the same interview, Larkin also told Haffenden: "John Kemp is uncomfortable because he's working class, but I made him working class to give him some inadequacy, some equivalent of my stammer. I was sort of professional middle class" (Haffenden, 116).

Within one year after the publication of *Jill*, Larkin published in 1947 his second and last complete novel *A Girl in Winter*. He first entitled it as 'The Kingdom of Winter' but when at the time of its publication Alan Pringle of Faber and Faber felt uncomfortable with this title, he switched to the present title of the novel—the title, he said, that was in his mind while he was writing it (he had in mind yet another queer title, 'Frosty Answer') and Pringle clung to this second title. Larkin began writing *A Girl in Winter* in January 1945 just after *The North Ship* was accepted by the Fortune Press for publication. In fact the acceptance of *The North Ship* was a shot in his arms as a writer, and being emboldened by the Fortune Press Larkin started to write his second novel with confidence and speedily. Finishing the novel, Larkin sent it to various publishers, but Chatto & Windus, Secker & Warburg, Cape, and the Cresset Press rejected the novel. At last, Faber accepted it and they published it on 21 February 1947. Larkin dedicated the novel to Montgomery Bruce whose novel *The Case of the Gilded Fly* attracted him towards fantasy and who whetted his interest in pornography and also who earlier dedicated his novel *The Moving Toyshop* to him. In the dedication, Larkin wrote: "To Bruce, whose consistent critical enthusiasms and encouragements resulted in this book" (Motion, 116). Andrew Swarbrick writes that *A Girl in Winter* is a psychological novel built around its heroine Katherine's harrowing feeling of isolation. Swarbrick writes about the plot of the novel: "Its central character is Katherine Lind, a European girl exiled in England during the war. The novel reconstructs her pre-war adolescent association with an English family whom she visited after a pen-friend correspondence with the boy, Robin Fennel. Amidst confusing gestures and responses, her first visit had ended in an unsatisfactory advance from Robin. Now, some years later, she has just heard again from him, and the novel tells the story of the day she is due to meet him. It ends with her indifferently submitting to his seduction and, like *Jill*, gathers imaginative fore with images drawn from *The North Ship*" (Swarbrick, 1995, 29).

A Girl in Winter is a carefully constructed novel, having three parts—'the first and the third set within one day and the second part a "flashback" to an earlier period'. Let us fully quote a resume of the three parts done by Roger Day in his book *Larkin*: In the first part, Katherine with the Fennels, an English family with whom, as an adolescent, she had spent one summer. This first part of the novel is largely taken up describing her drab life and unlikeable colleagues, in particular her superior, Mr Anstey, whom she regards with thinly veiled contempt. This section concludes when Katherine receives a letter promising an immediate visit from Robin Fennel, the son of the family, and she is filled with misgivings for reasons she cannot quite identify.

The middle retrospective section recounts her adolescent visit to the Fennels at (she supposed) the invitation of Robin who is her pen-friend. The visit is in many ways painful for the young Katherine who feels confused by the correct, middle-class Fennel family and especially by the self-assured and meticulously, correctly pleasant Robin. Eventually she discovers that 'at some untraceable point she had fallen in love with him'...and, bewildered, she cannot work out why, having taken the trouble to invite her, he yet remains distant. It is Robin's sister Jane, a down-to-earth woman of twenty-five, who reveals that the invitation had not been Robin's idea at all but hers, simply to alleviate her own boredom. Disillusioned, Katherine is disappointed about her visit:

> She had come expecting to solve a mystery, and had found at the end there was no mystery to solve. From what she had been told, she had been invited partly out of politeness and partly to divert Jane's alleged boredom....

Jane and Robin are contrasting figures: he, as his sister puts it, is 'ordinary, down to the last button'..., and has his life carefully planned out for the foreseeable future. The older and more realistic Jane is shown in the final pages of this section making a compromise between her real feelings and practical alternatives by accepting an offer of marriage from a family friend whose relentlessly extrovert and unimaginative manner is well summed up in his surname, Stormalong.

"The third part of the novel returns us to the present with Katherine now expecting Robin's visit. First we are given an account of her taking stock of her life. As a refugee in England, she has contacted the Fennels out of loneliness. She realises that

> ...she had not been facing the facts. To live from day to day, as she had been doing, shut out the past, but it shut out the future too....

The winter of the title is not simply literal: it is a metaphor for her world which is 'like a painting of a winter landscape in neutral colours'. There is then a short episode in which Katherine returns a handbag to its rightful owner, a Miss Parbury, a somewhat pitiful spinster about to sacrifice her own chance of marriage to the unpleasant Mr Anstey in order to look after her ailing mother. In a row with Anstey shortly afterwards, Katherine is able to use this information to exact revenge for his rudeness. In the meantime, Robin has left a message cancelling his visit. At home, Katherine, reflecting on the events of the day, realises that there will be other 'Miss Greens, Miss Parburys, Mr Ansteys' but resolves that, for her, there 'would be no more Robins'.... She consciously adopts a stoical outlook:

> Life would be happy insofar as she was happy, sad insofar as she was sad. The Happiness would depend on her youth and health, and would help no-one....

Ironically, Katherine has no sooner made this resolve than Robin turns up at her door unexpectedly. Although both recognise, in the course of conversation, that they were never really friends, she allows him to stay with her for the night as 'an unimportant kindness'.... The novel ends with a lyrical passage about their dreams:

> Unsatisfied dreams rose and fell about them, crying out against their implacability,
>
> But in the end glad that such order, such destiny existed. Against this knowledge, the Heart, the will, and all that made for protest, could at least sleep...." (Day, 21-22)

The core themes of both *Jill* and *A Girl in Winter* are the same—isolation and creation of fantasia to supplant that isolation and ultimately somehow and somewhat compromising oneself with the reality. The feeling of isolation, that leads to the feeling of being an outsider, is very much a modern theme, and in this regard the two novels are truly modern. David Timms has found similarity between the two novels on the score that both of them define mature life as an adjustment between our will and the reality that is outside us. Timms writes: "Like

Jill, *A Girl in Winter* is a novel about maturing, coming to terms with the facts of our lives, accepting what is real, rather than depending on false expectations, to make living worthwhile" (Timms, 46). Kemp ultimately realised that his fantasy of his relationship with Jill could not give him solace of life and that he needed things like kissing Elizabeth to make life worth living. Likewise, Katherine realised that merely her fantasy that Robin fell in love with her was nothing and that she could somehow escape her sense if isolation only by sleeping with him, indifferently, stoically. *Jill* and *A Girl in Winter* may be said to be sister novels, in the sense that both illustrate Larkin's early theory about life that it consists of three successive essential components: innocence, loss of innocence in the rocky terrain of reality, and birth of true or mature self through experience or education. Andrew Motion writes that these two novels "were planned as the first two illustrations of Larkin's 'early theory that life consisted of three stages; the first representing innocence; the second its loss resulting in devastation; the third the struggle, after the desolation, to return to a truer and mature self: a sort of social history—his own'" (Motion, 159). If we believe that the two novels are fantasy instantiations of Larkin's theory of the emergence of true or mature self, we may dub them as what some call 'education novels'.

The similarity between *Jill* and *A Girl in Winter* may go even further. Andrew Swarbrick has found ventriloquism in both the novels: in the former, as we have said, Kemp ventriloquises while writing the diary of Jill; and in the latter, the narrator (Larkin) ventriloquises because he narrates 'from Katherine's centre of consciousness'. Also, the two novels are poetical. Larkin himself "commented that both his novels are really extended poems" (Timms, 44). Roger Day says that *A Girl in Winter* is more poetical than *Jill*, a fact that may point to the supposition since when he was writing these two novels, Larkin was unconsciously and tardily moving away from prose narratives to poetry, whatever other reasons of his leaving novel writing he may have pleaded later on. According to Andrew Swarbrick, the two novels are also similar in that both are intensely psychological so far as both try to eagerly scan the psychological attributes of their principal characters and to closely study their psychological moments. Similarity between the two novels may also be found in the fewness of characters in both of them. But, in any case, *A Girl in Winter*, says Davis Timms, "is a better novel than *Jill*, largely because of the stylistic improvements on the earlier work" (*op. cit.*, 51). Larkin himself also believed *A Girl in Winter* better than *Jill* though the latter sold much better than the former. In an interview given to John Haffenden in 1979 or 1980, Larkin said: "*Jill* has always had the edge over *A Girl in Winter* as far as sales go, which surprises me because that's a much more sophisticated book—written, shaped, a Virginia Woolf—Henry Green kind of novel. I took much more trouble over it" (Haffenden, 116).

Roger Day has been critical of the characterisation of *A Girl in Winter*. Day writes: "the characterisation is sometimes thin: Mr and Mrs Fennel are never more than cardboard figures, and Jack Stormalong whom the author evidently despises, is frankly hardly credible. The main character, Katherine, is puzzling: we are given her thoughts in great detail (indeed, we see most of the action through them) and yet she remains shadowy" (Day, 24). The opinions of two novelist friends of Larkin—Amis and Montgomery—deserve mention. Andrew Motion writes that Amis, whom Larkin showed *A Girl in Winter*, "was less than wholeheartedly enthusiastic about it. So was Montgomery" (Motion, 139). David Timms is censorious of some similes in the novel: "There is (still) the occasional redundant simile, as when Katherine's vacillating emotions are compared at length to a flock of birds swooping first to one corner of a field and then to another. Really, for a state already fully described, we do not need to be given an explanatory image that adds nothing new" (Day, 51). Andrew Swarbrick was also not happy with *A Girl in Winter*. His overall comment on the novel is this: "The novel is ultimately unsatisfactory because Larkin cannot decide whether he is writing a psychological portrait in the manner of Katherine Mansfield or a documentary social comedy in the manner of Kingley Amis" (Swarbrick, 29).

But, though, on the score of Larkin's wobbling between psychological approach and social approach while writing the novel, Andrew Swarbrick admitted that it "is more successful in pursuing a coherent strategy as a psychological study" (*ibid.*). David Timms highly praises the creation of the character of Anstey and writes that he is "a superb piece of satirical observation and tangible expression of character" (Timms, 52). Roger Day writes that "Like *Jill*, Larkin's second novel has its intrinsic interest and continues to attract readers" (Day, 24). But Larkin himself did never consider either *Jill* or *A Girl in Winter* a good novel. In an interview given to John Haffenden in 1979 or 1980, he said about the two novels: "...I don't think either of them is any good" (Haffenden, 116). Again, in another interview on Radio on 29 March 1984, i.e. one year before his death, Larkin very apologetically and with all humiliation said, "my novels really weren't novels, they were poems, long, diffuse poems, perhaps" (Timms, 3). Here, Larkin was perhaps characteristically more than modest about his works. For "The novelist Barbara Pym, whom he [Larkin] admired and helped get published and who became a friend in later life, speculated aloud in a letter to him: '...remembering *A Girl in Winter* one wonders why you didn't go on writing fiction, and regrets it. I suppose you were *too good* and didn't perhaps sell enough, and then you preferred writing poetry?'" (Day, 24).

No, Pym's conjecture about Larkin's switching from novel writing over to poetry writing was not correct. We shall say, why. But before that let us recall that at the beginning of this chapter, we did not answer the question why, in spite of his keen desire to be a 'great novelist' in his youth and in spite of his good deal of exercises in novel writing then, Larkin, after his only two successful novels, said goodbye to the vocation of the novelist and remained only a poet throughout the rest of his life. In the same year in which *A Girl in Winter* was published (1947), Larkin began his third fragmentary and unsuccessful novel, to be entitled *A New World Symphony* and continued writing it for several years, progressing like one who walks his unwilling way. He once wrote a few pages, then abandoned writing, only to take up writing after a considerably long passage of time. Forced writing was followed by languor and ennui, and languor and ennui was followed by forced writing, and this continued for some six years, and then, finally, Larkin shelved his unfinished novel for good. Three drafts of this novel (*A New World Symphony*) Larkin preserved, protected from anyone's intruding eyes: one draft consisted of 41 pages, another 56 pages and the third 95 pages. All the three drafts tell the same story.

Briefly, the story of *A New World Symphony* is like this. Sam Wagstaff, an inexperienced and uncouth youth, and Stella Piggott are expected to get married. On the Christmas Eve, Sam plans to take Stella, a small fair-haired girl with enquiring but distant expression, to the local Rugby Club dance. Though they are known to each other since their teens and though they are known soon to get married, their feeling for each other is lukewarm. While driving to the Piggott house to collect Stella, Sam knocks a girl off her bike and the girl is wounded. She cries and blood streams from her chin. This simple incident exerted a powerful influence on Sam's thought of marrying Stella: being pulled by the memory of the second girl, he hesitates not only to marry Stella but to marry any girl whosoever. Andrew Motion writes that Sam's hesitation at this point reflects Larkin's own jactitation about marriage: "Half of Sam wants to have 'a serious bash' at Stella, half of him can't be bothered, but the source of his confusion has nothing to do with desire. It's to do with marriage. His dilemma is the one Larkin himself had been confronting ever since beginning the novel. Sam thinks that if he marries he will re-create his parents' unhappiness; if he doesn't marry he knows he will feel sexually deprived" (Motion, 226). When on his way to the Club with Stella, Sam thinks these things, he altogether forgets the accident of the girl he knocked off and all about her. Ultimately Sam and Stella reach the Club and there are warmly received. Soon the drunk Porky Haines is evicted by Ales Chattaway. Angered at this, some members forcibly undress Alex, hand over his clothes to the cloakroom attendant, and taking the receipt from the attendant gives it to Stella. This scene is 'a crude parody of sexual encounter'.

However, "...when Sam finally dances with Stella he finds that his need for her flares up, threatening to engulf his fear that it will eventually lead him to the alter: 'By holding her low down in the back he could feel the alternate shifting of her hips, which was enough to send a sudden illumination all over him, making the dance a dead skin of behaviour it was time to cast. "Let's go and see if the car's still there", he whispered, and felt he had called right when Stella replied, "Be careful if it got stolen, wouldn't it?"'" (*op. cit.*, 226-27). This unfinished novel is concerned with 'sexual indifference', 'violence towards woman' and 'insoluble fear of marriage', things with which Larkin began it but in spite of long groppings for an appropriate ending for it that would weld all these into a finery he failed to come by.

This failure let him down, and made him disgusted with self and frustrated, and he abandoned forever his nascent career as a novelist. We may perhaps conjecture, considering the moderate success of the two novels of his early age, that had his third novel not proved aborted, flop, he might have grown into a novelist of great standing. In his later life, of course, Larkin seemed to invent other reasons behind his abandoning novel writing. Firstly, and this was his most cogent plea for leaving novel writing behind, Larkin said that "novels are about other people and poetry is about yourself" (Timms, 53), innuending that he desired writing about himself more than writing about other people. And secondly, because, as he wrote in *Required Writing*, "...it is harder to write a good novel than a good poem" (Day, 25), though he also wrote at the same place, "I consider the novel at its best to be the maturest of our literary forms" (*ibid.*).

But though Larkin did never look back to writing novels, after he miscarried his third novel *A New World Symphony*, his inherent turn of mind is very much reflected in many of the poems of his mature years, and that is why David Timms writes that his "novels are interesting for those who wish to come to a fuller knowledge of Larkin's verse" (Timms, 52). In the novel, the author generally paints a situation in detail to make it palpably realistic; so in so many poems has Larkin described appropriate situations in details to evoke pre-meditated emotions, so as to make those emotions believable and realisable, as we will see afterwards.

Larkin is not a rare author to try one literary form and then leave it to take up another, forever. Roger Day has cited the cases of G.B. Shaw and George Orwell: Shaw wrote six novels, got no appreciation, and then produced a good number of plays and became one of the great playwrights of English literature, and Orwell became a life-long journalist after writing three novels. But actually there are many renowned authors who switched from one form, that did not fully suit them, to another which they stuck to, or held fast to two or more literary forms, utilising this one or that as the nature of what were there in their minds called for. For instances of such authors, D.H. Lawrence began his writing career as a poet but ended it as a novelist, though he did never cease to write poems as well; Lawrence Durrell also began as a poet and ended as a novelist and, like D.H. Lawrence, did never stop writing poems; and, lastly, both William Faulkner and Aldous Huxley first published only poetry in their early years and then only novels in the rest of their lives.

The Less Deceived

5

Dithering, vacillating, fumbling helplessly with his third projected novel *A New World Symphony* for want of a vision about how the book should be finished, Larkin, as we have already said, after making three successive drafts of the fiction ultimately abandoned in 1953 forever his novelistic oeuvre and turned to poetic creations. And within just two years, by publishing his first of the three most celebrated collections of poems, *The Less Deceived*, he could prove that his novelistic dexterity might have fizzled out after *A Girl in Winter* but his poetic skill remain with him in tact. He dubbed his two published novels 'long, diffuse poems', perhaps meaning to say that he was a poet and nothing but a poet. Whether he was also a novelist of some standing is a different question, but certainly *The Less Deceived* proved beyond all doubts that he was a poet of great worth. *The Less Deceived* was published by the Marvell Press in November 1955, i.e. one year after *The Fantasy Poets No. 21* ('Pamphlet 21') was published, four years after *XX Poems* was published, and ten years after *The North Ship* was published. Of the 29 poems that *The Less Deceived* contains, 5 were earlier published in *The Fantasy Poets No. 21* (this collection comprises only these 5 poems) and 13 were earlier published in *XX Poems*, and one poem—'At Grass'—was included in both the earlier collections—*The Fantasy Poets No. 21* and *XX Poems*.

After the fiasco of *A New World Symphony*, considering himself incapable of producing any more novel and understanding that his dream of youth of becoming a 'great novelist' was not going to be materialised for sure, Larkin turned his aspiring gaze to poetry. But shining as a poet was also not a smooth sailing. True, he had published three collections of poems by the time he finally abandoned his unfinished novel—*The North Ship* (Marvell Press, 1945), *XX Poems* (privately published, 1951) and *The Fantasy Poets No. 21* (Fantasy Press, 1954)—but none of the collections could bring him recognition as a poet. On the contrary, he could not forget the 'hammer of blows of successive rejections' of his early poems by publishers, particularly the blows of the rejection of his *In the Grip of Light* (a collection of 25 poems) in 1947. He was perhaps dejected to reckon that till 1954, when he was thirty-two years of age, he could not turn out any collection of poems that could strongly claim recognition for him.

However, a ray of hope soon dawned upon him—George Hartley of The Marvell Press agreed to publish a collection of Larkin's poems. Larkin selected 29 poems for the collection, taking 13 from *XX Poems*, which he privately published (only 100 copies) in 1951 while in Belfast, Ireland (of these 13 poems two were from the unpublished typescript of a collection of poems that he had selected for publication, in 1947, under the title *In the Grip of Light*—'Wedding-Wind' and 'Going'); all the 5 of *The Fantasy Poets No. 21* (the poem 'At Grass' earlier appeared in *XX Poems*); and 12 other poems. Apart from the two poems that were culled from *In the Grip of Light*, cited just now—'Wedding-Wind' (dated 26 September 1946) and 'Going' (dated February? 1946)—, all the poems of this collection to be published by the Marvell Press (with the title *The Less Deceived*) were written or completed after December 1949.

Larkin sent Hartley the 29 poems for publication under the title *Various Poems*, but Hartley did not like the title and so urged Larkin to change it. To give the collection a new title, Larkin chose the original title of the poem 'Deceptions' of it—'The Less Deceived'. Larkin was not in favour of any change in the title of the collection; he changed the title only a little grudgingly, for he told his mother that the title 'Various Poems' had never been used by anyone. The title of this collection (*The Less Deceived*) or of the original title of the poem 'Deceptions' of this collection ('The Less Deceived') originated in scene i of

Act III of *Hamlet* where Hamlet, in 'vicious mock-madness' toys with Ophelia's love for him:

> Ham. ...I did love you once.
> Oph. Indeed, my lord, you made me believe so.
> Ham. You shouldn't have believed me; ...I loved you not.
> Oph. I was the more deceived.

Of course, in the poem 'Deceptions' (original title 'The Less Deceived'), the girl, as Larkin tells her, was not 'more deceived' like Ophelia but was 'less deceived', nevertheless Larkin certainly got the idea of deception from *Hamlet.* Ophelia was falsely deceived by Hamlet but the girl in 'Deceptions' was really deceived by the criminal. In the case of the girl, the criminal who raped her was more deceived than she because after raping her he found only 'fulfilment's desolate attic', for his fulfilment was but utter vacuity—because he was deceived by self that by raping her he would gain eternal and heavenly joy and that his hunger for such joy would be for ever quenched, and when after raping her he came out of his blinding illusion his self itself was reduced into smithereens like a million-part broken glass and he underwent relentlessly excruciating pain, while the girl was only cringing in grief, and so she was less deceived by himself. The title 'The Less Deceived' for the collection appealed to Larkin because the common purport of the poems of the collection is to show how we are being deceived by illusions of our making and what truth lies behind the veil of those illusions. However, while sending the alternative title 'The Less Deceived' to George Hartley of the Marvell Press, Larkin wrote to him the following in justification of his second choice of title: "I especially didn't want an 'ambiguous' title, or one that made any claim to policy or belief: this (The Less Deceived) would however give a certain amount of sad-eyed (and clear-eyed) realism, and if they [i.e. readers] did pick up the context they might grasp my fundamentally passive attitude to poetry (and life too, I suppose) which believes that the agent is always more deceived than the patient, because action comes from desire, and we all know that desire comes from wanting something we haven't got, which may not make us any happier when we have it. On the other hand suffering—well, there is positively no deception about that. No one imagines their suffering" (Swarbrick, 1995, 43-44) (Very curiously, here Larkin's philosophy of life shows some semblance with the quintessence of the *Bhagavadgita*).

Hartley also requested Larkin to write the blurb of the collection, *The Less Deceived*, which the latter though left incomplete and in draft. What Larkin wanted to emphasise in the draft was that the poems of the collection were *emotional* and *personal.* He wrote in the blurb: "...the poems of Philip Larkin have been increasingly well-known for their unusual combination of deep personal feeling and exact, almost sophisticated choice of words. This volume, the first collection of his work since 1945, contains poems previously unpublished together with others that have already helped to establish their author as one who, while no less witty and intelligent than his contemporaries, deals with emotion more simply and intensely than is common today" (Motion, 262). Larkin dedicated the book to one who very much deserved it—Monica Jones. Monica was the inspiration behind many of the poems of the book and lent yeoman's service to Larkin to get it published. In the dedication, Larkin simply wrote her name holding back everything else in his heart: 'Miss Monica Jones'. It is interesting to write that *The Less Deceived* was published following the eighteenth-century practice of publication: forms were sent out to possible buyers of the book with the promise that their names would be printed at the end of it. Thus 120 intending buyers were found, who subscribed a part of the price of the book to facilitate the publication. Ultimately 700 copies of the book were printed and 400 of them were immediately bound. The reception of the book was unexpectedly warm. The first lot of 400 bound copies were sold within weeks of the book's coming out of the press in November 1955. By April 1956, the second lot of 300 copies were also sold and in the August of the same year a paperback edition of 1,300 copies was published. By the next August a third impression of 1,500 copies was made, and soon a fourth and a fifth impressions were required. *The Times* included the book 'in its round-up of the year's outstanding books'.

The reviews of *The Less Deceived*, on the heel of its publication, were also highly heartening. Andrew Motion writes:

"*The Times Literary Supplement* was anonymously cautious but encouraging; the *New Statesman* was enthusiastic; and Donald Davie, Anne Ridler and Roy Fuller, among others, produced praising pieces later in the spring. For the rest of 1956 and into the following year, articles and appreciations followed at regular intervals. Most of them concentrated, as Larkin hoped they would, on the book's emotional impact and its sophisticated, witty language—and the poetry-buying public soon took notice. So did the academic community, especially after F.W. Bateson, the English Fellow at Corpus Christi College, Oxford, had writen about the book in *Essays in Criticism*, urging people to 'Come buy!'" (*op. cit.*, 269).

Larkin's first collection of poems *The Less Deceived* was published in 1955, i.e. between the publications of J.D. Scott's article 'In the Movement' in *The Spectator* in 1954 and Robert Conquest's anthology *New Lines* in 1956. Naturally, therefore, the question may arise if Larkin was a Movement poet or not. Larkin always protested being thought to belong to any definite poetic movement or to any specific group of poets, but, yet, some critics reckon him as a Movement poet. However, we shall deal with the question whether he was really a Movement poet in a later chapter; for the present we may only say that in response to Conquest's request Larkin sent him eight poems for publication in *New Lines*, the anthology that touched off The Movement and that all the eight poems were earlier included in *The Less Deceived*. Those eight poems are: 'Maiden Name', 'Church Going', 'I Remember, I Remember', 'Skin', 'Born Yesterday', 'Triple Time', 'Toads' and 'Lines on a Young Lady's Photograph Album'. P.R. King says that through *The Less Deceived* Larkin was certainly related to The Movement, though his relation was but 'casual, not causal'. Quoting Peschmann, King writes: "What particularly links Larkin with The Movement in *The Less Deceived* is its fundamental honesty to experience: a clear-eyed unillusioned view of contemporary living and its problems, and a refusal to sentimentalize them; the whole couched, for the most part, in a language instantly recognizable as the colloquial idiom of our day, free from pedantry, grandiloquence, or recherche phrase" (King, 4).

As we have already said, *The Less Deceived* contains 29 poems, arranged with 'great care' following Larkin's own choice of sequence of the poems of his collections. In an interview with Larkin in 1979 or 1980, John Haffenden asked him, "Do you take great care in ordering the poems in a collection?" and Larkin answered: "Yes, great care. I treat them like a music-hall bill: you know, contrast, difference in length, the comic, the Irish tenor, bring on the girls. I think 'Lines on a Young Lady's Photograph Album' is a good opener, for instance; easy to understand, variety of mood, pretty end. The last one ['At Grass'] is chosen for its uplift quality, to leave the impression that you're more serious than the reader had thought" (Haffenden, 122). Here, Larkin was certainly referring to *The Less Deceived*. In any case, Larkin invariably places one of the most important poems of a collection at the beginning of it and one at the end. However, in this chapter we shall discuss only 12 poems from that collection. These are: 'Lines on a Young Lady's Photograph Album', 'Wedding-Wind', 'Coming', 'Reasons for Attendence', 'Next, Please', 'Wants', 'Church Going', 'Toads', 'Poetry of Departures', 'Deceptions', 'I Remember' and 'At Grass'. Let us discuss these poems below.

1

Lines on a Young Lady's Photograph Album

This poem was dated by Larkin 18 September 1953, though, as Andrew Motion tells us, it was began on 17 August, and completed on or in the neighbourhood of 18 September of that year, and it was first published in *The Fantasy Poets No. 21* (Pamphlet No. 21) in 1954 and then in *The Less Deceived* in 1955. The young lady of the poem was the real Winifred Arnott, one of the six women who came into the life of Larkin and ruffled it. She was a trainee librarian in Belfast University Library. Since he saw her, Larkin was attracted to the young beauty, but he could not be very intimate with her because he was considerably older than her, and because she soon left Belfast to complete her training in London, where she got engaged to one Bradshaw. Larkin used to call her 'sweet Winifred' though she mildly protested. The sweet impression that Winifred left on the screen of Larkin's memory did not fade out so soon, even after her marriage, for the poem 'Maiden Name' that he wrote in 1955, six months after her marriage, "expresses Larkin's lurking sense of betrayal" (Swarbrick, 1995, 48) from her end.

Andrew Motion writes about the source of this poem: "The precise source for 'Lines on a Young Lady's Photograph Album' is easy to trace, even though Larkin altered some details. 'I mea', says Winifred, 'there were in fact two albums not one, there's not a picture of me wearing a trilby hat (though there is one of me in a beret and moustache for Rag Week). On the other hand, I'm afraid to say, there's definitely my double chin, he got that right. And there's also one of me bathing.' Behind such details, and behind the feelings which make them precious, lies another, less obvious source. By covertly admitting to the pleasure it takes in fantasy, the poem connects with the other pictures Larkin liked to gaze at: the photographs in pornographic magazines. The sex life they entail—solitary, exploitative—is a crude version of the pleasure he takes in the album" (Motion, 234). Therefore, the 'you' in the poem certainly refers to Winifred Arnott, to whom the poem is addressed—Winifred, the 'real girl in a real place, / In every sense empirically true!' David Timms writes that this present poem has its predecessor in C. Day Lewis's poem 'The Album': "Lines on a 'Young Lady's Photograph Album' has a literary antecedent in C. Day Lewis's 'The Album'. Both poems start from the experience of looking at snapshots in an album, both poems are addressed to the subject of the photographs, and both lead to a reflection on how the past affects us in the present" (Timms, 76). The poem comprises nine stanzas, each stanza invariably containing five lines rhyming a/b/b/a/b.

In the beginning stanza, Larkin tells Winifred Arnott that after much persuasion she agreed ('yielded up') to let him see her photograph album. When he opened the album he was beside himself, perplexed, crazy ('distracted') to see her supreme beauty. He saw the glazy photographs of her different ages, framed with dull ('Matt') gold-coloured or white coloured border, are fixed with the dense dark ('thick black') pages of the album. The pictures are so much delicious ('confectionary') and glamorous ('rich') that Larkin becomes breathless to stare at these inspiring or salubrious ('nutritious') photographs ('images') of hers. In the second stanza, the poet (Larkin) describes some of the pictures of Winifred in the album. He says that his moving or unfixed eyes ('swivel eye') eagerly or hungrily look at ('hungers') a particular assumed attitude ('pose') of Winifred in a photograph and then at another assumed attitude of hers in another photograph. In one picture she has done her hair like the tails of pigs ('pigtails') and she is tightly holding in her grip ('clutching') a cat that is unwilling to yield to her grip ('reluctant'). In another picture, which was taken after she graduated ('girl-graduate'), she is wearing a coat with borders of fur or thick and soft hair of animals, and is appearing attractive ('sweet'). In the third photograph she is, as if, plucking ('lifting') a broad-petalled ('heavy-headed') rose from under 'a structure of cross-barred or lattice work' ('trellis') that props the rosier or rose tree, and in the fourth photograph she is wearing a kind of soft felt hat, known as trilby hat.

In the third stanza, Larkin says that those photographs of Winifred ('that') are a little agitating or stimulating ('Faintly disturbing') to him in more than one way, because from all her perspectives or angles, i.e. from all of her poses or attitudes in those photographs ('From every side') she is affecting or slackening ('strike at') his self-control, that is he is being mentally and physically attracted to herself. The poet is also not minimally ('Not least') affected (this time in a negative sense) or disturbed, or getting his self-control slackened or his peace broken ('disquieting') due to the presence of a bevy of youngsters ('chaps') who appear in the photographs to be lazily ('At ease') sprawling or dangling or hanging ('toll') around her when she was young ('your earlier days'). The poet affectionately ('dear') tells Winifred that those youngsters generally ('on the whole') do not belong to the social stratum ('class') from which she comes, i.e. they belong to a social class lower than her own.

In the fourth stanza, there is a new movement: here, instead of gazing at the beauty of Winifred in the photographs, the poet is wondering at the trashiness of photography itself.

Apostrophising at photography ('O, photography!'), he says that no genre of art is as imitating, exact, or trustworthy ('Faithful') as photography, and so no genre of art is as frustrating, depressing, or worthless ('disappointing') as photography. Photography is most trustworthy but most despairing because it, for instance, truly reproduces or copies ('records') uninspiring ('Dull') days as such and as nothing else; because it exactly reproduces fake and forced smiles ('hold-it smiles') as fraudulent, deceitful; and because it will not wipe out or cover up ('censor') any flaws or patches in the face ('blemishes') like left-out marks of lotion, etc. ('washing-lines'); and also because it will not remove or hide from the background (perhaps in the photograph of Winifred) such obnoxious or disconcerting things as the boards displaying the advertisement for distemper or 'watery vehicle giving body to the pigment in case of painting' manufactured by the company whose name is 'Hall's-Distemper'. In the fifth stanza, Larkin's diatribe against photography continues. He says that photography shows the disinterested or unwilling ('disinclined'; see also 'reluctant' in the second stanza) cat, in the grip of Winifred, as unwilling or disinterested and not otherwise, i.e. photography is not showing the cat as interested in (the beauty of) Winifred. And, if anybody has a double chin, like Winifred has ('when it is'), photography reproduces that faithfully with a mark of shadow, as in the case of her picture in the album. But now Larkin ceases his diatribe and wonders (and apostrophises) that in spite of photography sincere exactitude in reproductions, which is artistically 'disappointing' (fourth stanza), in the case of Winifred's photograph, its frankness ('candour'), honesty and exactitude in reproduction have bestowed upon her face an uncommon and bemusing elegance ('grace'). Moreover, Larkin wonders (and apostrophises) that the honesty and exactitude of reproduction in her photograph insuperably ('overwhelmingly') insists ('persuades') him to believe that the girl in the picture (Winifred) is not a replica or reproduction of a real girl but is itself a 'real girl', existing in a 'real place'.

The sixth stanza begins with the same stupefying wonder of Larkin at the overwhelming verisimilitude of the photograph of

Winifred. He mulls over the fact that from all aspects or considerations the girl in the picture is palpably ('empirically') a real ('true') girl and not a fiction of the mind—a girl presently existing before him. But the very next moment, Larkin is haunted by a doubt. He raises the question: is the girl (Winifred) in the photograph a real being of the present or are she and everything else around her merely ('just') a fantom of the bygone days ('*the past*')? The poet, Larkin, is seeing in the photograph of Winifred flowers and a gate at a distance ('Those flowers, that gate') and parks, opaqued by fog, and parked motor vehicles in the proximity, and he is thus mentally wounded, hurt meditating that all these things are for him merely memories of the past ('Simply by being over'). He tells the Winifred of the photograph ('you') that she squeezes and wounds his heart ('Contract my heart'), i.e. she makes him grieve, now by being appearing ('looking') as a being of the past or being an archaic thing ('out of date').

At the beginning of the seventh stanza, Larkin repeats that he really grieves because Winifred is now only a being of the past, only a memory ('Yes, True'). But, says Larkin, the ultimate or fundamental reason ('in the end') of *our* crying ('we cry') is not only that we are separated or excluded from the past ('exclusion') but also that we are no more attached to the past and so are free from the past—independent of the past—and, therefore, the separation ('It') renders us free and enables us to grieve uninhibitedly, willingly ('leaves us free to cry'). Larkin means to say that after Winifred's marriage to Mr Bradshaw or after his being rejected by her, a long time ago, he is now emotionally independent of the tenter hooks of his love for her and so can uninhibitedly cry for her, recalling his past association with her, as people ('we') generally do. (Notice that here Larkin is not speaking only about his own grief but about any one else's.) He knows that his past or his friendship with Winifred in the days gone by ('*what was*') would not come back and says that he is reasonably ('justify') crying or that his grief is natural, as people's past never comes back and tells them that their grieving ('Our grief') is only natural, though he or any man may very loudly ('hard') cry like a dog ('yowl') and the cry traverses ('across') the length of time that separates ('gap') the present ('eye': Larkin is presently looking at the photograph of Winifred) from the past ('page', i.e. the leaf of the album on which the photograph of Winifred of bygone days is attached).

Therefore ('So'), i.e. because he is now free to cry, Larkin, in the eighth stanza, says that he has now only one option: to mourn the lost past of Winifred ('You'), i.e. to grieve for his friendship with her that is now lost to him as it is now well a thing of the past, though he knows that by no freak or caprice of fate or nature ('chance') his mourning for her will bring into being any favourable after-effect ('consequence')—the after-effect in which she will go back to her magnetic beauty of earlier youth. Larkin is grieving for the loss of the young or earlier Winifred whom, in her photograph in the Album, he is seeing as riding a bicycle, all balanced against a fence. He is also fancifully speculating ('wonder') if she would notice, discover, or locate ('spot') him while he is thus thievishly ('theft') gazing at the particular photograph ('this one') in which she ('you') is bathing (actually, in a lake or pond). In the ninth or last stanza, Larkin says that, in brief, or to sum up ('In short'), all the photographs of Winifred in the album, taken together ('to condense'), show a past time or past life of Winifred ('past') that neither he nor any one else can now partake of ('share'). Larkin says that even the person, whosoever he may be, to whom she may belong in the future, i.e. whom she may take as her husband ('No matter whose your future') will not be capable to partake of, or enjoy, her past life (that Larkin enjoyed). In a particular photograph Winifred looks quiet and tranquil ('calm') and unemotional ('dry'), and that particular photograph is showing her ('holds you') like a celestial being ('like a heaven'), and also in that photograph ('there') she is showing or remaining ('lie') as beautiful ('lovely') as she really was in her young days, i.e. there have been no changes in her beautiful look in the photograph during all these intervening years ('Unvariably'). And lastly, Larkin says that with passage of time ('as the years go by') the distance between her past and his present is continually widening or prolonging, and so she is gradually seemingly getting reduced in size (as an object looks smaller and smaller as it continues to recede: 'Smaller'), but, all the same, her image, to him, is becoming ever brighter and brighter ('clearer').

'Lines upon a Young Lady's Photograph Album' may immediately bring to one's memory the lines of W.B. Yeats's poem 'Among School Children', where a flock of children, sitting staid in a class-room and thus working as a photograph, triggers in Yeats's mind the recollection of the emotion-charged images of the beloved Maud Gonne from across a long passage of time gone by:

> I walk through the long schoolroom questioning;
> ....
> ....the children's eyes
> In momentary wonder stare upon
> A sixty-year-old smiling public man.
>
> I dream of a Ledaean body, bent
> Above a sinking fire, a tale that she
> Told of a harsh reproof, or trivial event
> That changed some childish day to tragedy—
> Told, and it seemed that our two natures blent
> Into a sphere from youthful sympathy,
> Or else, to alter Plato's parable,
> Into the yolk and white of the one shell.

Andrew Swarbrick is very perceptive when he writes that 'Lines on a Young Lady's Photograph Album' shows some common traits of Larkin's poetry: "This, the opening poem of *The Less Deceived*, contains a number of features typical of Larkin's poetry. There is first the *creation of a speaking voice* which makes us feel that the poet is addressing us directly. We find, too, a *development of thought and attitude* in the poem as ideas are taken up, modified and concluded. There is a characteristic movement from the *particular to the general*: from a specific situation (the poet browsing through a young woman's photograph album) there grows a general reflection on the significance of the experience. The *tone of voice varies from idiomatic, off-the-cuff light-heartedness to a more serious and thoughtful exploration of meaning*" (emphases added)

(Swarbrick, 1986, 22). The speaking voice is clear to us since the very beginning line where Larkin addresses Winifred as 'you'. He, next, addresses photograph ('Your candour' in the fifth stanza) and lastly speaks to us from the seventh stanza ('we cry', 'It leaves us free to cry', etc.). Larkin begins the poem with a trifling scene: he persuades Winifred to hand over her album to him and then he somewhat gloats over her photographs. But soon he *thinks* that photography is a faithful but disheartening device and *nostalgically* ruminates over the past. So he develops thoughts and assumes an attitude. In the poem, Larkin obviously proceeds from the *particular* simple incident of his gazing at Winifred's photographs and arrives at the *generalisations* that photographs are frustrating truths and that the past may be miniaturized but certainly it does become more perspicuous. And, as is the wont of Larkin, he begins the poem like the drawing-room conversation with 'idiomatic, off-the-cuff lightheartedness' but ends it all the more seriously, musing on passage of time and nagging memory.

'Lines on a Young Lady's Photograph Album' has been quite dramatic, having implied asides, changes in attention, shifts in tone, and change in attitude. David Timms writes about the poem: "The poem is dramatic. This is apparent not only in the unspoken *asides* to the girl, and in the *explicit directions* to this or that photograph, but in the way the poem constantly *shifts tone and mood*" (emphases added) (Timms, 77). The asides that Timms points out occur in parentheses in the third stanza ('Faintly disturbing, that, in several ways') and in the eighth stanza ('without a chance of consequence'). The explicit change of directions is obvious in more than one ways. Firstly, Larkin himself says: 'My swivel eye hungers from pose to pose—'; secondly, from the subject of Winifred's photographs he moves on to the subject of photography itself, and then, thirdly, to the subject of time and memory. The changes in tone and mood are immediately clear. As told earlier, Larkin begins the poem somewhat facetiously but closes it on a serious note, and so his tone and mood at the end of the poem are quite different from what these are at the beginning of it. Andrew Swarbrick writes that the poem even startlingly begins with a dramatic situation: "The poem's opening immediately implies a dramatic situation—not, that is, a situation of tense excitement, but simply one in which the presence of another character [that of Winifred] is suggested" (Swarbrick, 1986, 22). But the poem is dramatic also and above all these because in it Larkin is addressing the women (Winifred) who is supposedly present before him ('At last you yielded up the album'). In addition of being dramatic, says Swarbrick, the poem has 'lyrical plangency' (Swarbrick, 1995, 50)—lyrical, of course in the modern sense of the word, i.e., in the sense that the poem expresses the poet's very intimate, personal feeling and mood.

Andrew Swarbrick has found two puns in the poem: one on the word 'Lines' in the title of the poem, and one on the word 'lie' in the third line of the ninth stanza. Of the first word, Swarbrick writes: "the 'Lines' are the poem but also the lines of age which will befall both the poet and the woman [Winifred]" (Swarbrick, 1986, 23). And, of the pun on the word 'lie', Swarbrick writes: "The poem ends with a compliment, not quite to the woman [Winifred], but to the image of her, a compliment silently qualified by the pun on 'lie' (a pun Larkin would use at least twice more, in 'Talking in Bed' and 'An Arundel Tomb')" (Swarbrick, 1995, 50). The punning on 'lie' comprises two meanings of the word—'to be in a horizontal or nearly horizontal posture' and *to deceive or mislead*. Steve Clark has found in the poem a suggestion or allusion of sexual seduction at the very beginning of the poem: 'At last you yielded up the album, which, / Once open, sent me distracted.' Clark writes: "There is obviously an implied seduction where 'At last' a yielding occurs that sends the narrator 'distracted': notice how 'once open' becomes an explicit image of sexual availability" (Regan, 115). Steve Clark has also discovered hints of Larkin's voyeuristic motive in the line 'My swivel eye hungers from pose to pose—' (*op. cit.*, 115-16). Larkin's sexual and voyeuristic hunger is expressed through dietary terminology: 'glossy', 'thick', 'confectionary', 'rich', 'choke' and 'nutritious', and we know that in psychoanalysis there is a relationship between dietary hunger and sexual hunger.

Larkin begins the poem with a particular incident, his gazing at Winifred's photographs in an album, but at about half way through the poem, to be exact in the fourth stanza, he for the moment swerves his train of thought from the topic of Winifred's photographs towards the topic of photographic imaging and dwells on it till the sixth stanza. Photography is sometimes taken to be a kind of art, but Larkin abhors to call it an art because it cannot ideally or imaginatively transmute an object but merely creates an exact, self-same image of it. Photography or the photographic process of creating images of objects, says he, is certainly trustworthy, believable, and exactly for this reason 'disappointing', impliedly because no image of objects, either whose flaws have not been removed or covered or which has had no touch of ideality, can provide us with happiness or can be treated as art. Andrew Motion, in his article 'Philip Larkin and Symbolism', writes in this regard: "Photography, the poem says, depends for its charm and success on depicting 'real' people in a 'real' place, and on being 'in every sense empirically true'. But it is exactly for these reasons that Larkin will not accord it the status of 'art'—which, he implies, depends on allowing the imagination free and potentially transfiguring play" (Regan, 52-53).

But the topic of photography or the photograph of Winifred is not the central topic of the poem; it is rather a digression; the focal topic or theme of the poem is Larkin's experience—his emotion and nostalgia—stimulated or evoked by Winifred's photograph, though the title of the poem superficially suggests that it is about her photograph. David Timms very rightly says that in the poem "Larkin recreates not the photographs, but the experience of looking at the photographs in the presence of the young lady" (Timms, 77). What is this experience of Larkin? The experience or knowledge of Larkin is that the flow of time is ceaseless and that a frozen or framed past memory sometimes remains very bright and lively, though in cameo form, and affects us more keenly than does a recent one. The past may be miniaturized but then it becomes 'clearer' and more appealing. But as in spite of our feeling nostalgic for the past we cannot reach, it gives us pain all the more.

The leaning towards anonymity that is a common feature of Larkin's poetry is obvious in 'Lines on a Young Lady's Photograph Album'. In the poem, the speaker, in fact, is not Larkin himself but a 'dirty old man who will pinch a bathing photo'. Moreover, in the poem, Larkin is scathingly mocking at his lechery when he says: 'My swivel eye hungers from pose to pose—'. Andrew Swarbrick says that 'Lines on a Young Lady's Photograph Album' signals future changes in Larkin's poetry: henceforth, he suggests, his poetry would be like photography—'Faithful and disappointing'. Swarbrick writes that since this poem, as Larkin solemnly says, "like photography, his poetry will aim to be 'as no art is, / Faithful and disappointing'" (Swarbrick, 1995, 49). This means that henceforth his art will be 'artless', anti-romantic, non-aesthetic, and in this sense this poem has a kinship with the poetic principles of the Movement. But how does the poem fare? According to Steve Clark, the "poem succeeds in establishing the relation of the 'swivel eye' to 'nutritious images' as central to the process of desire" (Regan, 117). But the value of the poem is not only this much. In fact, in the poem Larkin has been enough successful in conjuring up an appropriate situation for evoking his desired painful and nostalgic feeling due to evanescence of things and relations and viscosity of memory. Really, not for nothing is Larkin himself appreciative of this poem. He said that the poem is "easy to understand, [having] variety of mood, pretty end" (Haffenden, 122).

2
Wedding-Wind

This is the second poem, in order of sequence, in *The Less Deceived*, the first one being, as we have said, 'Lines on a Young Lady's Photograph Album'. It was dated 26 September 1946 and was first entered in the typescript of *In the Grip of Light*, then was published in *XX Poems* in 1951, and only then was included in *The Less Deceived* in 1955. It may be pointed out here that only two poems of *In the Grip of Light* were afterwards published in *XX Poems* and then in *The Less Deceived*, and these two are: 'Wedding-Wind' and 'Going'. 'Wedding-Wind' is a nostalgic narration of a woman of her happy experiences during her wedding day and wedding night and of her dubious expectations in the future. Andrew Swarbrick takes this poem to be romantically inspired and to be one of 'the most obviously "personal" poems' of Larkin written under the cover of a mask. Swarbrick writes: "Perhaps the most obviously 'personal' poems (though not necessarily 'confessional') in *The Less Deceived* are those dealing with romantic involvement. Of these, the earliest is 'Wedding-Wind' which was completed in September 1946 when Larkin was involved with Ruth Bowman. It is one of the very few occasions in the whole of Larkin's work when he clearly writes other character: It's worth recalling that in 1946 Larkin regarded himself primarily as a novelist [whose vocation is to write of other characters]. The poem imagines the feelings of a farmer's wife on the day after her wedding" (Swarbrick, 1995, 44). Another poem that Larkin wrote while he was enjoying intimacy with Ruth Bowman and wrote it four years afterwards under the cover of a mask is 'No Road' ('Since we agreed to let the road between us / Fall to disuse...').

'Wedding-Wind' reflects Larkin's hesitancy towards his getting married. His parents' not-very-happy conjugal life left an indelible impression on his mind, which always restrained him from taking an affirmative decision on marriage. For long, he faltered in giving word to Ruth that he would marry her. This poem reflects such an unsettled state of mind about the institution of marriage, and this is reinforced by what Larkin wrote in his diary five months previous to writing 'Wedding-Wind': "Five months before writing this ['Wedding-Wind'], sitting in the library in Wellington one afternoon, Larkin had scribbled in his pocket diary: 'At 1.45 p.m. let me remember that the only married state I intimately know (i.e. that of my parents) is bloody hell. Never must it be forgotten.' Now he was once again easing open the door through which Ruth might come into his life and settle down with him" (Motion, 151).

The dramatic poem 'Wedding-Wind' was written about ten days after another dramatic poem, 'Two Guitar Pieces'. 'Wedding-Wind' consists of twenty-four lines, which are divided into two stanzas, the first stanza comprising ten lines and the second stanza fourteen. Only a few lines rhyme with other lines very irregularly. This twenty-four-line poem may be divided into two parts: the first part, consisting of seventeen lines, is merely descriptive; and the second part, comprising seven lines, states the speaker's three fundamental questions of hers relating to the future of her married life (indicated by three question marks).

The speaker of the poem, a woman who was married (into a farmer's family, having horses and chicken) the previous day, says that throughout the day of her marriage wind blew and throughout the night it blew more forcefully, strongly ('high wind'). At night the wind blew so strongly that the door of the shanty in which horses were kept ('stable') was swinging and repeatedly striking against the wall with very loud sounds ('banging'), and this required her husband ('he') to go to the shanty (which supposedly was at a distance) and shut or fasten the door. While going to the shanty to close the door fast, her husband left her behind, and she was sitting in the candle-lighted house or hut dully or sadly and was listening to the sound of the rain outside. Then she was, as if seeing the reflection of her face in the coiled or contorted burning candle-stick (which may be a symbol of penis), and she was seeing nothing else besides, i.e., all her attention was glued to the candle-stick. When her husband came back, he told her that the horses in the stable became disquieted, excited, stirred up. Hearing this, the woman became sorrowful ('sad'), deploring that in that night any man or any beast—like those horses—should be deprived of ('lack') the sort of pleasure or delight ('happiness') that she was that night enjoying with her husband.

Then ('Now') in the morning, after her wedding night, she finds all things of the surround entangled or twisted with one another due to the wind that blew very strongly in the previous night. Her husband, at that time, went to see the pools of water ('floods') (outside their hut) due to the heavy rains of the previous night. And carrying a broken ('chipped') bucket ('pail') of water to the enclosure for chickens ('chicken-run') and setting it down for the chickens to drink, she is now gazing at them. At this time, the wind is pushing ('Hunting') across clouds and forests, and beating ('thrashing') her apron against her body and also winnowing the garments that are dangling from a tightly stretched rope ('hanging cloths on the line') in the sun meant to be dried. The woman now asks herself three questions. The first question is this. She says that her happiness (due to her marriage) has, as if, been externalised and transformed by the wind ('this bodying-forth by wind / Of joy') into something like a string around which her actions or works are revolving ('my actions turn on') like beads or balls move or circle round a string ('like a thread / Carrying beads'). This means that she is performing works ('beads') moving around the string of her joy ('thread'). Now, her first question is: will she be able ever to carry on with her ('Can it be borne') this very happiness? She, next, says that at this moment this (happy) morning (the morning is here personified) is staying with her in the bed ('morning shares my bed'), and this morning is staying in such a manner that it seems it will be staying with her eternally ('perpetual morning'). And now her second question is: will she be allowed to sleep ('Shall I be let to sleep') with this eternal and happy morning? That is, will she be able to enjoy sleeping happily in the bed till morning every day and unendingly?

The woman's third question is rather complex. She calls her first immense or unbounded happiness after marriage a novel lake of happiness ('new delighted lakes'), and she imagines that her husband has gone out to see not really a lake of pool of rain-water but a novel lake of happiness ('new delighted lakes') (notice that 'lakes' is plural: 'These new delighted lakes'). She thinks that both she and her husband are now drinking the water of their (personal or particular) lakes of happiness, by genuflecting ('kneeling') at the edges of the lakes, like cattle do, and thereby quenching their thirst of happiness. She thinks or believes that water is quite noble or bountiful or (spiritually) invigorating ('all-generous waters'). Now, her third and final question: if nothing else can destroy ('dry up') their happiness—if nothing else can evaporate the water of their lake of happiness—can death (personified) kill them and thus destroy their happiness (or will their happiness continue to remain with them even after their demise)? And can death (personified) bring to an end ('conclude') their wont of genuflecting by the edge of the lake of happiness and drink to their satiety the spiritually invigorating water of the lakes of happiness?

As we have said, the poem may be divided into two parts. The first part of 17 lines merely describes a newly married, woman's wedding-day and wedding-night and also the morning following the wedding-night. The setting is a suburban farm house with horses in the stable and chickens in the run (enclosure meant for chicken). The first part very aptly describes the express new joy of the recently married woman. Her joy is obliquely suggestive of its sexual origin, the suggestion having worked through psychological symbols of 'twisted candlestick' (symbol of phallus), restless horses (symbol of erotic excitement or arousal), 'water' and 'floods' (faintly suggestive of birth or procreation), and 'delighted lakes' (suggestive of female genitalia). The 'waters' in the last line of the poem may also (subsidiarily) refer to spirituality, like 'water' does in the poem 'Water'. Of course, the word 'water' in the poem 'Wires' faintly suggests sexuality, as it does in 'Wedding-Wind'. That water is associated with sexuality may be evident from the fact that one sometimes derives sexual pleasure while urinating, which in psychoanalytic terminology is called urethral eroticism (Rycroft, 174). The second part of the poem, consisting of the last seven lines of it, qualifies the nascent joy or happiness of the newly married woman with her doubts about the continuity of her happiness in her and her husband's lives and also after their demise.

In the poem (as also in its title), the term 'wind' is central and works as a controlling image or symbol, as the word is vitally significant also in the poems 'Absences' and 'Mr Bleaney'. The word 'wind' is employed five times in the poem, perhaps to emphasise its importance. Wind, again, is present in 'Talking in Bed'. In all these three poems—'Wedding-Wind', 'Absences' and 'Talking in Bed'—wind is presented as a disruptive, sundering, violative, destroying agent or force. So wind is negatively omenous. Andrew Swarbrick is quite perceptive when he writes: "As we have seen, from his earliest work the wind is in Larkin's poems as a disruptive and destroying force ('Wedding-Wind', 'Absences', 'Mr Bleaney')" (Swarbrick, 1995, 109). But, according to Swarbrick, the wind in 'Wedding-Wind' is not suggestive of 'indifference and arbitrariness', as in the other poems, but of 'an ambivalent expression of joy' (*op. cit.*, 32).

'Wedding-Wind', like 'Two Guitar Pieces', is a dramatic monologue in the style of Robert Browning and Robert Frost. *The Concise Oxford Dictionary of Literary Terms* (1996) defines dramatic monologue as "a kind of poem in which a single fictional or historical character other than the poet speaks to a silent 'audience' of one or more persons. Such poems reveal not the poet's own thoughts but the mind of the impersonated character, whose personality is revealed unwittingly: this distinguishes a dramatic monologue from a lyric, while the implied presence of an auditor distinguishes it from a soliloquy" (Baldick, 62). Following this definition, we can certainly identify 'Wedding-Wind' as dramatic monologue, for in the poem not Larkin but the newly married woman speaks to an implied auditor and expresses the state of her mind that is being harassed by doubts about the perpetuity of her and her husband's newly gained happiness. The newly married woman is of course the mask of Larkin. 'Wedding-Wind' (particularly the first 17 lines of it) narrates the incidents of the woman's marriage-day and of the marriage-night and also of the following morning, and in this sense the poem is narrative. Further, in the poem Larkin speaks in the fictional voice of a woman (ventriloqually) and so we may say that the poem bears the impress of the novelist. And this is so perhaps because Larkin, who wanted to be not so much a poet as a great novelist, was still struggling with novel-writing in the year 1946, the year in which 'Wedding-Wind' was written.

'Wedding-Wind', like 'The Explosion', has an experiential surprise for us at a time when we are not at all prepared for it. The surprise is not there in the narrative part of the poem but in the three urgent and vital questions of the newly married woman presently buoyed up with contentment and joy. The joy of the woman, though, is not absolute, for a thin shadow of doubt as to its perpetuity hangs over it.

Her three questions about her present joy are incessantly gnawing at her consciousness: will she be enjoying this joy perpetually, will she be permitted to sleep in bed perpetually till (such a lovely) morning as today, and will she and her husband be able to enjoy such delight or happiness perpetually? In fact, her three questions amount to only a single question: whether her nuptial joy and happiness will remain with her perpetually. The mood of the woman is, therefore, not clear but umbrageous; and her attitude towards marriage is ambivalent. Her ambivalent attitude certainly reflects Larkin's own opposing emotional attitude towards the institution of marriage. Andrew Motion writes about the ambivalcnt mood or attitude invoked in the poem: "'Wedding-Wind', (too,) in spite of its excitement and fulfilment, offsets its 'happiness' with a barrage of incredulous questions and an admission that the speaker [the newly married woman] is 'sad' because other people and animals cannot share her contentment" (Regan, 37).

Vivid descriptive imagery is a striking feature of the poem. Larkin graphically delineates the blowing of the wild and fierce wind: the wind's banging of the stable door, its crusing through clouds and forests, its beating the woman's forecloth against her body, and its lashing out at the cloths dangling from the stretched rope in the sun. The poem is studded with a few apt metaphors: 'the wind / Hunting through clouds and forests' (like a hunter chasing his game), the wind 'thrashing / My apron' (like farmers beat crops against planks) and 'this perpetual morning shares my bed' (as a husband perpetually shares his wife's bed). There are two memorable similies in 'Wedding-Wind': 'this bodying-forth by wind / Of joy my actions turn on, like a thread / Carrying beads' and 'Our kneeling as cattle by all-generous waters'. In the former, the woman is comparing her domestic works with the beads of a rosary and her joy with the thread that runs through the beads. She means to say that as the beads of the rosary smoothly move around the thread so her domestic works are done around her joy, i.e. happily. In the second simile, the woman likens her and her husband's squatly sitting on the edge of their pool of happiness (i.e. passing their conjugal life most happily or enjoying happiness) with cattle's squatting on the brink of a lake and drinking its invigorating or life-giving water.

Most of Larkin's poems suffer from doubt, hesitation or ambiguity (like he himself did), and this is quite evident in 'Wedding-Wind' as well. Andrew Swarbrick writes about the newly married woman's dubitating state of mind as we find it in this poem: "The poem shows Larkin working on a different vein from 'Lines on a Young Lady's Photograph Album', able to create a depth of feeling in the emotions of a newly-married woman and allowing his meaning to grow suggestively out of images rather than directly stating it. Although the poem seems to portray the woman's exultant joy, there is also a lurking sense of threat. The woman is for a time alone in her wedding-night when her husband has to shut the door blown by the wind and she is left 'stupid in candlelight... / Seeing my face in the twisted candlestick, / Yet seeing nothing'. The image is slightly macabre and conveys something sinister about her sudden loneliness. This confused mixture of feelings is also felt in her being 'sad / That any man or beast that night should lack / The happiness I had'. Later, the wind is 'hunting' and 'thrashing' dangerously, and the suggestions of boundless love at the end of the poem are in fact expressed as rhetorical questions. What Larkin captures in this poem are the ambiguous feelings of a woman on her wedding-night: her joy, but also her fears and vulnerability" (Swarbrick, 1986, 24-25). What Swarbrick has here perhaps misinterpreted or partially interpreted is that the woman's questions are not merely 'suggestions of boundless love' but also her radical doubts about that wished for 'boundless love'.

However, this is a relatively rare poem of Larkin, in the sense that whereas most of his poems were written about the life in contemporary British metropolis or suburbian towns, only in a very few poems of his do we find pastoral or farming scenarios, and 'Wedding-Wind' is one of them. The rural or pastoral setting of the poem is very aptly drawn with a minimum number of strokes of the brush, bringing to view only a few objects: stable, horses, floods, cloths hung on line for drying in the sun, and lakes. The evoked lyricism and heightened emotion of the poem have enormously added to its beauty, so much so that its appeal lingers in our memory even long after we have quite forgotten the text of it. But, however, this poem has failed to attract the attention of James Booth, who has rejected it as 'artificial' (Swarbrick, 1995, 44).

3
Coming

For at least one thing this is a distinctive poem and it is this that this is not a poem in which, as is normally done in a Larkin poem, a statement is made, but is a poem in which 'longer evenings' are celebrated. This poem, therefore, may be called a celebration poem. This poem is also distinctive for its rare lyrical intensity, for its tinge of romanticism, and for its sense of contentment that is very rare in Larkin canon. It is this poem, again, where Larkin's well-known confession that his childhood was a 'forgotten boredom' occurs. This poem, 'Coming', may be called a companion poem of 'I Remember, I Remember', in that in both the poems Larkin speaks about his childhood; in that, therefore, both the poems are autobiographical. The similarity between these two poems of course ends here, and then the difference between them becomes noticeable. 'I Remember, I Remember' is a lugubriously melancholic poem, but 'Coming' is one of Larkin's very few poems that describes a rare and fleeting moment of happiness of his in an atmosphere and surround of hope and romance, though he is not quite oblivious of the fact that his childhood had been a tale of boredom—a tale that he has suppressed into his subconscious mind. The 19-short-line poem 'Coming' was dated by Larkin 25 February 1950. It was first published in *XX Poems* and then in *The Less Deceived.*

Larkin begins the poem very realistically. He says that now the evenings are procrastinating, dilatory ('longer') (notice that the poem was written in the last quarter of February when the sun had already covered about one-third of its way to the equator), and the sun-light, that is yellow, i.e. not white or bright, and cold (because the winter has not yet departed) is flooding or washing ('Bathes') the quiet top-most parts ('serene/ Foreheads') of the houses or buildings. One bird of the species of throstle or mavis or storm-cock or song-thrush ('A thrush'), being enveloped or camouflaged by sweet bay trees ('laurel-surrounded') weel inside ('deep') the defoliated ('bare') garden, is singing. The singing of the bird is giving the impression that the throat of the bird has recently been cleared of all films or obstructions, so that its tune or melody is quite clear ('fresh-peeled voice'). And the song of that bird is, as though, astonishing the buildings that are constructed with bricks ('brickwork').

The poet, Larkin, delightfully says (notice the repetition of line no. 10) that soon spring will come, and so—though his childhood was a story of boredom, which he is now forgetful of ('whose childhood / Is a forgotten boredom')—he is feeling that even now (in his adulthood) he is, as if, a mere child (i.e. romantic). He is feeling not like any child whatsoever but like the child who has, as if, encroached upon, or reached, the state or territory ('scene') of adulthood where (or when) people have to compromise ('reconcile') themselves with the unchildlike or unromantic or unfriendly reality of life ('Who comes on a scene/ Of adult reconciling'). In such a state of his mind and in such a (romantic) environ, the poet cannot understand anything but that everybody is uninhibitedly and volubly laughing with great happiness ('can understand nothing / But the unusual laughter'). And seeing everyone uncommonly ('unusual') laughing in happiness, he himself begins ('starts') to feel happy, too.

This short poem comprises in its brief fold an autobiographical element, an insinuation of romantic sentiment, a touch of the poet's puzzlement at the complexity and opacity of the reality, and, more than all these, a suggestion of his love of nature. The mood in the poem is bright, and yet the poem betrays Larkin's nagging and painful memory of the 'boredom' of his childhood. It is only in this sense that the poem bears an autobiographical element. In the poem, Larkin seems to be dancing at the prospect of imminent advent of spring: notice the repetition of the verse 'It will be spring soon' and notice the mark of continuity or mark of muffled wonder at the end of the repeated line that stops with a dash: 'It will be spring soon—'. Suggestions of the spring are not insufficient in the poem: prolonged evenings, light of the declining sun washing the silently standing buildings, a thrush singing in melodious tune from her shy grove in the thinly foliated garden. The poet's eager attention to the oncoming spring speaks abundantly about his moment of romanticism. It is to be noted here that 'Coming' is a very rare poem where we find Larkin in his very uncommon mood of happiness and romanticism. But his moment of joy and romanticism is alloyed with the ineluctable painful memory of his childhood boredom and also by his befuddled state of mind due to the intricacy and incomprehensibility of the universe and the relationships among human beings. The poet cannot understand either the universe or the intercourse among people: he 'can understand nothing'. And lastly, this brief poem, briskly though, features Larkin's love of nature that he is said to have acquired from Thomas Hardy. Larkin's romantic mood and his joy in this poem are inspired by nothing else but the beauty and sweetness of the spot of nature that is the setting of the poem: the particular fading glow of evening, a twitering thrush hidden behind the screen of laurel boscage, and the thrush's gratifying melody.

'Coming' very positively compares with 'Spring' which—and this is very striking to notice—Larkin wrote about two months after he wrote 'Coming', to be exact, on 19 May 1950. Both the poems were first published in *XX Poems* and then in *The Less Deceived*. Andrew Motion writes that in both the poems, Larkin betrays a happy mood: "...'Coming', candidly describes [his] happiness.... And in 'Spring', although he describes himself as 'An indigestible sterility' the season has 'least use for', this allows him to see it 'best', and recognise it as 'earth's most multiple, excited daughter'" (Motion, 189). But the similarity between the two poems is to be found more elsewhere—in both the poems being nature poems. We have already said that 'Coming' may be deemed to be a nature poem in so far as it betrays Larkin's love of nature. Roger Day writes about 'Coming': "It might be called a 'nature poem', and in a way, it is, since it directly celebrates the lengthening evenings, the coming of spring and birdsong, but its real subject, as in most 'nature poems', is the mood and feelings of the speaker" (Day, 41). The mood and feelings of the speaker that Roger Day here refers to are the mood of joy and happiness, and the feelings of a child ('Feel like a child') who has enough of the power of free imagination and who is not yet compelled to reconcile with the dry—as dust and incomprehensible reality. With a child's power of free imagination, the nature poet accosts nature, and like him he feels, and like his mood his own mood develops with joy and wonder. In 'Spring', Larkin describes nature more elaborately than in 'Coming'. Most of the 14 lines of 'Spring' deal with the natural elements: green shadow, 'awakened grass', calm clouds, songs of birds, sun lights, 'branch-arrested mist of leaf', park, 'untaught flowers', 'race of water', etc. In 'Coming', Larkin 'starts to be happy' and in 'Spring' he means to say that his vision is 'mountain-clear' and his needs of natural beauty are 'immodest', though in the former poem he has not forgotten his childhood boredom and as an adult he has to compromise with the hard reality, and in the latter poem he considers himself as an 'indigestible sterility'. Therefore, we may legitimately call these two poems nature poems.

In 'Coming', Andrew Swarbrick has found lyrical intensity, but Roger Day has noticed not only that but all the common qualities of the poems of Larkin. Day writes that in this poem, "Qualities seen in other Larkin poems are present—lucidity, spare but telling choice of detail and, particularly characteristic, highly original choice of certain words as striking as they are immediately appropriate. For example, the bird's song is described in a vivid metaphor as 'fresh-peeled' suggesting that the music is like fresh fruit (a peeled apple?)—a striking use of synaesthesia. The song is then imitated in the repeated line about the coming of spring. (Larkin uses this rarely.) Here, the repetition neatly divides the poem into scene and speaker" (Day, 42). This short poem presents us with an appropriate instance of Larkin's great poetic-technical acumen. Firstly, in it he has employed two very powerful images that work as framed paintings: 'Light, chill and yellow, / Bathes the serene / Foreheads of houses' and 'A thrush sings, / Laurel-surrounded / In the deep bare garden'. The three phrases or catchwords of the poem are memorable, marvellous: 'Laurel-surrounded', 'fresh-peeled voice' and 'forgotten boredom'. Further, the repetition or refraining of the line 'It will be spring soon' to emphasize the imminence of the advent of spring and the poet's romantic hope and joy is subtle and ingenius.

4

Reasons for Attendance

In *The Less Deceived*, there are three poems, out of a total twenty-nine, that have direct reference to physical union between man and woman, and these three are: 'Dry-Point', 'Deceptions' and 'Reasons for Attendance'. 'Reasons for Attendance' was dated 30th December, 1953 and was first published in *The Less Deceived.* It is a dramatic poem, where Larkin first assumes a persona and then tears it off and presents his own voice. Superficially, the poem may seem to relate to sexual partnership between man and woman, but in actuality it delivers the message that not only in the matter of sex but in every other matter whatsoever happiness is mutual—that none can enjoy happiness in solitariness, that even in art, for instance, enjoyment depends on sharing, and that loneliness or isolation and happiness are absolutely contradictory concepts. Not only that, the message is that none can realise · his individuality uninterruptedly, without others intruding his being, i.e. "a stable, coherent, unified 'individuality' is an illusion" (Swarbrick, 1995, 57). In the poem, the speaker is an individual voice that speaks in the first person. When Larkin wrote the poem, he was perhaps suffering the "wriggling torments during his engagement to Ruth Bowman" (*op. cit.*, 56), being apprehensive that *if he married her he would lose his individuality*, though all at the same time he could hardly think of negating her attraction. His vacillating, wavering attitude towards his proposed marriage to Ruth is quite reflected in the poem. The poem is of twenty lines, which are divided into four stanzas, each stanza consisting of five lines. The rhyme-scheme of all the stanzas is a / b / a / b / b.

The poet is being called by the loud and commanding ('authoritative') sound of the trumpet to witness for a while the (amorous) performance of some dancers (both male and female) who are all below the age of twenty-five and who are dancing in a lighted house or room whose windows are made of glass panels. The poet is attracted ('draws') to the performance and sees that the dancers are always changing their places or their feet ('Shifting'), attentively or carefully ('intently'). He observes that the faces of the girls are suffused with extra blood or that the faces of the girls are ruddy or reddened (due to shyness) ('flushed') because the young men are gazing at them ('face to flushed face'). And he notices that the dancers are dancing, with religious or stately somberness ('Solemnly'), to the beatings of the drum that are bringing happiness to them ('on the beat of happiness').

But the poet is not certain that the dancers are happy; he says that it may be that he is only imagining ('fancy') that they are happy ('so')—or it may be that he is only guessing that they are happy ('—Or so I fancy'). He is guessing ('sensing') that they are happy because he is seeing the moisture ('sweat') on their exposed skin of their bodies and the vapour ('smoke') coming out of their hot and moistened bodies. (The 'sweat' and 'smoke' on their bodies are due to their excessive physical movements or dancings, which are an indication of their happiness.) He is also guessing or fancying that the dancers (male dancers, to be exact) are happy because they are enjoying the astonishingly ('wonderful') touch ('feel') of the girls, i.e. the female dancers. (At this moment, the poet is witnessing the performances of the dancers staying outside the dancing hall and looking through the glass-window.) He now asks himself why he is keeping outside the hall of dancing ('Why be out here?'). He does not answer this question of his; he, contrarily, raises a counter question to himself: why should he go inside the hall of dancing ('But then, why be in there?'). (In this way he is debating with him.) He is certainly being attracted by the prospect, once inside the dancing hall, of getting carnal satisfaction from the girls ('Sex, yes'), but he asks himself why he should positively respond to the lure of carnal satisfaction—he asks what sort of satisfaction or happiness carnality can deliver to him ('but what / Is sex?'). He says that, so far as his knowledge goes ('as far as I'm concerned'), the notion ('to think') that most ('the lion's share') happiness can be gained only by sexually conjugated people of opposite sexes ('couples') is absolutely wrong ('sheer / Inaccuracy').

(The allurement of carnality does not attract the poet.) He says that what attracts him ('calls me') is rather the raised-up-in-the-air ('lifted') harsh-sounding ('rough-tongued') 'cone of the trumpet' ('bell'). In the parenthesis, he says that one may, if one likes ('if you like'), call the 'lifted, rough-tongued bell' or its sound (modulated according to a pattern) a creative imaginary work of beauty ('Art'). He says that the particular, distinct, single sound ('individual sound') of the trumpet persuades ('Insists') him to believe that like it (the single sound) he himself is also an individual person, i.e. not a corporate being ('I too am an individual'). The trumpet sounds ('It speaks') and the poet hears that sound ('I hear') individually, singly (not along with others or like others, because his auditory receptors are quite different from those of others). Other persons may also hear the sound of that trumpet ('others may hear as well'), but they will not hear the sound so that along with them he will also hear the sound without the function of his own ears ('But not for me'), i.e. to hear the sound he has to employ his own ears, individually. Likewise, it is not possible that when he hears the sound, others also hear it without the aid of their ears ('nor I for them').

The poet says that in the same way when he enjoys happiness it is only he who enjoys the benefit and not others; and when others feel happiness it is only they who are feeling happiness and not he ('and so / With happiness'). It is for this ground, says the poet, that he is keeping outside the dancing hall ('Therefore I stay outside'), believing that hearing the sound of the trumpet or feeling happiness cannot be shared with any other person ('Believing this'). On the other hand, the dancing young men inside the hall ('they') are scrimmaging this way and that to catch hold of each other, like the players tussele for catching the ball in a Rugby football match ('maul to and fro'), supposing that happiness can only be mutually shared by two persons, or that happiness can be achieved only conjointly by two persons ('Believing that'). And thus both the poet, outside the hall, and the young dancers, inside the hall ('both'), are happy ('satisfied'). Of course this is true only if none of the two—the poet or the outsider and the dancing youngsters or the insiders—wrongly understand that they are happy ('If no one has misjudged himself') or if none of them make a false statement ('Or lied') about their actual feeling or state of being.

The central meaning of the poem is somewhat veiled by the description of the situation—the youngsters dancing in a hall to the tune and beats of music and the poet observing that through the window, keeping outside the hall. The term 'Reasons' in the title of the poem—'Reasons for Attendance'—means the grounds for which the poet does not want to enter the dancing hall. The poem may be divided into two parts: the first part comprises the beginning six and a half lines of the poem, in which the poet describes the situation that gives rise to his slant or inclination towards the dancing fiesta in the hall with glass windows; and the second part consists of the rest of the poem, in which he describes his wavering between his wise to go inside the hall and his decision not to go—to stay outside. In the first part we see the poet viewing the amorous spree of dancing among the young men and girls through the fenestra from outside the hall. He imagines, or rather fancies that the male dancers there must be happy because they are sensing the amorously exciting touch of the girls. When he thus fancies, he obliquely suggests his desire to go inside and mix with the dancers to be happy. Not only that, but the sound of the trumpet also emphatically invites him to enter the dancing hall. So, the poet has two *reasons for going inside the hall and attending to the dancing fiesta* (notice the title of the poem: 'Reasons for Attendance'): one, in answering to the insistent call of the trumpet; and two, to get a feel of, or have sex with, the girls dancing there, *for happiness*.

In the second part of the poem, the poet turns about on his earlier two grounds for going into the hall. Here he produces two other contrary *reasons against going inside the hall and attending to the dancing fiesta*: one, he does not believe that sex is the greatest source of happiness ('to think the lion's share / Of happiness is found by couples—sheer / Inaccuracy, as far as I'm concerned.') and also that sex is the only source of happiness; and two (he now perceives the call of the trumpet in a different way—as an image of individuality), the bell-shaped up-turned mouth of the trumpet persuades him to be an individual, to respect individuality, and not to surrender it, for instance, to a girl to share sex or happiness with her. But, in the second part, the poet is not constant in his conviction; he flags, wavers; he doubts his own conviction that he can be happy all right with his devotion to individuality—being an individual, pure and simple—without sacrificing it by way of enjoying sex with a girl; and he doubts his own belief that the couples of the dancers are not getting real amorous satisfaction or happiness because they are sharing it among them, and so are sacrificing their respective individualities.

The trumpet's sound or 'voice' is similative of the double desires of the poet. The trumpet has two voices, or the single sound or voice appears to the poet as double—two voices with two opposite meanings: one voice calls him to enter the hall and witness the amorous behaviour of the dancers from closer quarter, or to mix with them for the enjoyment of sex; the other voice dissuades him to do that and persuades him to keep his individuality (it must be precious) and so to stay outside the hall. The poet of course tilts to the second voice but not without having a mind of waver—to lean to the opposite voice. He prefers to respond to the second voice of the trumpet, because he thinks that he will be truly happy with his undiminished individuality and not with shared sex. The poet calls the sound of the raised up mouth of the trumpet art, hesitatingly though ('if you like'), and thinks that like the trumpet he will produce his own individual voice, i.e. he will pursue the vocation of the artist, who works individually or as a solitary human being with all happiness, and thus he will also be happy. But behind his supposed happiness in smug individuality lurks his concealed fear of loneliness, and also his true motivation towards sexuality, that is revealed through the obliquely leering expression 'wonderful feel of girls'. Andrew Swarbrick says that in 'Reasons for Attendance' the speaker (the poet / Larkin) is being pulled in two opposite directions (like in many other poems of Larkin): "The 'voice' of 'Reasons for Attendance' has all the appearance of reasonableness until the end when the poem's strategy of subversion is revealed. In fact, the central voice of the poem is the trumpet's which on the one hand, 'loud and authoritative', strikes 'the beat of happiness' and on the other is the 'rough-tongued bell/ (Art, if you like) whose individual sound / Insists I too am individual'.... It is between these two opposing attractions, the one sexual and communal, the other solitary and vocational, that the speaker is poised" (Swarbrick, 1995, 55).

Roger Day says that the speaker of the poem seems to be an old, lascivious, self-critical, rough and surly person. Day writes about the speaker: "How do we see the speaker? His tone seems to me almost blustering, that of an older man who has missed opportunities and who is bluffly determined not to see it as a loss. Notice, for instance, how the 'wonderful feel of girls' (hinting at lasciviousness in the observing speaker) is set against the derisive 'they maul to and fro' to produce a comic ambivalence" (Day, 36). David Timms, who believes that this is a 'personal' poem (or autobiographical poem), says that the speaker of the poem is Larkin himself. Timms writes: "In 'Reasons for Attendance', Larkin plays the academic university librarian, just old enough to feel out of touch with the students with whom he deals" (Timms, 86).

The concluding two words of the poem, 'Or lied' expresses with appropriate emphasis the speaker's indecision or ambivalence or ambiguous intention. In the concluding couplet of the poem, the speaker arrives at a conclusion ('both are satisfied') and immediately negates it ('If no one has misjudged himself. Or lied.'). Roger Day writes about the concluding two words: "Larkin has explained why the poem ends with the devastating qualification 'Or lied'. These two words are intended to correct any false impression of certainty, and this ambiguity, the 'built-in' comment, is an inverted contribution to 'truth' by questioning, unmasking people's assumptions. They produce an effect also found in 'Wants'...—the implication that possibly neither way of life produces real happiness" (Day, 37). However, 'Reasons for Attendance' is a poem of ironic self-dramatization. The poem's modulations are very subtle, its view is slant or opinionated, and its language is conversational or colloquial. The caesura in the last line of the poem is a distinctive feature of it.

5

Next, Please

'Next, Please', a poem that is built up on the depressing concept of death, may be taken to be central to Larkin's pessimistic philosophy of life, that he took up, as in this poem, also in such others as 'Maturity' (1951?), 'Wants' (1950), 'Triple Time' (1953), etc. The poem was written on 18 January 1951—at a time when Larkin was around 29, when, we may suppose, he had already tasted the bitterness of life and seen the seamy side of it. He published his last novel *A Girl in Winter* four years ago and his till then only collection of poems *The North Ship* was published five years back, and neither could he write another novel, in spite of all efforts, nor could he publish any further collection of poems. Moreover, by then he had lost his father and had found love of women unrewarding. So, it was not so unnatural for him then to be pessimistic, particularly because he was naturally introverted, defeatist, and was frequently given to brooding over death. 'Next, Please' features this pessimistic turn of his mind. The poem was first privately published in *XX Poems* (1951) and then in *The Less Deceived* (as the seventh poem of it). It consists of six stanzas, each stanza having four lines, rhyming a / a / b / b. The title of the poem, according to Larkin's sister Kitty, "is a phrase he [Larkin] dreaded hearing as a child whenever he reached the head of a queue at school or in shops: it meant he would shortly have to speak, which would be embarrassing because of his stammer" (Motion, 208).

Larkin begins the poem disapproving our always being very eager to wait to see what good things may happen to us in the future and thus developing ('pick up') within us the bad habit of expecting only good things or incidents for us in the future. We always think that some good things or incidents are day after day coming to us or are going to happen to us ('approaching'). We always think in this way till the moment when, standing on a high and steep bank or promontory ('bluff'), we see at a distance an array of little and visible ('tiny, clear') and dazzling ships ('Sparkling armada') carrying hopes or promises of fulfilments of our desires coming closer to us ('draw near'). Impatiently we see the ships as coming very slowly ('How slow they are?'), and it seems to us that they are spending time unnecessarily or wasting time ('how much time they waste'), because they will not agree to accelarate their speed ('Refusing to make haste!').

Nevertheless ('Yet still'), those ships ('they') persuade us to hold out or endure, and wait ('leave us'), holding up in our hands stems without roses ('wretched stalks'), which symbolise our despair ('disappointment'), and we welcome those ships by waving the naked or bare stems. We do this because ('for') there is nothing that forestals or stems ('balks') the approaching of the ships (near us). Each one of the ships is expected to carry for us very satisfactory hopes or lucks ('big'). Each one of the ships is decorated ('prinked') with brass-works, so heavily that under the weight she is inclining ('leaning') downwards or sideways. Each rope of a ship is being clearly seen as having an unfurled flag of promise ('lagged') and the carved or embossed figure of a woman under the bowsprit ('figurehead') of each ship has her nipples ('tits') made of gold, and each ship is projected ('Arching') towards where we are standing in expectation ('our way'). But none of the ships reaches any port or shore and fastens herself to it ('never anchors'). Again, if for a while a ship seems to be existing *now* ('present'), the sooner she seems to be existing in the *past* (such are those illusory ships of hope). And this illusoriness or deception those ships maintain just till we die ('Right to the last').

We think that each ship ('each one') will haul or anchor herself ('heave') near us and then unload or disembark all the good hopes or satisfying fulfilments ('All good'), that she has carried, for us ('into our lives')—everything that belong to us, or all we are entitled to ('all we are owed'), because ('For') we are waiting for those things with all religious earnestness ('devoutly') and because we are waiting for those things for a great length of time. But we come to understand, at a certain stage of our lives, that we all are mistaken ('But we are wrong') in expecting the arrivals of these ships which are supposed to carry hopes or fulfilments for us.

Only a single ship, and no other ship (which we are not waiting for), is searching, or closing in, for us ('seeking us'). That ship has its sail coloured black ('black- / Sailed'), and we are unacquainted ('unfamiliar') with her. The ship is dragging or drawing with a rope ('towing'), behind its back, or after herself, an enormous silence in which not even chirping of birds is heard, i.e. a lifeless silence or the silence of death. And in the foamy track left behind ('wake') by the ship there is no generation ('breed') or nothing bursts forth, like creatures are born by breaking the shells around them ('break'), i.e. there is no life behind, or in the trail, of the ship—because it is the ship of death.

The image of ship is a stock image of Larkin that appears in such other poems of his as 'The North Ship', 'Ultimatum', 'Absences', etc. In fact, some of the images of 'Ultimatum', the poem that Larkin wrote in 1940 (28 November), including the image of ship, reappear in his other later poems. Andrew Motion writes: "'Ultimatum' contains images and ideas which were to remain important to Motion throughout his life. 'The Ship' in the third line appears again in 'The North Ship', in 'Poetry of Departures', in 'Next, Please' and in 'How Distant'; 'docks' and 'seagulls' return in several of the poems he wrote in Belfast and Hull" (Motion, 34). The image of dock ('bluff') and seagull ('birdless'), beside the image of ship, of 'Ultimatum', are present in 'Next, Please'.

The theme of the poem is drawn from the poet's stock-in-trade: deception and death. Deception occupies the first four stanzas of the poem, and death only the last stanza. The poet says that we develop the habit of always anxiously expecting some good things to happen to us but ultimately we are frustrated. This idea is expressed through the extended metaphor of our viewing from a high cliff on the shore of the sea the slow approaching of a fleet of ships bearing, we eagerly expect, freights of good lucks for us, but at the end of our 'waiting so devoutly and so long' we are disappointed to find that 'we are wrong' in our expectation. But, nevertheless, we soon over again begin to wait for that fleet of ships that we dimly perceive at a distance, and thus we are endlessly being deceived for fault of no one else's but ours—being deceived because—here we repeat—no ship brings any freight for us. This idea occupies the first five stanzas of the poem. In the last stanza, the poet says something different. He says that we are of course not always deceived, because one ship certainly brings freight for us—the freight of death. In sum, the poem, taken as a whole, deals with the futility of life that promises much, but all its promises ultimately prove deceptive, counterfeit; save that it fetches for us only one ultimate thing—our inevitable extinction, nullity, death.

'Next, Please' may be taken as a dimly or distantly autobiographical poem. Larkin, as we know, understood life to be a long waiting for a sequence of deceptive promises, ending in the certainty of our absolute and irreversible extinction. And this is the central theme of the poem. It is in this sense that we may call this poem autobiographical. Symbolism is a distinctive feature of this poem. The dominating or controlling symbol of the poem is that of ship, that we expect as carrying for us the freight of fulfilments, but which ironically brings for us only one thing—death. The symbol of ship also works as the central or controlling symbol in 'The North Ship', a poem with five (almost independent) parts: 'Legend', 'Songs', 'Fortunetelling', 'Blizzard' and 'Above 80 Degree North'. In the first part of 'The North Ship', subtitled 'Legend', the word 'ship' occurs four times and the term is employed there as a symbol of death, as in 'Next, Please'. In 'Legend', the three ships were rigged for 'a long journey' over the 'unforgiving sea', and these two metaphors obviously point to death. The image of the ship negotiating the high waters, roughened by fierce wind, occurs in the four other parts of the poem, where also the ship symbolizes death. Besides, in 'Songs' and 'Fortunetelling' the images of sea, sea voyage and birds occur as they do in 'Next, Please'.

David Timms says that, like 'Dry-Point', 'No Roads' and 'Wires' of *The Less Deceived*, 'Next, Please' of the same collection is also built around an emotional concept. Timms writes about this poem: "'Next, Please' opens with a statement of emotional concept with which it is concerned:

> Always eager for the future, we
> Pick up bad habits of expectancy.

The poem goes on to elaborate the concept through a metaphor. We watch for the future in much the same way as someone might watch for ships from a cliff, or to use the poem's word, a 'bluff'. The word is intended to carry both its meanings here: a promontory, but also a pretence. As we watch, the ships approach like hopes—slowly, but growing clearer all the time. In the poem, the ships are glittering sailing vessels, with ornamented figure-heads—the objects of our desires are always more attractive before they are realised. When they are realised they begin to pale; the ships reach us, but do not anchor. They turn, and recede once more into the distance. Larkin is making the point that our hopes are never fulfilled, but that, when they are fulfilled, the fulfilment is only temporary. Fulfilment, in the words of another poem, is often 'desolate attic', and the reason lies as much in the structure of time itself as in our feelings. Present time is instantaneous" (Timms, 70). 'Next, Please' is not only pessimistic, it has also a sense of anger at the series of frustrations of our repeated expectations, as Andrew Swarbrick observes. The despair and frustration that visit us from time to time, Swarbrick believes, gradually hardens us and we grow more and more mature, as Larkin tells us in 'Maturity'.

6

Wants

This ten-line poem is one of Larkin's very short poems. It comprises two stanzas of five lines each, and in each stanza he states one of his innermost wants or desires: in the first he wants loneliness, and in the second extinction. But behind these his two wants there is, in fact, a single want—the want or desire of oblivion, i.e. he wants to be forgotten by everybody. As 'Coming' is Larkin's brightest poem so 'Wants' is his gloomiest. The poem may be called both existential poem and escape poem. The poem was dated 1st June, 1950. It first appeared in *XX Poems* and then in *The Less Deceived.*

In the first stanza of the poem, Larkin says that in spite of the superficial glittering attractions of life ('Beyond all this'), what we most hanker after is solitariness, loneliness ('the wish to be alone'). Even though ('However') we are invited through invitation-cards to attend some social functions at night ('the sky grows dark with invitation-cards'); or even though we follow the commendments or injunctions of religious books in our marital or conjugal relationships ('the printed directions of sex'); or even though we enjoy being photographed, as a family or as a nation, under the national flag unfurled on the pole ('flagstaff'), i.e. we enjoy being citizens of a state or enjoy our nationality, etc.—('the family is photographed under the flagstaff—') we actually do not desire all these and such other social things (recall 'Beyond all this') but desire only one thing —solitude (recall 'the wish to be alone').

In the second stanza, the desire of Larkin is graver and more serious, gloomier and more dark. He says that though we attend to routinised social functions ('Beneath it all'; recall 'Beyond all this'), we desire to be effaced, i.e. we wish our existence or being itself be erased, obliterated ('desire of oblivion runs'). Larkin says that in spite of our being tricked to be excited ('artful tensions') of different social ceremonies and functions throughout the whole year ('the calendar'); in spite of our being hopeful of the prospect of our life insurance policies ('life insurance'); in spite of there being the powerful attraction of pre-arranged ('tabled') ceremonies of fertility, i.e. religious observances in expectation of progeny, on particular dates of the calendar ('the tabled fertility rites'); and in spite of all our medical measures, involving huge amounts of money, to avoid death ('costly aversion of the eyes from death—'); i.e. in spite of all our happy social observances and all our apparent confidences and hopes, says Larkin, what we really desire, or what wish crosses our minds or traverses our veins ('runs'), is the total effacement, erasement of our being or existence itself ('Beneath it all, desire of oblivion runs').

The poem, in a few words, states Larkin's covert wish to die, to get his existence totally effaced. Life and social observances, to him, are our formalised, mechanized, instinctual behaviour. He thinks that we live only by social customs, instincts, and false hopes. Of course, he wants to participate in social observances, wishes to fulfil his instinctual drives, and hopes to be happy in the future, but all these are his merely half-felt, half-understood and superficial wants, wishes and hopes. What he earnestly, urgently and direly wants is his total effacement, obfuscation, extinction. Andrew Motion writes that in no other poem has Larkin exposed his fundamental wish to die, his 'desire of oblivion'. Motion writes about Larkin: "It is the only time [i.e. in this poem] in his [whole] work that he makes this unqualified appeal [of getting totally effaced, of dying]—elsewhere death is variously whined or withstood, never simply welcomed" (Motion, 189). We have said that the poem was written in June 1950. Andrew Motion informs us, through his book *Philip Larkin: A Writer's Life*, that during the time when the poem was composed Larkin actually felt extremely saddened, depressed. By that time his euphoria over the success of his two novels fizzled out, his strong attraction towards Ruth became greatly reduced, and he pathetically fumbled with his prose work—with new novels. Add to this his switching over from under the literary influence of the romantic Yeats to the darkly pessimistic literary influence of Hardy. All these perhaps contributed to the moribundity of 'Wants'.

Roger Day has raised a very pertinent and important question and then has answered it: "Is the pessimism of this poem intended to convey a whole attitude to life? It could be argued that it expresses only a particular mood and that Larkin's thought is altogether more tentative..." (Day, 35). Day, further, writes that the particular syntax and other elements of 'Wants' have contributed abundantly to the arousal of emotion in the poem. For instance, Day writes, "The impression of weariness and the futility of trying to escape are brought out by the use of unrhymed lines and repeated syntax suggesting lassitude ('however we follow...' 'However the family') and by the way in which each stanza is framed by the reiteration of a bare statement" (*ibid.*).

7

Church Going

This is undoubtedly one of the best poems of *The Less Deceived*, and also of all Larkin poems. The poem is the longest of all the poems of the collection, and is 'much anthologised and widely admired'. David Timms says that 'Church Going' "is arguably Larkin's best poem, and undoubtedly his best known, most anthologised, and most discussed" (Timms, 79). Timms further writes about this poem: "It is certainly a central poem in

Larkin's works, and is as important a statement of the mid-twentieth century consciousness as Arnold's 'Dover Beach' was of the mid-nineteenth. In a widely-read survey of modern literature, *The Modern Writer and His World*, G.S. Fraser called 'Church Going' 'the Movement's prize poem and a poem with claims to greatness'. It is certainly the best and most important poem in *New Lines*, and it certainly has claims to greatness" (*op. cit.*, 81-82).

The poem was dated 28 July 1954 and was first published in *The Less Deceived*. The poem perhaps could have been published earlier in the *Spectator* but the magazine "on receiving 'Church Going' lost the manuscript for a year" (Motion, 242). This 63-line poem is divided into seven stanzas, each stanza having nine lines, rhyming a / b / a / b /c / a / d / c / d. Larkin was always very keen on linguistic and prosodic excellences of his poems and devoted much labour on their drafts. In this regard, his care and labour around 'Church Going' is certainly noteworthy. Anthony Thwaite writes about the time and energy Larkin spent on the poem: "'Church Going', began on 24 April 1954, went through twenty-one pages of drafts, was 'abandoned on 24 May 1954.', and then resumed and completed in July of that year" (Thwaite, 1988, xvii). The fervent reception that he enjoyed can be guessed from at least three facts: firstly, not long after its publication in *The Less Deceived*, the poem was included in Robert Conquest's *New Lines* (1956); secondly, in 1958 Anthony Thwaite, a great admirer of Larkin's poems, requested him to read 'Church Going' and two other poems of the poet in his 'Young British Poets of Today' programme on BBC (and Larkin agreed); and thirdly, in the memorial service of Larkin the poem was selected for recitation by Jill Balcon, C. Day-Lewis's widow.

In the poem, Larkin says that once he visited a church while no ritual was going on inside it (and understandably while there was nobody within it). He entered the church, being certain that no ritual ('nothing') was 'going on' inside it, and after he had already gone into the church, its door automatically slammed shut ('thud shut') behind him. Then the church seemed to be a different church ('Another church')—different from a church inside which rituals were going on. Inside the church, Larkin saw such things as a mat, covering the floor; seats for the church-goers; stones (presumably carved); 'little books' (understandably, copies of the bible or of mass-books); litterings ('sprawlings') of flowers, meant for Sunday congregation ('cut / For Sunday')—flowers which had by then turned nearly brown (from red or purple) due to passage of time; some utensils or ceremonial tools and vessels made of brass; and some other objects ('stuff') at the sacred site of the hall ('Up at the holy end'). Larkin also noticed a small sleek 'organ' or piano (for playing on when masses were to be chanted). The hall is so taught or emotionally strained ('tense') and fetid, frowsy or mouldy (perhaps due to the smell of partially fermented wine) ('musty') that the silence within it cannot escape the notice of anybody ('unignorable'). And for how long that sort of silence was prevailing ('Brewed') within the hall no one but only God knows, i.e. only God knows how long ago those who gathered inside the church, after drinking partially fermented wine, to participate in a religious function, had left the hall. Larkin wanted to show respect to the church but as he was not wearing a hat ('Hatless') he could not do that by taking off his hat. So, as an alternative means of showing respect to the church Larkin took off the clips (devices for 'gripping or clasping, or holding things together') of his bicycle by which he went there, in an unbefitting manner ('awkward').

Larkin then paced towards ('Move forward') the church's receptacle for holy water ('font') and ran his hand or palm along the edge or over the brim of the font (and thus perhaps felt the smoothness of it). After that, from near the font where he stood ('From where I stand'), the roof of the church appeared to him to be 'almost new', and so he questioned himself: was the roof scoured, scrubbed, washed or cleansed, or was it refurbished or renovated ('restored')? He himself did not know the answer ('I don't'), but believed that someone else knew it. However, he then proceeded towards, and climbed, the raised platform or dias or reading-desk from which holy verses are read out, or lessons given ('lectern'); and there on the 'lectern' he found the Bible and hurriedly ran his eyes through, or silently read ('peruse'), a few long-winded ('large-scale'), rhetorical ('Hectoring') and emotional or poetic sentences ('verses'). And after reading those 'verses' he uttered (involuntarily, though) the words 'Here endeth' much more emphatically than he would want to ('than I'd meant'). The sound of his utterance was (mockingly or satirically) laughed at by its own resonances or reverberations ('echoes snigger briefly'). Larkin then went back to the door (to leave the church), but before going out he signed the attendance register or book and dropped an Irish coin worth sixpence into the charity-box as donation. He then thought ('Reflect') that it was not worthwhile to stop anytime on the way near the church ('place') and enter into it.

But, in spite of his thinking like that, Larkin actually ('in fact') frequently stopped there, i.e. near the church. And whenever he did stop afterwards near that place (to look at the church or to enter into it), as on that particular day or occasion, his stopping and visiting the church always ended in his being much befuddled or stupefied ('end much at a loss') as he had become on that particular day or occasion ('like this'), i.e. he could not make out if there was any utility in visiting the church. Each time he visited the church, thenceforth, he failed to understand ('Wondering') what he should seek in the church ('what to look for'). He also failed to decide or understand ('wondering') what he and the other people (of England) would convert all the churches (of England) into ('What we shall turn them into') after those churches would prove quite useless ('When churches fall completely out of use'). He also could not understand whether, when all those churches would be absolutely useless, the people would preserve ('keep') a few principal or leading churches ('cathedrals') eternally ('chronically') as exhibits ('on show'), along with such properties or assets of those principal churches ('their') as hides of animals on which sacred words were written ('parchment'), plates of metals on which also were written sacred words or names, and boxes containing consecrated cakes ('pyx') that were kept in 'locked cases'. And, further, he could not understand if the other churches ('the rest') would be given as tenancies or leased out ('let') to rain (for wearing off) and to folds of sheep (for grazing) without demanding any rental from them ('rent-free'), i.e. whether the rest of the churches would be left exposed to rain-water for being corroded and to sheep to graze upon their debris. Larkin asked if in the future people would avoid the notice of those desolated and ruined churches as omenous ('unlucky') phenomenon.

Alternatively ('Or'), Larkin asked himself, whether it might also happen that some women, with half-believing minds ('dubious women'), would bring their children, at night, to those desolated and dilapidated churches and ask them to touch particular stones of the churches for their well-being or bright future, or the women themselves would pick up and take away some ordinary stones from the debris of the churches ('simples') to their homes in the belief that those stones would cure carcinoma ('cancer'). Or, he further told himself, some women, being told ('Advised') by some knowledgeable persons, would come to those ruined churches and see the ghosts of their deceased loved ones as walking around them. Larkin was confident that belief in some sort of supernatural powers ('Power of some sort or other') would continue to seem to exist here and there ('seemingly at random') in alietory games, played by men, in their puzzling situations ('riddles'), but a day would come when the belief in supernatural beings (such as God), which are but false notions ('superstition'), would certainly go ('must die') as beliefs, in course of time, would not hold any more but go out of existence. Larkin asked, after superstitions, and beliefs in other things related to the superstitions ('beliefs'), and after even agnosticism about those superstitions ('disbelief') would cease to exist, whatever else of that ruined church would remain there? And he answered his own question by saying that after the superstitions, beliefs and disbeliefs would go, the debris of the church would remain as covered by grass ('Grass'), the concrete-covered path leading to the church ('pavement') would remain as shrouded by weeds, and there would remain around the church bushes ('brambles'), supporting projections ('buttress') of that church-building, and the sky overhead.

The church itself would then look like an amorphous mould or a ghost ('shape'), which would become less and less recognisable day by day ('each week'). And the people would then mostly forget the purpose for which the church had once been erected ('A purpose more obscure'). Larkin pondered over ('wonder') who might be the ultimate person that would visit the church ('to seek / This place'). He asked himself whether that last person would go to the church for spiritual purposes for which it stood ('for what it was'), or that last person would be one member of a band of antiquarians ('crew') who would inspect the church-building by tapping or striking it ('tap') (to determine, perhaps, the age of the building, the materials used in constructing it, etc.) and record ('jot') their findings, and discover ('know') what sorts of galleries there were over the ornamental partitions separating the choirs from the naves of the church ('rood-lofts') (*Chambers Twentieth Century Dictionary*, 1981, entry: rood). Larkin further asked himself if, after the dilapidation of the church, a certain dissolute tippler or boozer ('ruin-bibber') would go to the site of the church and boisterously ('randy') search the place for antiques, or whether someone, with uncontrollable habit of visiting the church during Christmas ('Christmas-addict'), would visit the site of the ruined church and bring to memory ('counting') the bygone hey-days of the church when men and women would assemble in the church and their fine strongly ironed accoutrement would rustle and fan the air ('whiff / Of gown-and–bands'), when 'organ-pipes' would be played on and incense ('myrrh') would be burned. Or, Larkin alternatively asked himself, whether the last person to visit the church would be a person like himself ('be my representative').

Larkin asked himself if that last person would be like himself in being disgusted with life ('bored') and ignorant ('uninformed') and also in knowing or understanding that the remaining belief in, or myth of ('silt'), spirituality or supernatural beings ('ghostly': 'ghostly silt') is no more in vogue ('Dispersed'). He asked himself if that ultimate man, nevertheless, like him, would incline to come ('tending') to the site of the church or the crossway near the church ('cross of land') (the word 'cross' here obliquely refers to Christianity) through the suburb that is covered with bushes or low trees ('scrub'). Larkin asked himself whether that last man, like himself, would go to the site of the church because the church ('it') had so long been holding the people (of the place or of the community) together or united ('unsplit') smoothly or evenly ('equably'), through such ecclesiastical functions that had been so long imperative on the occasions of marriage, birth or death, or because the people would think that (and believed that) such functions or rituals of the church ('thoughts of these') held them together, and also because the last man would understand that ever since the decline of those ecclesiastical functions or rituals related to marriage, birth and death, all the people ('what') became separated from one another ('what since is found / Only in separation'), and because he would understand that for this reason, i.e. for keeping the people together the church ('special shell') had been built. Larkin says that though he had no knowledge ('idea') about the value ('worth') of the decorated or dressed up ('accoutred'), stuffy and musty-smelling ('frowsty') church that seemed to be a house for storing corn ('barn'), he felt delighted ('It pleases me') to stand silently within or without the church ('here') and so ('Far') he had been waiting there.

Larkin says that he stood near the church in silence because the church was ('it is') a most valuable ('serious') house or structure on the earth which was also most serious, i.e. both the church and the earth or the world were to him most valuable things of life. The church was most valuable because in its atmosphere, with which spirituality had been mixed or infused ('blent air'), we all converge with all our instincts and motives ('compulsions') along with their entailed good and evil consequences ('all our compulsions meet'). There in the church, we realise or understand which instincts and motives of ours good and which are evil, what we truly are and what are not ('Are recognised'); and there in the church we take our instincts and motives as well as their good and evil, consequences as our fates or lots, i.e., there in the church all these, as if, appear before us as dressed up as our fates or lots ('robed as destinies'). And this at least ('that much') is the value or importance of the church, and this value or importance of the church, mused Larkin, would never become antiquated, effete ('And that much never can be obsolete'). Because ('Since'), a few ('someone') people would always be wondering ('surprising') to feel the desire ('hunger'), in themselves ('himself'), of becoming urgently aware of their instincts and motives and the consequences of those instincts and motives ('serious'). And thus becoming aware, those persons would tend or proceed to that church ('this ground')—the persons who earlier heard that the church ('Which') was the appropriate ('proper') place where one could become sagacious or sapient (about metaphysical, escatological, and ethical matters) ('to grow wise in'). And lastly, Larkin subjunctively added that those few persons would proceed or incline towards the church only if they notice a good many graves existing around it ('If only so many dead lie round'), i.e., only if they were convinced that men must die.

The title of the poem 'Church Going' is comprehensive in its meaning, but the probable different meanings of the title converge on one thing—religion, and in this sense we may say that the poem is about religion or about the decay of Christianity. Roger Day writes about the meaning of the title of the poem and its theme: "I would suggest that the title is a play on words with three meanings:

(a) 'going into churches'—like this visit;
(b) 'the church is going'—religion dying;
(c) 'going to church'—as people used to, and as they will in future.

The poem is, then about religion, its place in people's lives and the places where it is practised. Its basic assumption is that Christianity is a dying religion ('when churches fall *completely* out of use'—my italics) and that there will be an inevitable evolution in people's thinking. The power exercised by religion will pass to other activities. After belief, there will be superstition with 'dubious women'...acting irrationally..., but then 'superstition, like belief, must die'. After 'disbelief', churches will serve only a 'purpose more obscure'. What is this purpose? At this point, the argument [in the poem] which has been clear and certain becomes indeed obscure though no less certain: belief in supernatural religion is no longer tenable but there remains in humanity a need for seriousness in which to clothe...'our compulsions'. What are these 'compulsions'? They are 'marriage, and birth, and death'" (Day, 43). However, though the poem seems to talk much about religion, or rather about decay of religion, in general, or of Christianity, in particular, Roger Day believes that its general tenor is secular and humanistic, and, argues Day, this is clear from Larkin's use of the term 'dead one' rather than the term 'ghost', which smacks of supernaturalism, and from the humanistic concern spelled out in the concluding stanza—humanity's need of seriousness, expressed specifically through the use of the words 'serious', 'wise', 'robed' and 'grave'.

Roger Day's interpretation of the poem is corroborated by David Timms's interpretation. Timms writes: "The church,..., may decay, for 'Church Going' means church-going in the normal sense, casually visiting a church, and the going of the church; but if it falls into ruin, life will be poorer for it. Even in this case, though, Larkin feels that the place [the church and its precinct] will lure people, for we have a 'hunger' for what it represents, which will take us there, though unwittingly; and in fact, just this has happened to the speaker of the poem. The last stanza is the solution to the problem the poet poses himself at the beginning. Out for a bicycle ride, the poet stops at a church, and goes in to look round. He mocks what the church connotes for him, but in the face of this, thinks that something did make him stop. That something, he finally realises, is 'a hunger to be serious', which is satisfied by this building and what it truly represents" (Timms, 83).

The powerful vision of ruination in 'Church Going' is also present in 'A Stone Church Damaged by a Bomb', written in June 1943, and in 'Explosion', written on 5 January 1970. One may, therefore, naturally surmise some actual experience of Larkin of destruction behind the set of these three poems, an experience, it may be added, that remained fresh in his memory for a long time. Andrew Motion points his finger to the German bombing of Coventry, particularly around Manor Road where the Larkins lived, in 1940, the fall-out of which Larkin saw with his own eyes. The vivid impression of the destruction caused by the German bombing first found expression in 'A Stone Church Damaged by a Bomb', but, Motion conjectures, the impression intruded well into the other two poems. Motion writes: "The damage of 'A Stone Church Damaged by a Bomb' is assimilated into the larger ruination of 'Church Going'; the blasts around Manor Road echo underground in 'The Explosion'" (Motion, 1993, 50). But Larkin's experience of devastation due to German bombing was not the only material utilised in the narrative of the poem. In a conversation with John Haffenden in 1979 or 1980, Larkin told Haffenden about the original inspiration of the poem: "It came from the first time I saw a ruined church in Northern Ireland, and I'd never seen a ruined church before—discarded. It shocked me. Now of course it's commonplace: churches are not so much ruined as turned into bingo-halls, warehouses for refrigerators or split-level houses for architects" (Haffenden, 124).

'Church Going' breathes the depressed, frustrated and resigned religious consciousness of the average middle-class post-Second World War Englishman, who was passively observing the progressive ruination of the churches—the symbol of spirituality or Christianity—with repressed anger, perhaps. The poem also subtly refers to the economic slump or depression of the post-Second World War England. The speaker of the poem was hatless and he went to the church not by a car but on a bicycle. These two particulars of the speaker suggest the economic slump of the period. The absence of concern about the decline of spirituality that the poem suggests also points to the same time-frame.

'Church Going' is a monologue, in so far as in it the speaker (who is none else but the poet himself) speaks to himself. The poem begins with a religious pretension, but, in fact, it is not so much about religion as about man's secular need of engaging in something serious, to make his life serious or valuable. It is for this reason that the speaker says about the church: 'A serious house on serious earth it is'. The speaker is not concerned about the absence of religious faith (belief) or even of religious superstitions; what he is gravely troubled about is the spiritual vacuity that will come up after the existing remnants of belief and superstitions will cease to be. True, he is not pleading for retrieval of the lost religious faith but he is certainly urging us to understand that we do have a dire necessity of something like religion that will confer value on our life and thus make it serious.

David Timms writes that "'Church Going' is like 'I Remember, I Remember' in being about a person's feelings, thoughts and emotions in a particular situation, not just about what he can see and hear. The poem is not about churches directly, but about certain man with a certain disposition, visiting a church at a certain time" (Timms, 84). Superficially, the poem seems to be lacking in emotion, but a closer study of it will reveal that the speaker of it is certainly emotionally charged: he has realised with grave concern that in the absence of the churches our demand ('hunger') for the value or 'seriousness' of our lives will irreducibly and helplessly suffer. This is not a mere intellectual deduction, this is also emotionally surcharged. Davis Timms writes about the emotionally imbrued speaker of the poem (i.e. the poet): "He walks around to the font, looks at the large bible, and parodies the manner of the vicar or lay reader. But having done so, he finds he has emotions that remain unsatisfied: he feels that there is something he has missed, but he cannot quite see what it is. He stopped at the church, he went in, he mildly ridiculed the connotations of the place—but why did he stop at all?... He cannot have stopped for the shabby flowers, the musty hymn books, the big bible; but these things have their function in the poem. They are what the church contains—but they are only its visible contents. They contrast with the more important things the church has 'held unsplit' for so long: births, marriages and deaths, which are its real history" (*ibid.*). This understanding or realisation of the speaker triggered emotion in him. Timms further says that 'Church Going', like 'Lines on a Young Lady's Photograph Album', is a dramatic poem. In fact, Larkin himself suggested that there is dramatic posture or disposition of mind in the speaker of the poem. Timms writes: "Speaking of 'Church Going', Larkin said: 'I think one has to dramatise oneself a little.' I have pointed out how this is true of 'Lines on a Young

Lady's Photograph Album' as well as 'Church Going', poems that are not generally recognised to be dramatic" (Timms, 85). Timms further writes that many of Larkin's poems "are dramatic in the sense that they present a slant view of his opinions, through just such a persona as the one in 'Church Going'" (*op. cit.*, 86).

'Church Going' is full of contradictions, from the beginning to the end. The speaker of the poem has no respect for the church and yet he takes off the clips of his bicycle 'in awkward reverence'; he is 'uninformed' or ignorant about the church (or Christianity) and yet well knows such things as 'font', 'parchment, plate, and pyx' and 'lectern', and seems to be conversant about the customs inside the church (he pronounces 'Here endeth', signs 'the book' and drops 'an Irish sixpence' in the donation box). He does not personally believe in religion but complacently trusts that churches will continue to exist amongst people to spiritually inspire them, and to provide solace to the life-weary. Roger Day feels that there is a contradiction, or at least ambivalence, between the second stanza of the poem, where the speaker appears as a perfect 'preacher', and the last stanza, where the speaker seems a secular 'rhetorician'.

The diction of the poem quite accords with the canon of *Lyrical Ballads* in being colloquial and 'unpoetic', and yet the 'precise use of language' in the poem has earned the appreciation of Roger Day and many others. David Timms is highly appreciative particularly of the concluding stanza of the poem. Timms writes: "This stanza has a weighty sonorousness: the alliteration within the lines, the careful balance of each around the caesura, the slightly heightened diction, and above all the measured stresses of the metre—here, all the lines are end-stopped by punctuation or by sense—emphasise the seriousness, to use the poem's word, of the conclusion. No other poem in the Movement anthologies seriously adopts this diction, is so emphatic in its statement, or uses such words as 'forever' or 'destinies' without satirical intent. The final stanza is an unreserved affirmation of the importance of the central events in human life..." (Timms, 82). The 'central events' that Timms speaks of, as Larkin has explicitly stated in the poem, are 'marriage, and birth, / And death'. Andrew Swarbrick praises not just the final stanza but the 'final stanzas' of the poem, in particular, as well as the whole poem, in general. He writes about 'Church Going': "Much anthologised and widely admired, its rhetoric is in fact all too palpable, complacently modulating from facetiousness to gravity. Those stately final stanzas, with their elevated vocabulary and solemnly end-stopped lines, whilst they satisfyingly express the 'hunger' to be 'more serious', also set about disguising uncomfortable notions. The solace of churches, they assert, is in 'our compulsions' being 'robed as destinies'. The image, compelling as it is, actually suggests that the appeal of church ceremony involves an illusion. The arbitrary, provisional and circumstantial, the 'compulsions' of birth, marriage and death, are euphemised as 'destinies'. The undisturbed rhetoric of the poem represents a kind of wish-fulfilment, a desire to ritualise the randomness of life, to make chance look like order.... If 'Church Going' is less 'devious', it is because it is determined to gloss over its more disturbing questions" (Swarbrick, 1995, 66-67).

Lastly, as we have said, 'Church Going' is a very popular poem of Larkin. But why is it so popular? Roger Day answers the question. He writes: "One obvious reason is that, ..., it is very accomplished verse. In addition, it is consciously serious in a way that no one has difficulty in recognising and, in expressing experiences and impulses common to many people, it appeals to an uneasily secular age. It also claims, implicitly, to reflect the attitude of that age" (Day, 46).

8

Toads

Larkin's contemporary poet Ted Hughes was, so to say, a poet of the animal world, for he wrote as many poems on the sub-human kingdom as no other poet has yet done, not even D.H. Lawrence. But Larkin has only three poems where he has merely utilised creatures as central and controlling images: 'Toads', 'Toads Revisited' and 'At Grass' (in which the central image is that of horses). 'Toads' was written on 16 March 1954, and was first published in *The Less Deceived*. It is one of the eight poems that Larkin selected for publication in Robert Conquest's *New Lines* (1956). 'Toads Revisited', which was written in 1962 and was published in *The Whitsun Weddings* in the same year, may be called a companion poem of 'Toads'. 'Toads' consists of 36 lines, which are divided into 9 stanzas, each stanza consisting of 4 lines. The simple rhyme-scheme of the poem is a / b / a / b . The poem was written at a time when Larkin already moved away from his early lyricism and romanticism, and consequently, the poem has become realistic in tenor and prosaic in diction.

In 'Toads', Larkin has identified himself with toads, and has comically expressed his disgruntlement with the stereotyped life of the personnel or 'toads' of quotidian sedentary office-works, which is his lot. Larkin's similising an office personnel with a toad is crassly comical but appropriate, for if we look at a staidly sitting office-bearer with his gaze pathetically and resignedly glued to the piles of files on his cabinet, his plight of itself brings to our mind the image of a frog squatting somewhere and vacantly staring at something in the distance, while bellowing its belly for respiration. The toad may also be taken as a symbol of the modern man. In the extremely busy and demands-laden modern world, we are, as if, squatting despairingly with a huge hill before us of files of urgent demands and duties to be cleared. In this sense, the toad squarely reflects the image of the modern man. The image of the toad perhaps naturally came to Larkin because as a librarian in Belfast in Ireland in the early 1950s, he had also before him a heap of files he used to stare at like a toad. He could not then understand the meaning of such a life as his which was so much weighed down by the load of urgently pressing heaps of files to be monotonously and disinterestedly cleared (notice also the similitude between the pronunciation of the two words 'load' and 'toad'). It may here be pointed out that Larkin was not at all quizzical in picking up the critter toad as a symbol, because the toad had long been in human consciousness in many parts of the world, though not as a symbol of duty-laden despairing humanity but as related to hallucinatory beatific experience. The poet Robert Graves, for instance, in his Introduction to

New Larousse Encyclopedia of Mythology writes that "...a Central American stone-sculpture, a Toad-god sitting beneath a mushroom, means little to mythologists who have not considered the world-wide association of toads with toxic mushrooms or heard of a Mexican Mushroom-god, patron of an oracular cult; for the toxic agent is a drug, similar to that secreted in the sweat-glands of frightened toads, which provides magnificent hallucinations of a heavenly kingdom" (Hamlyn, vii).

However, in the first stanza of the poem Larkin compares the unrelievable burden of his huge amount of monotonous works with a toad, which is 'a toothless tailless amphibian that walks or crawls instead of jumping like a grog' (*Chambers Twentieth Century Dictionary*, 1981, entry: toad). He says that the burden of his office-works is, as if, sitting on its hams or heels, like a toad, while its hams or heels are resting on his life itself. He then questions himself why he is allowing ('let') the toad of his works thus to sit on his life, i.e. why he is allowing the load of his office-works weigh his personal life down? He asks himself if he cannot use his intelligence as a pitchfork—a fork for thrusting hey on the ground or a tuning-fork—to catch hold of the toad and throw it off his shoulder ('drive the brute off') or off his burdened life. In the second stanza, Larkin expresses his discomfort due to, and abhorrence for, the toad or the load of his office-works. He says that the toad sits on him six consecutive days of a week and disturbs the peace of his mind or the creativity of his mind ('soils') with its debilitating and annoying work-loads ('poison'). Larkin wonders and grieves that the toad can sit on him, i.e. he has to drudge in the office simply because he gets a pittance with which he foots some of his bills, or with which he meets some of his expenditures ('just for paying a few bills'). He says that the amount of his drudgery or labour is not commensurate or proportional with the amount of money he receives for that: the former far exceeds the latter ('That's out of proportion').

In the third, fourth and fifth stanzas, Larkin compares his life with the lives of some other people in other professions or occupations. In the third stanza he says that many people ('Lots of folk') earn their living ('live on') by utilising their intelligence ('wits')—such people as influence others with rhetorics ('Lecturers'); and as behave like sycophants or deceivers, articulating words lispingly like a child (pronouncing 'th' for 's' or 'z'), and artificially, with a view to achieving a particular motive by thus influencing others ('lispers'). There are also people like scamps or worthless fellows ('Losels'); foolish and clumsy persons (lob) who seem to be sweet (lolly) and who are like thick gruel (loblolly) ('loblolly-men'); and bumpkins or awkward rustic people ('louts'); all of whom go on living by (somehow) employing their (minimal) intelligence (in deceiving others), and none of whom die as destitutes, or in penury ('end as paupers'). Again, there are many wandering people who have no permanent habitats (such as Gypsies and other nomadic people) and so temporarily live on some lanes of towns and then move on to other lanes for living ('live up lanes') and who, having no kitchens, carry on their portable ovens ('fires') couched in buckets. They consume whatever they luckily come by ('windfalls') and also young pilchards that are tinned in oil ('sardines'). These people, nevertheless, do not grumble with the kind or quality of their life but seem to be happy ('seem to like it'). Larkin further says (in the fifth stanza) that the children ('nippers') of those people go about barefoot, for those people cannot afford to buy shoes for them, and the wives of those people are pitiable ('unspeakable') because, due to malnutrition, they are as lanky or thin ('skinny') as cross-breeds of greyhounds and spaniels or terriers, employed as racing-dogs ('whippets'). But, though these people are extremely poor ('and yet'), they somehow go on living, and they never really go without food.

In the sixth stanza, Larkin wishes ('Ah') that he were enough courageous to relinquish the drudgery of his job telling his boss or employer in a loud and angry voice ('shout') that he did not care a straw or tuppence for the petty allowance of money ('*pension*') that he receives from the boss ('*Stuff your pension!*'). The word '*Stuff*' very significantly refers to a part of Prospero's speech in Shakespeare's *The Tempest* (Act 4, scene I): 'We are such stuff / As dreams are made on.' Here Prospero means to say that we are an 'insubstantial matter', and so Larkin, in the poem, wants to say that the pension or money that he gets from the office is an 'insubstantial matter' or almost nothing to him. The reference to Shakespeare becomes crystal clear when Larkin lowers his voice and admids to his weakness saying 'that's the stuff / That dreams are made on'. But he cannot do that, i.e. he cannot leave his job or the petty allowance, because, he satirically says, he knows very well that he can bear, or fancy meeting, the expenditures on his necessities only with that petty allowance ('that's the stuff / That dreams are made on'). In the seventh stanza, Larkin presents us with a further reason for his not being able to relinquish his job. He says that he cannot resign his occupation also ('too') because ('For') there is something (Larkin's urge or will to work) that is very much ('sufficiently') like a toad ('toad-like'), and that toad-like something is sitting inertly or irrevocably within him ('Squats in me'). [Here one has to notice that in this stanza Larkin is speaking not of the earlier toad or the burdensome lots of works he has to do in office but of 'something sufficiently toad-like'. For our convenience, let us call the former toad 'outer toad' and the later toad or 'something sufficiently toad-like' 'inner toad'. The 'inner toad' is Larkin's inner compulsion or sense of morality that obliges or coerces him to perform the works.] However, Larkin says that the *hams* or *hocks* ('hunkers') of that 'something sufficiently toad-like' or the inner toad are as weighty or burdensome or depressing or painful as niggardly luck or bad luck ('heavy as hard luck'), and the hams of the inner toad are also quite devoid of warmth or are very cold, i.e. his inner compulsion to work is very unemotional, dry-as-dust ('as cold as snow'). And that inner toad or inner compulsion would not let him talk flatteringly or cajolingly or coaxingly ('to blarney') to persuade others for receiving ('way to getting') glory or honour, a beloved or a woman for sexual satisfaction, and money ('The fame and the girl and the money')—all the three (gifts) at the same time ('All at one sitting') [The word 'blarney' derived from "*Blarney* Castle, near Cork, where a stone difficult to reach confers the gift on those who kiss it" (*Chambers Twentieth Century Dictionary*, 1981, entry: blarney).].

In the last stanza of the poem, Larkin says that he does not mean to tell us ('I don't say') that either of the two toads—the outer toad and the inner toad—is the embodiment or the representative of the other ('embodies'), that he does not mean to tell us that the outer toad is the expression or embodiment or representative of the inner toad's urging or conscience or moral sanctions ('spiritual truth'). He only says that as he has both the toads, i.e. as he has both the external compulsion to do his office works, it is very difficult for him ('hard') to ignore either of the two compulsions or forces ('hard to lose either, / When you have both').

'Toads' verily reveals a trait of Larkin's personality: perception of contradiction or dialectics in life and his embedded ambivalence. Nothing could he do with a single motive. He, for instance, of course preferred women but he was funky about marriage. Such an ambivalence is present as much in 'Toads' as in 'Reason for Attendance' and 'Poetry of Departures'. Larkin wanted to transcend the contradictions he came across life but it was hard for him, and so he preferred to passively embrace both the opposing terms of life and thus strike a somewhat balance. Andrew Motion writes about Larkin's resignedly accepting attitude towards the contradictions of life: "Transcendence was no good: he must accept that failure and success, misery and happiness, confinement and freedom could not be separated from each other" (Motion, 237). Such a pair of contradictory terms are there in 'Toads' that Larkin, after weighing the pair of contradictory term against each other, accepts them both. In 'Toads', the pair of contradictory terms are his freedom on one hand and his conscience on the other.

Larkin had two clear and independent identities: he was a librarian and he was a poet. The librarian in him required him to bear the drudgery of clearing heaps of files from day to day, but the poet in him urged him to escape that drudgery and be poetically creative. In the poem, at first he produces arguments in favour of his leaving that drudgery that is *sitting on him* like a toad. But immediately afterwards he contradicts himself saying that he has an inner urge or conscience that is 'sufficiently toad-like' and that is *sitting within him* to constantly persuade him to perseverantly discharge his duty of clearing files in order to enjoy fame, girls, and the other benefits of money, without having to do sycophancy. Between these two contradictory options Larkin's ambivalence works. But ultimately he decides that neither of the two can he reject, nor can he reject both of them to achieve transcendence, and so embraces both of them, saying that none of the two can be a substitute for the other: 'it's hard to lose either, / When you have both'.

Andrew Swarbrick, in his *The Whitsun Weddings and The Less Deceived by Philip Larkin*, has analysed the poem threadbare, adding his very perceptive comments stanza by stanza. About the first two stanzas, he writes: "The imagery conveys a mixture of disgust and anger but its comic exaggeration suggests that this is an explosive outburst of somebody releasing pent-up feelings knowing that they are not entirely reasonable. The following three stanzas continue with this tone of exasperation" (Swarbrick, 1986, 32). Swarbrick further writes about the rest of the poem, from stanza six to stanza nine: "The sixth stanza marks a shift in tone as the speaker draws to a recognition of his true condition. He admits to a lack of courage 'To shout *Stuff your pension!*', knowing that for him it is a fantasy, the stuff of dreams. For he has absorbed too completely the work-ethic and now the 'toad' is part of his nature, leaving him free only to hanker after the fruits of success: 'The fame and the girl and the money'. But there is once more a suggestion of disapproval here, for these are the cliched images of pulp-fiction won by those who 'blarney', who deceive others and perhaps themselves into thinking that such success is possible or even desirable 'All at one sitting'. Again, what is proposed as an object of envy is in fact qualified by a fundamental disapproval. Only if we catch this note of self-criticism can the suddenly-complex final stanza fall into place, for by the end of the poem, the speaker has come to realise that working and not working are not alternatives but complementary. Whichever way you choose, you will always desire the way you rejected, either because of its freedom or its security. To choose one way entails not commitment but only the suspension of choice, for the alternative is always available. To work or not to work is neither more nor less admirable than its alternative. But for the poet, 'It's hard to lose either / When you have both', because his discontent with the daily grind of work leaves him free to enjoy prospect of rebelling whilst enjoying the security of work. This honest self-appraisal which ends in an admission of complacency (he knows he will not give up work but can thereby enjoy the temptation of doing so) reconciles the two sides of his personality in a grudging acceptance of habit and routine" (Swarbrick, 1986, 32-33).

Swarbrick says that 'Toads' like 'Poetry of Departures', 'explores our capacity for self-delusion'. About the functions of the poem, he writes: "The poem's form is that of a debate which brings together conflicting desires and impulses in an effort to arrive at the truth about the poet's nature. It shows a rationality which refuses to take things at face value and which strips away layers of illusion with self-critical honesty, and this is one of the hallmarks of Larkin's poetry" (*op. cit.*, 33). Elsewhere, that is in his book *Out of Reach: The Poetry of Philip Larkin*, Swarbrick writes about the poem: 'Toads' is a poem about desire and necessity, and (again) its language betrays the fact that the speaker's 'argument' is settled in advance. The poem is light-hearted, but the use of half-rhymes throughout gives it a nervous, fidgety edge of seriousness" (Swarbrick, 1995, 65). 'Toads' may be conceived of as a paean to liberation from quotidian drudgery of life, particularly from enforced slavery of office works. How cringing such works are may be guessed from Charles Lamb's essay 'The Superannuated Man', where Lamb terms his retirement from India House in 1825 'my deliverance'.

The poem may be found to contain an autobiographical element. Larkin was a librarian, having to clear ever-undiminishing heaps of files, as well as a poet, always desiring leisure for creative works. So he had an internal conflict which is reflected in the poem. He was a university librarian and perhaps jealously noticed the easy-going life of the university lecturers, and this may be clear from the third stanza of the poem. But Larkin could not slink out of his duty right away because of his strong conscience. In 'Toads' this conflict between his wish or desire of freedom and his constricting conscience that urges him to be quite dutiful remains unsolved, only to be solved, eight years afterwards, in 'Toads Revisited' where he resignedly implores the 'toad *work*' (of 'Toads') to keep company with him till his death: 'Give me your arm, old toad; / Help me down Cemetary Road.' The comic element of the poem pervades throughout it, except the last stanza. There are slangs in the poem such as 'folk' (stanza 3) and 'nippers' (stanza 5), and cliches such as 'out of proportion' (stanza 2), 'at one sitting' (stanza 8), etc. And, as has been said, the form of the poem is that of a debate, in which Larkin is speaking like an actor in a drama—in a very colloquial language. However, 'Toads' is one of Larkin's best known and popular poems, especially "for its expression of the constricting weariness of work and the apparent attractions of carefree liberation from routine" (Swarbrick, 1986, 32).

9

Poetry of Departures

This poem deals with the same subject as in 'Toads': 'that of choosing between a life of adventurous freedom or ordered dullness'. And like in 'Toads', here also Larkin criticises both the options and then resignedly but realistically embraces his present dull life at home, calling the other option idealistic, illusory, and impracticable. Roger Day considers this poem "a witty yet serious poem about a man's very ordinary, perhaps humdrum life" (Roger, 40). 'Poetry of Departures' is the 19th poem of *The Less Deceived*, and there in the collection it occurs very appropriately immediately after 'Toads', probably for the reason that the subjects of the two poems are the same. Further, as Andrew Swarbrick says, like 'Toads' 'Poetry of Departures' is also Larkin's 'comic disgruntlement' (against self). And, we may add, 'Poetry of Departures' is at least tangentially autobiographical like 'Toads'. It may be noted that the two poems were written one close on the other's heels: 'Poetry of Departures' was written on 23 January 1954 and 'Toads' was written two months later on 16 March 1954. Andrew Motion dubs these two poems as Larkin's 'most memorable poems' (Motion, 136). The poem 'Poetry of Departures' consists of four stanzas, each stanza consisting of eight short lines. The rhyme scheme of the poem is a / b / c / b / a / d / c / d.

In the beginning stanza of the poem, Larkin says that we occasionally hear that somebody ('*He*') gave up ('*chucked up*') everything he had been possessing and thus got disentangled from all his moorings with domestic and social lives ('*just cleared off*'). Such informations are not received first-hand or directly from a person who knows it for sure or has seen the person chucking up everything, but fifth-hand, i.e. from a person who has heard of the news from another person, and that another person got the news from yet another person, and so on, which simply means that the information is dubious, is but a hearsay or a gossip. Such informations or news are always brief, succinct—they do not details—like tombstone inscriptions ('epitaph'). And each time we hear such a hearsay our comment ('voice') will appear to be very clear ('will sound / Certain') in suggestion that we appreciate or praise ('approve') the fearless or courageous ('audacious'), purging or spiritually elevating ('purifying'), and radical or fundamental ('Elemental') decision ('move') of relinquishing all his possessions behind for ever and thus converting himself into a free soul.

In the second stanza, Larkin approves of the actions of such persons ('they') as thus leave behind all their possessions for purging themselves and making themselves free souls ('And they are right, I think'). Larkin says that it is a fact that we all detest, loath home and being at home (throughout our lives, doing domestic and social duties). He also says that he, too, abhors remaining confined in his apartment, and also detests the rubbish or worthless things or upholstery ('junk') which he had once particularly chosen and brought into his apartment or room—such things as 'good books' and 'good bed'. Larkin further says that he also loathes his absolutely regulated life ('my life, in perfect order'). The last line of the second stanza is linked with the third stanza.

In the third stanza (along with the last line of the second) Larkin says that when he hears ('hear it said') that a certain person ('*He*') deserted or left behind ('*walked out on*') the whole host of the things in his possession ('*the whole crowd*'), or deserted all people without honouring their request not to go away ('*walked out on the whole crowd*'), he becomes (i.e. the news of that person's leaving everything behind and going away makes him) so elated and vigorous that fresh blood circulates to the surface of his body, particularly of his face ('flushed') and he gets excited ('stirred'). He becomes as vigorous, with fresh blood in the surface of his body, and excited as ('like') when he would possibly hear someone tell him that at a certain time in the past a woman put off her dress (and he would have been sexually provoked, inflamed) ('Like *Then she undid her dress*') or when someone would possibly address him as 'bastard' or speak to him in a very obnoxious language ('Or *Take that you bastard*'). Larkin now asks himself if he is certain or confident ('Surely') that if that person, who is rumoured to have escaped his home leaving behind everything in his possession, really did so ('if he did') he (Larkin) can do the same, too ('Surely I can, if he did?'). But when the idea of leaving behind his home, or leaving behind his possessions, duties and obligations comes to Larkin's mind (he turns about from his earlier position when he vouchsafed that the idea of escaping home was positively exciting to him) his earlier enthusiasm or excitement for escaping his home, etc. subsides and he becomes composed ('Sober') and turns perseverent and hard-working ('industrious') and dutiful. This means that Larkin is not really interested in the placidity, inertia and secured comfort of the life of a sinecure, however much ephemerally elated he may be at the prospect of such a life, but in the industrious, conscientious and dutiful domestic and social lives. True, he is not interested in the dull monotony of the routine life of the office but he is also not to be allured by the crass adventurism. He wants the life of industry and responsibility in so far as it is to be found in office and in domesticity.

The last line of the third stanza is also linked with the fourth or final stanza, as the last line of the second stanza is linked with the third stanza. However, in the last stanza Larkin says that he would escape from his office and home and live like a tramp or a gypsy in the carefree wide world outside immediately ('But I'd go today') and certainly ('Yes') begin to live braggingly ('swagger') the life of vagrants or nomads who easily, promptly, and very smoothly move continuously from one living place to another, as they walk the ways spread over with round nuts ('Yes, swagger the nut-strewn roads'). Or, says he, he would immediately leave home and office (or the monotonous duties of them) and escape into the carefree and adventurous world outside stealthily squatting ('Crouch') in the forecastle of a ship or the 'short raised deck at the fore-end of a vessel' ('fo'c'sle'), with uncropped or unshaven face ('Subbly') but with all gentleness, warmth and happiness of heart ('goodness'). But no, he would not do either of the two: he do either of the two if the two options were not so much unnatural, crassly adventurous, extremely romantic, idealistic or unpragmatic ('if / It weren't so artificial'). Larkin calls these two alternative means of living a life (that of the tramp and that of the stowaway) regressive, intentionally (and illusively) undertaken ('a deliberate step backwards'). He says that such two alternative lives are quite away from the true life or real life, and that the true life consists of such routine activities and occupations as collecting books and chinawares and such other articles ('Books, china'). Larkin calls such a life model life, desirable life ('perfect'), and says that the two alternative lives are just an attempt to make illusory, showy, exhibitory mode of living ('To create an object'). Of course, he says that the life, which he calls model life or perfect life, is rebukable, reprovable, detestable ('Reprehensibly perfect'), and yet he would stick to it, and will not embrace either of the two illusory lives.

The title of the poem is somewhat peculiar, but there is certainly justification behind it. The moot-point is the word 'poetry' in the title: why poetry in departures? The reason is that poetry resides in imagination and there is imagination in the departures from the monotony of office life or of domestic life—the departures in which one finds the nomadic life of the gypsies or in which one proceeds towards an unknown destiny stealthily hiding in the forecastle of a ship. Roger Day says in fact the same thing. He means to say that in the poem Larkin mulls embracing "something which is probably only true in the imagination. This is where the meaning of the title [of 'Poetry of

Departures'] becomes relevant: the illusion of being able to leave unsatisfactory reality for a better, liberating alternative is pretty, artificial and unreal—what many consider poetry to be" (Day, 41).

The tenor of the poem has two stages: in the first stage Larkin seems to be carried away by the lure of the illusion of a better life to be achieved by adventurously escaping from the monotonous, humdrum quotidian life, and in the second stage illumination suddenly dawn on him that what he wants to achieve by escaping is but illusory, and so he retraces to the same monotonous, humdrum quotidian life, though it is blatantly unsatisfactory, realising that only such a life is true, and so if he sticks to it he will not be deceived. Both 'Toads' and 'Poetry of Departure' deal with the same subject—the attractive, inviting life of illusion *vis-à-vis* the dull, monotonous and dissatisfying life of truth, and the poet's' resignedly accepting the latter. Andrew Swarbrick writes the meaning of 'Poetry of Departures' and about the identity between it and 'Toads': "The man who cavalierly throws everything up and 'lives on his wits' (as 'Toads' puts it) is caught in the very same illusion as the speaker who keeps 'The good books, the good bed, / And my life, in perfect order' ['Poetry of Departures']: both believe that a perfect life is possible. Both lives are artificial, evasive, a deliberate step backwards from the truth that life is always dissatisfying and to act otherwise is 'reprehensible'. There is no poetry (romance, escape) in 'departures', except in our idealistic and illusory view" (Swarbrick, 1986, 34).

Roger Day finds a sort of 'imaginary rebellion' of Larkin in 'The Poetry of Departures' against wistful romanticised life away from pragmaticism and the truth of life (which he persuades us to accept stoically). Day writes: "I see this [poem] as a witty yet serious poem about a man's very ordinary, perhaps humdrum life. It begins with a contrast drawn between the speaker's present life ('I detest my room') and an imagined alternative ('He walked out on the whole crowd'). He reflects on his tedium, made bearable partly by means of an imaginary rebellion and partly by an exercise of intelligence rather than feeling—that is, by first imagining a different kind of life, and then judging it not only as unreal, but unreal in the same way as his present life. But the final irony is the realisation that the alternative existence can be accounted for in just the same stereotyped way as his present life" (Day, 40).

In 'Poetry of Departures', Larkin bitterly mocks at idealism and romanticism as well as at himself. Firstly, he satirises one's romantically escaping his home or his responsibilities saying that such escapade is 'purifying' and 'Elemental'. Next, he mocks at the carefree popinjay tramp and the stowaway, saying that the tramp 'swagger the nut-strewn roads' and the stowaway 'Crouch in the fo'c'sle'. And lastly, Larkin levels his gun of satire at himself. He says that rather than embracing the life of romantic adventures he would humbly accept the real life, the humdrum quotidian life and keep himself somehow going on by collecting books, chinawares, etc. Evidently, the poem appeals to the brain and not at all to the heart: it argues and satirises, but never arouses our emotions. Andrew Motion has found some echoes of Larkin's 'Ultimatum' (1940) in 'Poetry of Departures'. He says that some of the images and ideas of 'Ultimatum' remained with him throughout his life, and they reappeared in some of his later poems, including 'Poetry of Departures'. For instance, the idea of, or desire for, escaping present life and the image of escaping by ship are present in both the poems. Motion says that in 'Poetry of Departures', as also in 'Reasons for Attendance', Larkin, in fact, innuendoes to his own personality suggesting himself that he naturally needs passivity and solitude (Motion, 237).

As is usual, Larkin has employed *colloquial* and conversational language in this poem, and has freely used cliches very profitably—for humorous and satirical effects. The first three and a half stanzas of the poem are as if a debate and the concluding three lines of it are the conclusion. In this sense the poem is very much syllogistic or logical in form. However, appreciating the construction of the poem, Roger Day writes that "It is a natural complement to the essentially conversational style of the poem. Larkin manages to contain the cliches within a recognisable form by abandoning regular line length and, for the most part, rhyme, but keeps a careful control over the basically iambic rhythm and introduces full rhyme only at the end of each stanza to pull the preceding lines together. This full rhyme, especially in the final stanza, reflects ironically on the artificial 'perfection' of each of the two ways of life. Larkin introduces colloquial speech into his verse for various purposes: here it serves as a kind of Aunt Sally, comically expressing stock actions and sayings which are then exposed as mere fantasy" (Day, 41).

10

Deceptions

It was this poem that perhaps suggested the title of the collection of poems, *The Less Deceived*. The subject of the poem Larkin got from his study of a case of rape, that took place in the 19th century, in Henry Mayhew's book, *London Labour and the London Poor*. In his book, Mayhew wrote that a woman was first drugged to unconsciousness and then raped, after which she came out of her unconsciousness, suffered from remorse and wanted to commit suicide. However, ultimately she refrained from killing self, and having no home of hers and no means to live by, she then went to her aunt as a dependent. Andrew Swarbrick gives some more information about Mayhew's narration of the incident: "Henry Mayhew's documentary study of the London poor was published in 1861. In it, Mayhew gives the story of 'a woman of over forty, shabbily dressed, with a disreputable, unprepossessing appearance'. She was the daughter of a Dorsetshire tenant-farmer who visited London when she was sixteen. She was enticed by a stranger feigning illness into a brothel where, after consuming drugged coffee, she was raped. She was briefly the man's mistress but inevitably fell into prostitution. Mayhew records her as saying, 'You folks has honour, and character, and feelings, and such can't understand how all that's been beaten out of people like me. I don't feel. I'm used to it'. She went on: 'I don't want to live, and yet I don't care enough about dying to make away with myself. I ain't that amount of feeling that some has'" (Swarbrick, 1995, 57). In such cases, we naturally feel sympathetic only for the woman victims and never for the perpetrators of the fornications, but in this poem Larkin very uncommonly feels sorry not only for the victim but also for the criminal victimiser. He is sympathetic towards the woman because she had been deceived by the man, and he is sympathetic towards the man, perhaps more than he is towards the woman, because the man is more deceived than the woman, by self. The logic of Larkin's uncommon sympathy for the victimiser is this. The man had wanted absolute pleasure ('fulfilment's...attic') from sexual act with the woman. But after he had done the act he found the act void of pleasure—the sexual desire was fulfilled but happiness he did not find. Firstly, because his love (or, rather, sexual act) was not reciprocated by the (unconscious) woman and so he felt lonely or desolate during the act. Secondly, because sexual pleasure continues only during sexual act, and after the act the pleasure is followed by 'absence of pleasure', which is not very different from pain. It is for this reason that Larkin says that the rapist or the deceiver was, in fact, more deceived than the woman, i.e., the woman was less deceived than he. And, further, it is for this reason that Larkin is more sympathetic to the rapist than to the woman, for the rapist greatly suffered from post-coital self-delusion.

The original title of 'Deceptions' was 'The Less Deceived', and when Larkin entitled the collection of poems in which it occurs *The Less Deceived* he changed the title of the poem to 'Deceptions'. The poem was written on 20 February 1950, the year in which were also written such other poems as 'Dry-Point', 'Spring', 'Wants' and 'If, My Darling', and was first published in *XX Poems* (without any title, in April 1951) and then in Larkin's first mature collection, *The Less Deceived*. This 17-line poem was a favourite poem to Mrs Margaret Thatcher, the Prime Minister of England. Once in 1980, when Mrs Thatcher told Larkin at a certain reception that she was an admirer of him, he promptly demanded of her a line to be quoted from his poem, and she too forthwith recited 'All afternoon her mind lay open like a drawer of knives' from the poem 'Deceptions'—a slightly changed version, though. This seventeen-line poem consists of two stanzas, the first stanza containing nine lines and the second stanza containing eight. The first stanza of this iambic pentametric poem is built on the rhyme scheme a / b / a / c / d / c / e / d / e and the second on the rhyme scheme a / b / a / c / a / b / a / c.

In the first stanza, Larkin tells the raped woman, who is present in his imagination or memory, that though the incident of her being raped took place long ago (in the 19th century) ('Even so distant'), he ('I') can quite feel ('taste') her affliction or sorrow ('grief'). He understands that the man who raped her ('he') forced her to swallow the sorrow or affliction which was acerbic and poignant and which, as if, had barbs or shafts ('stalks'). While the raping was in progress, sun-light flickered in the room (in which the raping took place) (understandably through window) from time to time ('occasional'), and this sun-light imprinted on her person the fact of her being raped, as in a book or newspaper facts or ideas are printed ('The sun's occasional print'). Outside the room and along the street, wheels of vehicles (which promptly carried lively human beings) gave out from time to time sudden ('brisk') and short-lasting ('brief') sounds of agony, indicating that they were in distress or anxiety ('Worry of wheels'). (The wheels gave out sounds of agony because, as if, they were anxious about, or pitiful for, the miserable plight of the woman being raped.) The place of the street where the wheels of vehicles made agonized sounds ('Where') led the street to the other direction—to the direction in which jolly bridal convoys or fleets of vehicles accompanying brides veered ('bows the other way') (suggestively in contempt of the room in which the woman was being raped, for, henceforth the hypocritic morality of the Victorian London would count her as a prostitute) ('Where bridal London bows the other way').

The sunlight that entered the room in which the rape was being perpetrated was powerful ('tall') and widely influential ('wide'), and it would not answer anybody's questions about the rape ('unanswerable'). And that sunlight would not let the humiliation or shame of the woman go, i.e. the sunlight would like the humiliation or shame remain with her like a blemish or mark of healed wound ('Forbid the scar to heal'). [Or, the people would be enlightened ('light') about the incident of the rape—the people who were multitudinous ('wide') and proud of their (sham Victorian) morality ('tall')—and they would not forget the shame or degeneration of the woman and would consider the shame as an indelible slur on her ('Forbids the scar to heal').] And the sunlight (or the multitudinous people) would also publish the rape from place to place ('drives') so that the shame of the woman could not be kept a secret ('Shame out of hiding'). That very day seemed to the woman to be slow in passing out ('unhurried day'), and throughout the seemingly slow-moving day she was fully conscious ('Your mind lay open') of the pains of barbed shame, as if her mind was a drawer of chest containing sharp knives ('like a drawer of knives').

In the second stanza of eight lines, Larkin tells the woman that her memory or the memory of her being raped has been forgotten ('buried') by successive generations of crowds or people ('Slums') during the long passage of time ('years'). (And then he expresses his reactive feelings about the woman raped and the rapist man. In such a case of raping, we generally become sympathetic to the victimised woman, and never to the victimising man, but here Larkin feels more sympathetic for the man than for the woman.) Larkin tells the woman, who is present to his imagination, that he would not be bold enough to console her had he been present at the site where she was raped ('I would not dare / Console you if I could'). He admits that her pain and sorrow were very natural and were equal to the amount of her suffering ('exact'), and that beyond this he cannot say anything else ('What can be said, / Except that suffering is exact'). He says that when ('where') one is overtaken or overpowered ('takes charge') by his own sexual urge ('Desire'), his decisions or calculations about the moral implications of his action of raping a woman ('readings') will naturally go astray ('grow erratic'), and that further than this he has nothing more to say. Larkin says this because ('For'), as he tells the woman, she would scarcely ('hardly') be mindful ('care') to understand or believe that during the time when her modesty was being violated by the rapist on that bed, she was, in fact, rather less cheated or cozened ('deceived') by the rapist that the rapist was cheated by his own desire or urge for happiness to be had through sexual gratification (because sexual gratification is immediately followed by despair, or by intenser urge for such gratification). Larkin says that the rapist hurriedly ('breathless') climbed up the flight of stairs unsteadily ('slumbling') (because he was hot with sexual desire and very eager to promptly gratify that desire) to the uppermost storey of the house and rashly entered into ('burst into') the skylighted room on the roof ('attic') where he wanted to fully gratify ('fulfilment's') his sexual lust. [The expression 'stumbling up the breathless stair' may also mean the act of coitus, and the expression 'burst into fulfilment's desolate attic' may also mean orgasm and the sense of loss that follows it immediately (Rodway, 100).] But after his fleshy enjoyment, the rapist was quite disillusioned to find that he could not have achieved happiness through his carnal action (because sexual enjoyment is not possible if the acts of one of the partners is not appropriately reciprocated by the other, and in this case of coitus the woman was quite unconscious) and that he was joyless and forlorn ('desolate') in the room which also seemed to him joyless and forlorn (because it seemed to him that in that room it was only he who was present, the woman being quite unconscious).

As already said, Larkin got the subject of this poem from his study of Mayhew's anthropological book *London Labour and the London Poor*, where he came to know of the rape of a woman after she was drugged to unconsciousness. Larkin has used a confessional sentence of the woman, as he found it in that book, as the head-note of 'Deceptions': "'*Of course I was drugged*, and so heavily I did not regain my consciousness till the next morning. I was horrified to discover that I had been ruined, and for some days I was inconsolable, and cried like a child to be killed or sent back to my aunt.'—Mayhew, *London Labour and the London Poor*" (Rodway, 97). According to Allan Rodway, the poem has two themes: uselessness of pity, in the case of the victimised woman; and self-punishment, in the case of the victimiser man. The woman had already been subjected to sexual exploitation, and so no amount of pity can help her in any way. The woman was certainly *deceived* by the man and so one should expect pity from Larkin for her, but Larkin says that the man was more deceived than the woman, not by her but by himself, and so Larkin is pitiful for him. Cannot Larkin feel pity both for the man and the woman? No, because pity must show itself for either of the two contrary beings—the wronger and the wronged. Pity for both is inconceivable, for, in such a case, commiseration for the one accompanies anger against the other. Further, as Larkin tells us, the man is more deceived—as said, not by the woman, of course, but by self—and so naturally one should be pitiful for the man. The suffering, too, of the man is greater than that of the woman; because whereas the suffering of the woman was inflicted upon her by the man, the suffering of the man was caused by himself—self-inflicted pain is always greater. But this is not to say that Larkin has no compassion for the woman, and, in fact, he begins the poem commiserating her: 'I can taste the grief'.

The wronger, the perpetrator of the crime was more deceived by himself because he could not achieve what he wanted to—happiness through sexual act with an unconscious woman—for two reasons. Firstly, sexual satisfaction much depends on reciprocation of signals of positive feeling by the partners, but in this case the woman neither had the positive feeling nor could she reciprocate. Secondly, the perpetrator certain had in mind his gaining of pure, unqualified happiness from sexual act with the woman, without having any afflictive entailment or consequential pain. But he was ignorant of the fact that every sexual act ultimately ends in a sense of loss, despair, ennui or misery. So, the perpetrator was quite disillusioned and deceived by self. On the other hand, the woman neither desired any happiness nor was she conscious during the carnal act. And so the question of her being disillusioned does not arise, though, of course, she was cheated or deceived by her wronger. It is for this reason that Larkin says that the victimiser was more deceived than the victim, and so the former's suffering was greater than the latter's, and, further, it is for this reason that Larkin is more compassionate for the man than for the woman.

Though in this poem Larkin speaks only about the particular man being deceived by self, the purport of the poem (or, what is the same thing, of Larkin) is not particular or specific but general. Larkin, through this poem, means to say that everyone of us is being deceived by self, or that life itself deceives us to a man, that while living all of us suffer the illusions of life all through, because though at each step of life we become disillusioned, we become preys to the illusions of life over again all the same and immediately afterwards. We become deceived or disillusioned because we desire happiness or something like that from life, and so Larkin very obliquely wants to suggest that we should live on our lives without desiring anything, leave alone happiness, from life.

However, Andrew Swarbrick has found an uncommon and unfamiliar moralistic tone in the poem in that, according to Larkin, in the particular case raping one should be more compassionate for the self-deceived, disillusioned man than for the woman who was cheated and violated by him while she was unconscious. The question of justification of Larkin's moral position is open-ended, debatable, but it is also a fact that in most cases, if not in all, along with the victimised the victimiser too suffers, for no victimiser can well achieve what he wants to from his act of victimising another person. Swarbrick writes: "The poem ('then') passes a moral judgement on the experience it describes. Is Larkin right to feel that the victimiser is in fact the greater victim of his illusions? It is certainly a challenging view which makes the raped girl the lesser victim. Perhaps we might say that Larkin is not so much callous (about the girl) as moved to compassion for the plight of humanity emblematised by this incident: one suffers at the hands of another whose own suffering lies in a deception leading to an endless cycle of disillusionment" (Swarbrick, 1986, 36). Larkin is not callous about the woman, and this is quite clear from the first two lines of the poem: 'Even so distant, I can taste the grief, / Bitter and sharp with stalks, he made you gulp.' He is, though, not clangorously compassionate and consolatory to her, and this is because he is rightly aware that consolation would be no compensation to her. In fact, as Swarbrick tells us, the charge of callousness about the victimised woman was framed by a critic against Larkin, but Swarbrick, in his *Out of Reach: the Poetry of Philip Larkin*, has squarely rebutted the charge. Swarbrick writes: "One critic ends her discussion of the poem thus: 'In sum, I do not think that one can have it both ways: Larkin as detached poetic observer and Larkin as sympathetic to human suffering...the callousness which [the poem] exhibits and the sadism which it in part condones ought at least to be seen as problematic—and as a limitation in Larkin's art'. This states the problem, but fails to consider that the poem knows it is problematical, that Larkin concerned to show how sympathy can never compensate for suffering and that identifying with suffering is fraught with potential moral dishonesty" (Swarbrick, 1995, 57). In the poem, Larkin frankly and deliberately avoided this dishonesty, telling the woman: 'I would not dare / Console you if I could. What can be said, / Except that suffering is exact'. The word 'exact' here may have a spiritual significance. It means 'to force out', 'to compel payment of', 'rigorous', etc., and so we may say that the woman's suffering was 'rigorous' enough for her spiritual alleviation, or that her suffering was a sort of payment which she was compelled to make against her spiritual upliftment, or that her suffering forced out the spirituality that was dormant in her.

But though Swarbrick defends Larkin's insouciance or lack of concern about the suffering of the woman, he mounts a fierce attack on his *einfuhlung* or empathy with the perpetrator of the crime. Swarbrick writes: "The poem makes its readers uncomfortable. For we too are victims of the woman's rebuke: 'You falks as has honour, and character, and feelings, and such *can't understand* how all that's been beaten out of people like me'. The poem refuses to traffic in easy sympathy and instead admits to a more *shameful* identification with the man violently imprisoned in desire and the delusion that desire can be fulfilled. Where 'Reasons for Attendance' makes its strategy of subversion explicit in the final volte-face it performs, 'Deceptions' gradually discloses its own *treachery* in extending sympathy from the victim to the perpetrator (*my stresses*)" (Swarbrick, 1995, 59). But, all the same, Swarbrick admires the craft and poetry of 'Deceptions'. In his *The Whitsun Weddings and The Less Deceived by Philip Larkin*, he writes about 'Deceptions': "The argument of the poem may be debatable, but the writing is admirable. The first sentence puts us into the scene with a piercing dramatic immediacy before the longer sentence explores the girl's feelings. Her sense of exposure and vulnerability is caught in the insistent, all-embracing light, 'unanswerable and tall and wide', when all she wants is darkness and oblivion; this diffusive image is followed by the clarity and sharpness of her mind being like an open drawer of knives. And the second stanza, although it shifts our sympathies towards the man, still recognises the woman's suffering: 'out on that bed' makes her isolated, cast adrift, with a suggestion of disgust for 'that bed'. The final image expresses with simple economy what the experience signifies. The man struggles exhaustedly 'To burst' upon the object of fulfilment but finds instead a 'desolate attic', a sudden emptiness in which he, like the forlorn girl, is also abandoned. And in 'Dry-Point', the attempt to satisfy our desires only reminds us of our true condition: lonely, disconsolate, doomed to dissatisfaction" (Swarbrick, 1986, 36).

And Allan Rodway has the following in praise of the artistic craftsmanship of the poem: "Technically, the poem is masterly. Every word is a normal everyday word, every phrase and sentence in perfectly ordinary syntax, the rhythms those of natural self-communing speech. There is no trace of ostentation or preaching, so the reader is prepared to trust the poet, to go along with him in what seems an unpretentious honest exploration: what was it like? And how is it to be placed? The rhyming is strict, but the many run-on lines render it unobtrusive, and the iambic pentameter is subordinated to speech-rhythms (though it is never at odds with them). Together, rhyme and meter are just evident enough to 'frame' the piece as an artifact, an object of disinterested interest. It combines form with informality; and in that the verse seems a perfectly natural embodiment of the content, it is an example of organic form without free verse" (Rodway, 99).

Our discussion on this poem would remain incomplete if we do not at least make a passing reference to Graham Holderness's very interesting 'essay', or rather dramatic conversation on this poem. Through this dramatic conversation, Holderness has demonstrated the great value of entertaining the possibility of critical pluralism of the poem 'Deceptions'. The small body of *dramatis personae* of this dramatic conversation comprises the following characters:

CLEANTH, a formalist
RAYMOND, a Marxist
KATE, a feminist
COLIN, a poststructuralist
CECIL, a chair

The scene of the conversation is "A seminar room in an institution of higher education. Around a circular table sit several teachers of English. Books and papers on the table in front of them. The rest of the room is filled with an audience of teachers and students" (Regan, 83). And the time of the conversation is a late afternoon of an early October.

Cecil touches off the conversation saying that four colleagues will 'give brief papers offering contrasting perspectives on...an interesting poem by Philip Larkin', and immediately afterwards falls asleep. Then Cleanth reads the poem 'Deceptions' aloud and presents his critical observations on it. He says that the poem is not about *anything* at all, leave alone about a girl who was drugged and raped, and that through the poem Larkin creates an art by transforming the imagination, or the *memory*, of the victimised girl into an agonising experience of a *real* girl being observed as a subject of utter victimisation. Cleanth says that in the first half of the poem (i.e. the first nine lines of it), Larkin has been quite successful in depicting the despicable and pitiable condition of the woman, and thus in arousing our sympathy for her. But, says he, in the second stanza of the poem he has shattered what he successfully constructed in the first. He says: "The second half [or stanza] of the poem is a denial of the first, a betrayal of the achieved reality of art, a failure of the poetic imagination. Everything that was in the first half realised in precise, but images, is here translated into lifeless abstractions: 'your mind lay open like a drawer of knives' becomes 'suffering'; the imagery of wounding and violation and 'bitterness' is translated, strongly, into the abstraction 'desire'; where previously the poet was concerned to dramatise the exactness of an imagined experience, here he takes refuse in the detached activity of 'reading'. Larkin's attempt to dramatise the man's experience fails by comparison with the achieved realisation of the woman's; and the attempt again to link emotion with physical surroundings—'breathless stair', 'desolate attic'—seems merely mechanical in comparison" (*op. cit.*, 86). Cleanth, therefore, rejects the poem: "Ultimately the poem is an imaginative failure, precisely because Larkin was not content to let the poetic drama, the enacted realisation of a wholly imaginary experience, speak for itself. The impulse to tamper, to explain, to reflect and philosophise, to intervene with some deliberate, willed intention, finally destroys the poem. A poem should not *mean*, but *be*; and what damages this poem is the poet's reluctance to let it 'be', his determination to make it 'mean' something other than itself" (*ibid.*).

Raymond, the Marxist, presents his paper. In his paper, he contradicts Cleanth saying that the poem is 'very much *about* something'. He maintains that the poem "addresses people and situations we should have no difficulty in recognising as 'real'; it is rooted in that 'history' of which we are all (apart from Cleanth) 'mere creatures'; and it certainly contains a deliberate 'intention' which is that of forcing the reader to confront and become aware of unpalatable social realities" (*ibid.*). Raymond points to the head-note of the poem, the quotation from Henry Mayhew, and endeavours to push forward the point that the quotation carries within it the central idea of the poem that in a Dickensian world of 'extreme contrast between wealth and poverty' such cruelty and exploitation as the raped woman underwent are a 'reality', is only to be frequently expected. Raymond points out that Larkin is right in saying that both the woman and the man, both the victim and the victimiser, were preys to deception, which grows and sprouts only in a society where the few deceive and exploit the many to force them into poverty in order to make themselves wealthy. He says that in the Victorian underclass—the locus of the theme of the poem—where there is extreme poverty, everyone is a prey to deception, either the deception that is thrust on him (as in the case of the raped woman) or the deception that is of his own making (as in the case of the man who raped her). Raymond concludes that "This is the true importance of the poem, which consists in Larkin's recognition that every member of that oppressed Victorian underclass—not merely its most obvious casualties—was a victim of deception, blinded by ideological illusions to the real conditions of their lives" (*op. cit.*, 88).

Then, as is expected, Kate interprets the poem from the perspective of feminism to which she very much subscribes. Kate says that the poem is about the suffering of a woman at the hands of a man, i.e. it is about power-relation—the relation between a weak woman and a strong man. She accuses Larkin of favouring the rapist, himself being a masculine person. She admits that Larkin has shown sympathy to the deceived woman, but she censures him for exculpating the rapist, the perpetrator of the heinous crime, by treating the crime not as due to the man's contemptible will but to some unfounded abstract force or power which is beyond human control. She therefore stows the ultimate responsibility or the guilt of the crime on the shoulder of Larkin himself. She writes in her paper: "The real 'deception' constructed by this poem...is that attempt to shift the responsibility for this fundamental masculine crime onto some abstract power beyond actual men and women. Such a projection of guilt beyond the living criminal can only serve to blur the real power-relations—and to blur the real structure of moral responsibility—between men and women in this, or any other, society" (*op. cit.*, 90).

The last person to read out his paper is Colin. As a poststructuralist, he is particularly interested in language, or, rather in linguistics. Before listening to Colin's paper, we may very briefly acquaint ourselves with poststructuralism. To begin with, poststructuralism was born as a reaction against structuralism that claimed that its linguistic and cultural analyses were quite scientific. Structuralists, such as Ferdinand de Saussure, Claude Levi-Strauss, and the Russian narratologist Vladimir Propp, said that the meaning of any literary piece depends on some fixed, invariable abstract codes and conventions of a particular society, and so far as those codes and conventions are fixed, the meaning of any literary piece is fixed. On the other hand, according to the poststructuralists, such as Jacques Derrida, Jacques Lacan, Julia Kristeva, Michel Foucault, Lyotard and Deleuze, the social codes and conventions are not absolutely fixed, but are variable, and in so far as they are variable, the meaning of a literary piece is amenable to a plurality of interpretations. Now, as a poststructuralist, Colin believes that the poem 'Deception' is certainly about 'something', and that it yields to a variety of interpretation. Colin, however, understands that the poem is 'about language', about 'reality', about 'ideology' and about 'experience'.

Colin says that in the poem there are 'really four separate narratives within its structure': first, the woman's own story; secondly, Mayhew's narrative; thirdly, Larkin's attempt to represent the woman's experience; and fourthly, 'our narrative' (i.e. Colin's interpretation). He says that the poem is 'critical and self-reflexive', more complex than apparently may seem to be, and admits of a poststructuralist analysis. Colin, however, emphasises the linguistic aspects or elements of the poem and in his paper writes that in 'Deception' Larkin "recognises that the reality of experience he has been pursuing is simply not there: just as the woman's existence has been obliterated, so the effort to capture a reality beyond language is doomed to failure" (*op. cit.*, 92).

And as Colin closes his paper, Cecil, the chair, automatically springs up like a doll from his slumber and closes the seminar saying he is sure that everybody has been enlightened by the discussions and that 'we will leave here just a little "less deceived" than we were when we came in'. Then "*Polite, embarassed laughter* [of Cecil]. *A few whispered remarks, inaudible. Shuffling of papers. Scrapping of chairs. People begin to file out.* Blackout" (*op. cit.*, 93).

11

I Remember, I Remember

As in 'Next, Please', in this poem also Larkin creates a very interesting comedy out of misery. David Timms is very perceptive when he writes about this poem: "... 'I Remember, I Remember' deserves specific consideration because, besides being the kind of poem most often associated with Larkin, it illustrates his superb craftsmanship" (Timms, 79). Timms further writes that in this poem Larkin "reflects on his childhood, recalling everything that did *not* happen, in a parody of the standard Portrait-of-the-Artist-as-a-Misunderstood-Young-Man sort of autobiographical novel" (*op. cit.*, 3). 'I Remember, I Remember' obviously betrays the chief features of the poems of the Movement in being anti-wet, anti-romantic and anti-phoney. The poem mocks the cozy and nostalgic Lawrentian or Dylan Thomas-ish idea of childhood.

The title of the poem Larkin took from Thomas Hood's (1799-1845) poem 'Past and Present' that begins with the refrain, 'I Remember, I Remember' (though the purport of Larkin's poem parodys or mocks that of Hood's). Let us, for ready reference, quote below Hood's poem in full.

Past and Present

I remember, I remember
The house where I was born,
The little window where the sun
Came peeping in at morn;

He never came a wink too soon
Nor brought too long a day;
But now, I often wish the night
Had borne my breath away.

I remember, I remember
The roses, red and white,
The violets, and the lily-cups—
Those flowers made of light!

The lilacs where the robin built
And where my brother set
The laburnum on his birthday,—
The tree is living yet!

I remember, I remember
Where I was used to swing,
And thought the air must rush as fresh

To swallows on the wing;
My spirit flew in feathers then
That is so heavy now,
And summer pools could hardly cool
The fever on my brow.

I remember, I remember
The fir trees dark and high;
I used to think their slender tops
Were close against the sky:
It was a childish ignorance,
But now 'tis little joy
To know I'm farther off from Heaven
Than when I was a boy.

'I Remember, I Remember' was dated 8 January 1954, and was first published in *The Less Deceived*. The poem was one of the eight poems of Larkin which were included in Robert Conquest's *New Lines* that was published in 1956 and that helped to establish the Movement poets. The poem consists of 7 stanzas of 5 lines each and a concluding single line.

The occasion of the narrative of 'I Remember, I Remember' is a train journey like that of 'The Whitsun Weddings' that Larkin wrote four years after this present poem. In the first stanza of the poem, Larkin, the speaker of the poem, says that he was, on an occasion ('For once'), travelling by train towards England early in a new year when it was cold. The train was running not through the usual route but through a different route unfamiliar to Larkin ('different line'). The train stopped ('We stopped') at a certain railway station, when he was observing some men, 'with number-plates' on their breasts, running fast ('Sprint') across the railway platform towards their own houses or quarters ('familiar gates'). At this moment, Larkin could well recognise that the place was Coventry and so was extremely delighted ('Why, Coventry!') and he remembered that he was born there ('I was born here'). In the second stanza, Larkin says that he then greatly inclined out of the window of the train ('leant far out') and looked out like a person having a squint ('squinnied') to discover a particular familiar sign to assure himself that the place or the town to which he had arrived was really 'his' town, i.e., the town of Coventry in which he was born ('mine'). But he found that he was not yet certain ('I wasn't even clear') about the identities of the various places of the town ('Which side was which'). Larkin then asked himself, or tried to recollect, if from the particular place where the iron frame-works or grilles for keeping bicycles ('cycle-crates') stood ('standing') he and some other members of his family ('we') would each year start proceeding towards some other places at different times to spend the holidays ('hols').

In the third stanza, Larkin says that while he was thus trying to recollect his memories, the whistle of the train in which he was travelling was blown ('A whistle went') and the train started to move jactitating things on board it ('Things moved'). So long, coming away from his own seat, Larkin was keeping his head out through a window to see men and things of Coventry, but as the train began to move he went back to his seat and sat down ('I sat back') and was gazing at his boots. A friend of Larkin's meaningfully smiled at him, asked him if he belonged to that place (where the train stopped, i.e. Coventry), or if he received physical and spiritual sustenance from that place, like a sapling draws its sustenance striking its roots in the soil ('Was that,' my friend smiled, 'where you "have your roots"?'). Larkin promptly replied ('I wanted to reply') in the negative ('No'), telling him that it was only the place where he could not enjoyably or profitably pass his childhood, such that he can now say that he did not spend his childhood there but only remained confined within the four walls alone at that place ('Only where my childhood was unspent'). Larkin further told him that it was just the place from where he started his life or career ('j'st where I started').

In the fourth stanza, Larkin says that by this time, i.e. since he had recognised Coventry ('Why, Coventry!': stanza first) till this moment, ('By now') he imaginatively saw, or recalled the memory of, the place of Coventry in its exact and accurate details, and clearly ('I've got the whole place clearly charted'). Larkin at first recalled the memory of their garden at Coventry, where he did never make himself intensely interested, or make himself interested with religious zeal, in the flowers and fruits thereof, so much so that he would have been oblivious of anything else ('Blinding theologies'). And he recalled that there at Coventry a certain old person ('old hat') would not speak to him. And there in Coventry was that extraordinarily beautiful and lovely family that attracted Larkin and others ('we have that splendid family'). In the following stanza, Larkin elaborates on that family. He says that (in his young age) he would never seek refuse in that family for getting sympathy or compassion, or simply visit that family, when he would have been in a depressive mood (but only when he would happen to be delighted, jolly) ('I never ran to when I got depressed'). There in that family the boys were muscular and the girls had full breasts ('The boys all biceps and the girls all chest'). The family had a ludicrous-looking motor car made by the Ford company ('Their comic Ford'), and a farmstead for cultivation or pasturing, where he could really feel very natural and happy ('where I could be / "Really myself"'). Larkin told his friend that he would particularly show him that thicket of fern ('bracken') where he sometimes used to go and fearlessly or boldly sit ('The bracken where I never trembling sat').

In the sixth stanza, Larkin says that he would go to that thicket of ferns with all resoluteness to walk across it ('Determined to go through it') and reach that place where that particular girl used to lie on her back ('where she / Lay back'). And when he would meet her he would become very passionate ('burning') and everything seemed to him unreal ('mist'), so that everything seemed to him to be burning with passion and hazy with unreality ('all became a burning mist'). And then, his third-rate, irregular, burlesque verses ('doggerel') were not printed by the publishing houses ('those offices') in ten-point broad head or bold types ('Was not set up in blunt ten-point') and were not read by a certain famous ('distinguished') cousin of the mayor of the town of Coventry. In the seventh stanza, Larkin says that (as she did not read his verses and so could not realise the beauty and strong effect of them) the cousin did not meet his father ('didn't call') to tell him that she and others could discover in (the young) Larkin a future ('*ahead*') genius ('*gift*'), i.e. a very promising poet ('*There / Before us, had we the gift to see ahead*—'). Larkin was then wanted to tell his friend something more (suggested by the dash after the word '*ahead*') but the friend interfered and told him that from the expression of his face ('judging from your face') it seemed that he (Larkin) wished Coventry ('the place') to be in hell, i.e. he very much despised and damned his birth-place, Coventry (''ou look as if you wished the place in hell'). Then Larkin told his friend minchingly or hesitatingly ('Oh well') that he believed ('I suppose') that Coventry itself had no imperfection or wrong (that might have made his childhood unhappy). But Larkin also told him that nothing like what happened in his childhood while he had been in Coventry happens anywhere in the world, i.e., what happened to him during his young days in Coventry was extremely deplorable, miserable, regrettable ('Nothing, like something, happens anywhere.').

In 'I Remember, I Remember', Larkin has very comically drawn the ennui and vacuity of his childhood by enlisting some striking fragmentary recollections with a quite detached mood. In the poem, as Andrew Swarbrick writes, "he is able to define his childhood by its utter remoteness from the cliches popularly associated with it. Stereotyped images are summoned up in order to be discredited: he was not a child-prodigy, was not favoured by a conventionally lovable eccentric ('an old hat'), did not find shelter in the bosom of his family, was not surrounded by heroic brothers or beautiful sisters and did not discover a rural retreat (the phrase 'Really myself' stands exposed as an empty cliché). Neither did he experience the trembling intensity of a first love (again mocked by the cliché of 'all became a burning mist'), nor was he celebrated as a budding writer" (Swarbrick, 1986, 37). And Larkin extraordinarily sums up his list of cliches (and they are four, excepting the concluding line, all within quotation marks: 'mine', 'have your roots', 'Really myself' and 'all became a burning mist') giving vent to his pent up emotion gorging out of the memories of fallow, uninspiring childhood in the concluding master cliché 'Nothing, like something, happens anywhere'.

The poem is obviously autobiographical in so far it contains a glimpse of Larkin's 'boring', uninspiring, uneventful childhood.

In an interview with John Haffenden in 1979 or 1980, Larkin frankly admitted that his childhood was 'boring' and that it 'wasn't unhappy' but then he also 'wasn't a happy child' (Haffenden, 114-15). The autobiographical element of the poem may also have been suggested by the noticeably frequent employment of the nominative singular of the first personal pronoun 'I' in it ('I' has been used sixteen times in the poem of thirty-six lines). But, Andrew Swarbrick says that the 'I' of the poem "should be regarded as another subjective presence, another 'voice', rather than an unproblematic author" (Swarbrick, 1995, 61). However, 'I Remember, I Remember' may be compared with, or rather contrasted from, 'Coming' which Larkin had written four years earlier than it and which we have already discussed (see pages...). While 'I Remember, I Remember' is all too dejected, gloomy, 'Coming' shows a rare spark of delight and hope in Larkin ('It will be spring soon'). Secondly, while in 'Coming' Larkin says that his childhood is 'forgotten', in 'I Remember, I Remember' he repudiates his statement. 'I Remember, I Remember' also strongly contrasts from Thomas Hood's 'Past and Present', for, in the first place, where Hood's poem is soaked in facile sentimentality, Larkin's is blatantly anti-wet. Thirdly, and here falls the stress, where Hood recalls his romantic and idyllic childhood nostalgically with a sigh, Larkin insipidly looks back to his 'unspent' and vacant days when he was a child. But David Timms holds a different opinion. He writes: "It might be argued that Larkin too is sentimental, though sentimental at the other end of the scale, in making his childhood seem so dismal" (Timms, 80). Fourthly, Timms says that Hood's poem is definitely about childhood memories, about what happened in his (or the speaker's) childhood, but Larkin's poem is only about 'what did not happen' in his. Timms writes: "we must reflect that Larkin's poem is not about his childhood in the same sense as Hood's is. Larkin's 'I Remember, I Remember' is about just that—remembering is about the experience of looking back at childhood on a particular occasion. We have no evocations of what happened, or what his childhood home looked like. At that moment, when the train in which the poet is making a journey north, taking an unusual diversion, stops at Coventry, his birthplace, he can remember only what did not happen. His childhood contained none of the unusual formative incidents usually recounted in literary autobiographies or autobiographical novels" (*ibid.*).

Critics have highly praised 'I Remember, I Remember' both for its style of argument and technical excellence. It is conversational to a T, its language is perfectly colloquial and prosaic, but its rhyme-scheme is highly complex. Andrew Swarbrick shows us the subtleties in the argument or content of the poem: "Characteristically, the poem is a progress towards clarification and honesty. The comic exaggeration and ironic use of stereotyped language mocks the romantic view of childhood which sees in it an idyllic happiness and innocence. The mounting bitterness contained in the satire expresses an anger that childhood, like all time that is present, is 'unspent'. But the anger is also directed at the speaker himself, and like so many others, this poem of self-appraisal is also an act of self-criticism. For the poet is angry at himself for having entertained romantic illusions about his past which have to be cruelly dashed; after all, 'I suppose it's not the place's fault'. This bitterness is actually exaggerated, and this can be seen in the catalogue of romantic illusions. The simple negative of 'did not invent' and 'wasn't spoken to' is repeated with ever-increasing emphasis. This irony is progressively sharper in 'here we have that splendid family' and 'I'll show you, come to that' before the accumulating anger is broken off by the companion's interruption, 'You look as if you wished the place in Hell', which calms the poet into expressing his disillusionment in more subdued fashion. The poet's anger is caused not just by disappointment in his own childhood so much as by regret that it was nothing more than it was. Whilst rejecting the stock romantic cliches, he nevertheless wishes that childhood might be closer to what Hood's sentimental poem describes" (Swarbrick, 1986, 37).

Swarbrick writes about the prosaic and conversational language of the poem and its apt idioms, pedestrian diction, matter-of-factness and mockery: "The language of the poem is prosaically conversational, a finely tuned idiom in which all the nuances of feeling are caught. In particular, it shows up the preposterous conventionality of the cliches associated with childhood felt even in the phrase 'family hols', which seems to belong to a particular class in a bygone age. Against the background of colloquial, matter-of-fact tone and diction, phrases such as 'have your roots', 'Really myself' and 'all became a burning mist' are, as their quotation marks in the poem testify, absurdly pretentious. Mockery is also present in the hyperbole of 'Blinding theologies' the pulp-fiction argot of 'she / Lay back', the far-fetched detail of the doggerel set in 'blunt ten-point' (a size of print). The diction appears bluntly ordinary, but in a very sophisticated way catches the shifting moods of a speaking voice" (*op. cit.*, 37-38). David Timms calls the language of the poem 'straightforwardly conversational' and says that it perfectly accords with the theory of language of poetry that Wordsworth propounded in the Preface to *Lyrical Ballads*. About the language of 'I Remember, I Remember', Timms says that "Larkin perfectly achieves an idiom that is living and contemporary. And he does this without lapsing into flatness, as the marvellous last line [of the poem] proves" (Timms, 81).

The peculiar arrangement of the last line of the poem deserves special notice. The line—'Nothing, like something, happens anywhere'—almost works like the *envoi* of a sonnet—it summarises the whole argument of the rest of the poem in a cameo form. David Timms writes about it: "The last line is immensely powerful, partly owing to its felicitous phrasing, but more to its honesty. How often have we heard someone deride his birthplace? Larkin will not flatter himself by settling the shortcomings of his childhood on the place where it was spent. The line finishes the poem in completing its form, as well as being physically the last words. Though typographically tacked on to the end of the poem, the final line completes a complex, large scale rhyme scheme, which breaks across the seven-line stanzas" (*ibid.*). Tectonically, the poem is highly complex, indeed. The five-line stanza overlaps the next stanza, carrying the meaning forward. Timms says that "By rhyme, the poem is in four units, each unit having three rhymes—abccbaabc. The rhyme scheme, by joining stanza to stanza—there is no point at which the end of a rhyme unit and the end of a stanza coincide—unifies the poem" (*ibid.*).

The highly complex rhyme-scheme, it seems, Larkin has utilised in the poem quite deliberately to achieve some special effects, as may be understood from what Andrew Swarbrick elaborately writes about the rhyme-scheme and other poetic crafts of the poem: "The poem's rhyme-scheme is highly complex. Although the poem is divided into seven stanzas each of five lines and a final tail-line, its rhyming unit is actually one of nine lines so that the tail-line, so distinctively separated from the rest of the poem, is in fact integrated into the rhyming pattern. The nine-line rhyming unit [which is not completed at the end of a stanza but at the end of the fourth line of the immediately following stanza] is itself ornately symmetrical:

abccbaabc / deffeddef / ghiihgghi / jkllkjjkl

with rhymes in each unit revolving around two pairs of couplets. Apart from admiring the technical expertise involved in this, we ought also to ponder its effect. When overlaid on the stanza unit, the rhyming pattern is forever shifting, the rhymes occurring at different places within the stanzaic structure. This slightly puzzling displacement (we are vaguely aware of a regular rhyme-scheme on the first reading but cannot quite place it) helps to create precisely that nagging familiarity felt by the poet before recognising his home town and the disorientation he feels when identifying what did not happen there: the rhymes, like 'nothing', seem indiscriminately to happen 'anywhere'" (Swarbrick, 1986, 38).

12

At Grass

The collection of poems we have so far been discussing—*The Less Deceived* (1995)—opens with 'Lines on a Young Lady's Photograph Album' and closes with 'At Grass'. 'At Grass' also appears at the end of *XX Poems* (1951) and *The Fantasy Poets No. 21* (1954). Further, Larkin made manuscript drafts of this poem "available for publication in the celebratory issue of *Phoenix* in 1973" (Swarbrick, 1995, 37). All these may show the amount of importance Larkin attached to the poem. As we have said, Larkin peculiarly got the most important poems of each one of his collections printed at the beginning and at the end of it, and this formula immediately convinces us of the importance of 'At Grass'. It is certainly one of Larkin's 'most admired and best liked poems'. 'At Grass' was written on 3 January 1950. It was written at a time when Larkin, then 28, could hardly have been expected to ponder retirement or death, but he was lacerated by the progresively cooling down relationship between himself and his fiancee Ruth, and also by his perhaps fancied sense of 'regret, guilt, anger and disappointment'. 'At Grass' betrays a mood of release from all these negative affections. However, it may be pointed out here that there is a confusion at some quarters as to the date of composition of 'At Grass'. Both Andrew Motion and Anthony Thwaite believe that the date was 3 January 1950 (when Larkin should have been 28), but Andrew Swarbrick writes a different story. In his *Out of Reach: the Poetry of Philip Larkin*, Swarbrick writes: "'I wrote my first good poem when I was 26', said Larkin in an interview in 1973 (without identifying the poem). Peter Ferguson has suggested the reference is to 'At Grass', which a writer in *The Times Educational Supplement* for 13 July 1956 said (presumably Larkin) grew out of a newsreel film about a retired racehorse which Larkin saw in 1948 (when Larkin was 26). Andrew Motion dates things differently, with Larkin seeing the film on 3 January 1950 and writing the poem the same day (the day given as its completion date in the *Collected Poems*" (Swarbrick, 1995, 37).

The poem has an interesting history of origin, as narrated by Andrew Motion in his celebrated *Philip Larkin: A Writer's Life* (let us quote at some length): "Larkin began the new year [1950] with no hope of his life improving. The atmosphere in Dixon Drive [where he was then digging] was stultifying; the university [where he was serving], closed for the vacation, was forlorn; his friends were elsewhere. On the afternoon of 3 January he went to the cinema to try and divert himself.

Before the main feature started, he watched a short film about a racehorse called Brown Jack, which had been famous before the war. 'It was,' [he] remembered later, 'a film about, you know, "Where is Brown Jack now?" Where Brown Jack was now was at grass, quite happy, moving about, no harness, no jockey, nobody shouting the odds, simply cropping the grass and having a gallop when he felt like it.' As Larkin walked home that evening he found the story of the horse had 'for some reason' impressed him 'very strongly', and when he reached his room he wrote about it. The result was the poem 'At Grass', which for its filmic re-creation of actual details, its formal melancholy and graceful swoop into the familiar experience has become one of his most admired and best liked poems" (Motion, 187-88). The only other poem that Larkin wrote after watching a film is 'Faith Healing' (Haffenden, 126).

Ted Hughes has many poems on animals, so many that he may be called poet of animals, but Larkin has only two poems on animals ('Toads' and 'Toads Revisited' are not poems on animals): 'At Grass' and 'Pigeons'. However, 'At Grass' is a poem of five stanzas, each stanza comprising six lines. The perfect rhyme-scheme a / b / c / a / b / c runs throughout the poem.

The retired racehorses, to which Larkin, just in the beginning line of the poem, is drawing our attention, are now lonely, and are living in deprivation and dark oblivion, away from the glamour and fanfare that they once had enjoyed. Larkin says that those horses are now kept ('shelter in') under the cold shadow ('shade') of trees, and that they are hardly reflected in the eyes of an observer, or they scarcely come to the notice of an observer, i.e. an observer can very rarely see them ('pick them out'). But sometimes a whiff of wind tousles ('distresses') the tails and the manes of the horses and only when does the wind do this, do the horses become noticeable, and then the observer sees, for instance, that one horse is grazing ('crops grass') and moving about while the other is apparently gazing at him ('The other seeming to look on'). And when there is no more whiff of wind, the horses again become unnoticeable ('anonymous').

In the second stanza, Larkin says that though the horses are now unnoticeable ('Yet'), fifteen years earlier they participated in races, and possibly merely two dozen successful runs of a particular standard length of interspace, technically called 'distance', would be enough ('sufficed') to make them famous ('fable them'). (In the jargon horse-racing 'distance' means 'the space measured back from the winning-post which a horse, in heat-races, must reach when the winner has covered the whole course, in order to run in the final heat'.) Fifteen years ago, in the dim and mild sunlight of the afternoons ('faint afternoons') such things would come to one's notice as people gathering at the race-course to watch the races, wagering money on their chosen horses ('Stakes'), cups being awarded to the winner horses or their grooms or jockeys, and gentlemen (or, better, ladies) bearing with them the disadvantageous or discomfortable article of umbrellas ('Handicaps') to prevent even that dim and mild afternoon sunlight. And all these things—wagering, cups and parasols ('Whereby')—would skilfully or craftily ('artificed') curve ('inlay') on the late and jaded ('faded') but elegant ('classic') months of June the (celebrated) names the fames of the horses ('their names').

In the third stanza, Larkin says that silken flags would be unfurled or waved to start the race of the horses ('Silks at the start'). A huge number of people ('Numbers') would gather to see the race, many of them with umbrellas ('parasols'), occupying a wide space under the sky ('against the sky'). Many of those people would go there by cars, and (when they would leave behind the cars in the car-park to watch the race) the great number of cars, without their occupants ('Squadrons of empty cars') would be waiting outside the race-course. On the other hand, in the scorching sun ('heat') and in strewn grass ('littered grass') these race-horses would be awaiting their appointed races. Then, these horses would be brought in the race-course when the races would begin along with continual or non-stopped ('unhushed') and prolonged or protracted shouting ('long cry') of over-excited or extremely enthusiastic people who would be dangling, swinging or impending from the fencing. And then, the race being over, the shouting would cease ('subside') to give reporters, who were waiting in the street to collect information about the results of the races, to come in to take notes of the results, which would be printed in the columns of the instant newspapers, or which would be inserted in newspapers, while they would be in the process of being printed ('stop-press columns') (Stop-press are the 'late news inserted in a newspaper after printing has began').

In the fourth stanza, Larkin asks if now, after the lapse of fifteen years, the horses are painfully disturbed ('plague') by the memories of their glorious days fifteen years ago as presently they are being painfully disturbed by flies ('Do memories plague their years like flies?'). He is seeing the horses ('they') shaking their heads, which they are doing, he believes, perhaps to drive away the troubling flies, and so understands that they are jerking their heads in order to forget the recollections of their bygone splendid days ('They shake their heads'). It is the time when evening ('Dusk') is gradually closing in and surrounding the periphery or the edges ('brims') of the shades or umbrages ('shadows') (of the trees under which the horses are staying). All of those fifteen years, one after another ('Summer by summer'), have slowly elapsed ('stole away'), and the recollections of the 'starting-gates' from where the races used to begin, of the people who gathered to witness the races, and of their shouts of joy—all have vanished, excepting ('All but') only the fresh, lively or virgin pastures ('unmolesting meadows') of the race-course in which they are no more physically forced to run. Now, the performances of the horses in the races are forgotten, and the performances are only remaining ('live') in the records or registers of the race-course club along with the respective dates of the performances ('Almanacked') and the names of the horses.

In the concluding stanza, Larkin says that people ('they') have now forgotten the names of the horses, i.e. the names have escaped, so to say, the consciousnesses of the people ('Have slipped their names') (or the horses themselves have forgotten their names, i.e. the names to which they used to respond). Now, of course sometimes the horses stand comfortably ('stand at ease') or run very fast keeping all four feet off the ground ('gallop') for joy for sure ('for what must be joy') (because now they are not held by bridles), but nobody takes notice of them quite closely ('sees them home') with the help of a binocular ('fieldglass') (particularly when they rarely run fast) and nobody now curiously foretells ('prophesies') the length of time they (the horses) may need to reach the finishing point in races and compare their guess with the actual time they take to touch the finishing point by looking at and reading their stop-watches ('stop-watch prophesies'). Now, only two persons—the man who has the charge of looking after them, i.e., the horses ('groom') and the man's assistant ('groom's boy')—come to them in the evenings with bridles in their hands to confine or curtail their, i.e., the horses' freedom ('With bridles in the evening come') (this is a symbol of the oncomimg death—of the horses).

'At Grass' symbolically presents a verisimilar picture of man's pathetic state of existence in his old age, when he is quite forgotten by all others as a junk and abandoned to his supposedly gracious oblivion; no more do people recall his glorious past and no more do people become curious about him as earlier—he is simply left by them to his oncoming slow death; when man, nevertheless, enjoys a peculiar sense of contentment in his enforced terminal repose. Though in the poem Larkin is narrating the deplorable lives of a couple of abandoned race-horses in their senility, he is actually speaking of old people in their touchingly pathetic condition when they have irretrievably lost their physical as well as mental forte with which they once achieved distinction. The race-course suggested in the poem may symbolise our mundane life, the horses symbolise human beings, and the race symbolises the unrelenting struggle of our life. People certainly applause the successes that we achieve struggling throughout our active lives but they callously turn their eyes away from us when we fall into senescence and so into decrepitude, and forget us for ever and ever. However, Larkin says that even when we become somewhat immobile and are engulfed by oblivion, we may have at least one contentment: the contentment that we are no more whipped to run fast in our life to achieve glory by forces external to our selves, that is, we may have the contentment of being free beings, the contentment of enjoying freedom. The comparison between the old, jaded horses and humans in their senility is most appropriate and interesting. The pathos generated in the poem around the condition in senescence may be compared to that created by W.B. Yeats in the beginning ten lines of his 'The Tower':

> What shall I do with this absurdity—
> O heart, O troubled heart—this caricature,
> Decrepit age that has been tied to me
> As to a dog's tail?
> Never had I more
> Excited, passionate, fantastical
> Imagination, nor an ear and eye
> That more expected the impossible—
> No, not in boyhood when with rod and fly,
> Or the humbler worm, I climbed Ben Bulben's back
> And had the livelong summer day to spend.

However, the setting of the narrative of the poem is quite pastoral and idyllic, and, perhaps, also platonic, in the sense that it exudes a sort of transcendentalism, other-worldliness, or remoteness from quotidian experiences. The semblance of a story, involved in the poem, is demonstrably vivid, sensuous, and kaleidoscopic—the images employed pass along before our vision like a catena of tableaux, or like a cascade of pictures in a slow-moving celluloid reel. In short, the picturesqueness is unique and impressive. Tom Paulin says that the setting that Larkin has conjoured up in the poem is Edwardian, nostalgically Edwardian, as is suggested by such terms as 'Squadrons', 'littered grass', 'parasols' (metonymy of sunshine), 'meadows' and the implied term 'horses' which is the subject of the poem (Regan, 163). The poem is built upon nostalgia, and Larkin here has created the occasion for nostalgia by focusing on temporal and spatial distances. Stan Smith writes in this regard: "In 'At Grass', it [distance] is the very stuff of nostalgia, as the poem opens with a view of one-time racehorses reduced to anonymity by retirement. Spatial distance places the observer in a secure frame: 'The eye can hardly pick them out'. As the poem develops the image, by recalling a time when these horses were 'picked out' both by binoculars and by fame, it compounds spatial and temporal distance..." (*op. cit.*, 178-79). The anonymity of the horses, we are speaking of here, is very aptly suggested by Larkin in the poem by referring to them obliquely and imprecisely as 'them' ('The eye can hardly pick them out'). It is interesting to notice that in the poem, Larkin has also referred us to the subject of it—the horses—not directly, precisely, but quite obliquely: he has not used even for once the word 'horses' anywhere in the poem.

Andrew Swarbrick believes that the poem expresses no one's but Larkin's desire for anonymity, and that the horses of the poem 'stands for the speaker [i.e. Larkin himself] as icons of anonymity'. Swarbrick explains his point: "'At Grass' is another poem about oblivion, but this time much more maturely conceived than the lurking self-pity of 'Wants' [it is an irony that 'At Grass' was composed on 3 January 1950 and 'Wants' on 1 June 1950, and yet the former is more mature than the latter].... These horses [of 'At Grass'] has escaped their fables, their past, even their names. Remote now from nearly all human contact ('not a fieldglass sees them home...'), they stand for the speaker as icons of anonymity, patiently awaiting their end" (Swarbrick, 1995, 62). This anonymity coupled with the memory of glorious past generates deep pathos and copious sighs in us. The pathos begins to affect us right from the beginning line of the poem, 'The eye can hardly pick them out', and continues to do so till the end, and even thereafter as the concluding two lines ring on in our ears for some time after we have done with the poem: 'Only the groom, and the groom's boy' / 'With bridles in the evening come'. This pathos is, of course, somewhat alleviated by the relative, restricted freedom that the horses one day vainly desired but are now enjoying. The freedom of the horses is now curtailed though by their physical debility and by the fact that even now 'the groom, and the groom's boy' / 'With bridles in the evening come'.

David Timms writes that Al Alvarez has compared Larkin's 'At Grass' with Ted Hughes's 'A Dream of Horses' and has opined that Hughes's poem is 'more important' (he has not said 'better') than Larkin's (Timms, 73). But Andrew Swarbrick says that Alvarez has definitely judged Hughes's poem to be superior to Larkin's. Swarbrick writes: "...when Alvarez offers an account of 'At Grass' to show its inferiority to Ted Hughes's 'A Dream of Horses', he does so by ignoring the metaphysical status of the horses. 'His horses are *social* creatures of fashionable race-meetings and high style; emotionally they belong to the world of the R.S.P.C.A. [Royal Society for the Prevention of Cruelty to Animals].' By contrast, 'Hughes' horses have a violent, impending presence'. Quite so: this is because Larkin wants to honour the *otherness* of the horses, their non-human anonymity, their chastening unknowability, whereas Hughes and Alvarez want to appropriate them as psychologically expressive symbols: 'they reach back, as in a dream, into a nexus of fear and sensation'" (Swarbrick, 1995, 161). But David Timms does not agree with Alvarez. He says that "Alvarez is entitled to his opinion, but the method he uses to persuade others to his view, that Hughes's poem is more important than Larkin's, is suspect. He compares the objects in each poem, suggesting that 'At Grass' is less worthy of notice because the horses in it are less frightening than those in 'A Dream of Horses'" (Timms, 73). Without going deeper into the debate, we may hazard that Alvarez was a bit biased towards Hughes, and our hazard may be a little propped up by what Andrew Swarbrick means in the following sentence of his: "In 1962, the critic Al Alvarez published *The New Poetry*, a popular anthology introduced by another anti-Movement, and this time more specifically anti-Larkin polemic" (Swarbrick, 160).

The mood of the poem is that of serenity and contentment, and this is the most distinguishing feature of this poem among all the poems of Larkin. To recapitulate, *The Less Deceived* begins with 'Lines on a Young Lady's Photograph Album', which speaks of the speaker's (or Larkin's) disturbing desire and memory, and disappointment. He is, for instance, hungry for viewing more and more the beauty of the lady ('My swivel eye hungers from pose to pose—') and he is disappointed with her photographs, nay, with photography itself ('But o, photography! As no art is, / Faithful and disappointing!'). But in 'At Grass', with which Larkin closes the collection, he is tranquil and contented like the retired horses that 'stand at ease,

/ Or gallop for what must be joy'. Andrew Swarbrick elaborates on this point of 'At Grass': "The poem takes up Larkin's familiar themes of identity, time and memory, but in this poem he finds a peacefulness, a contentment in these horses that he cannot find in himself or in human life. In his memory, he recalls the time fifteen years ago when the racehorses were famous: the race-meetings, the 'Squadrons of empty cars' (arranged in straight lines of military exactness), the 'heat' which contrasts with the 'cold shade' in which they now shelter. Now, in their retirement, the horses have retreated from their former world and can gallop for no other motive than the sheer joy of it. Having relinquished their former world, they have relinquished with it their identities. They share an anonymous solitude; where in 'Wants' Larkin sought an isolated oblivion, these horses have found a kind of oblivion in their anonymity and absence of memory. They now live in a continuous present, unplagued by the future (the prophesies of the stop-watch) or memories of the past. They live, too, in a close harmony with nature, merging with the shade, now knowing the 'unmolesting meadows', caught up in the slow, regular rhythm of the groom's arrival each evening, and so they live harmoniously by having relinquished identity, memory, anticipation. Unlike man they have no illusions, fears, doubts, even though the evening may be drawing to its ultimate close. The poem portrays a repose, a contentment, which brings *The Less Deceived* to a peaceful close tinged with melancholy, for these horses possess a tranquility beyond humanity's grasp" (Swarbrick, 1986, 39).

Larkin's biographer, Andrew Motion, has all encomium for this poem which, he believes, 'has become one of his most admired and best liked poems'. Motion writes about 'At Grass': "The horses in the poem stand outside the drama of their lives—they are 'fifteen years' on from the races which turned them into legends—and if they remember anything it is success, not failure. They are secure in their achievement, enjoying a freedom which is beyond both curiosity and comment. Even the prospect of death is gentle: it is not a Grim Reaper but a groom with bridles (strictly speaking it should be halters) who comes for them at the end of their day.... Without taking its eye off the horses, 'At Grass' manages to suggest deep admiration for human lives well-lived and safely over. It is an envious poem which shows no trace of envy's corrosions. The feelings which produced it—regret, guilt, anger and disappointment—are consumed and transfigured into appreciation of 'what must be joy'" (Motion, 188).

However, to conclude our discussion on *The Less Deceived*, we may repeat that it was this collection of poems that first catapulted Larkin, all on a sudden, to a great height of fame, and that it was 'At Grass', the last poem in the collection that was written in 1950, that marks 'the start of a remarkably fruitful period' of Larkin's poetic career 'after the aridity of 1947-49'. After the great success of *The Less Deceived*, Larkin had to wait for no fewer than nine long years for producing another great collection, *The Whitsun Weddings*, that can vie its predecessor for acclamation, and with this contender we will be dealing in the next chapter.

The Whitsun Weddings 6

The Whitsun Weddings, a collection of 32 poems, was published by Faber and Faber on 28 February 1964. Larkin's relation with The Marvell Press that published *The Less Deceived* began to cool down since not long after the publication of the collection. Larkin complained that The Marvell Press 'was too slow to respond to orders. It couldn't distribute the books properly'. Further, the relation between Larkin and George Hartley, through whose agency Larkin got *The Less Deceived* published, was fast losing its warmth. It was during this time that Charles Monteith, the famous publisher of Faber and Faber, was inchingly coming closer to Larkin. Monteith joined Faber and Faber in 1953, became its director the next year, and its chairman in 1976, and remained as such till 1981. It was Monteith who first took up the task of publishing the works of William Golding at a time when they were being rejected by a number of publishers, and of the works of Seamus Heaney. Since the publication of *The Less Deceived*, Monteith used to write to Larkin at intervals and would now and again see him. In the beginning of 1963, the friendship between Larkin and Monteith deepened, which was an additional reason why Monteith, on behalf of Faber and Faber, accepted the manuscript of *The Whitsun Weddings* in June 1963 for publication. Seven months after the publication of *The Whitsun Weddings* in England, the collection was published in America by Random House, situated in New York.

About the reception of *The Whitsun Weddings* in America and England on its first publication, Andrew Motion writes: "In America, as had been the case with *The Less Deceived*, attention was modest and sales unspectacular (2,000 copies in two years, then a reprint of 1,500, in spite of an enthusiastic review by Christopher Ricks in the *New York Review of Books*). In England it was an immediate success: the first 4,000 copies were sold in two months, a further 3,000 in the next year, and two more reprints were ordered in the next six years" (Motion, 342). David Timms writes about the reception of the collection by both the reviewers and the public of England as well as of America: "The *Times Literary Supplement* and the *New York Review of Books*, the most widely read organs of literary opinion in Britain and the U.S.A., praised it highly. The *Times Literary Supplement* approvingly quoted Kenneth Allott's comment from the *Penguin Book of Contemporary Verse*: Larkin is 'the most exciting new poetic voice—with the possible exception of Dylan Thomas—since Auden'. The reviewer for the *New York Review of Books*, Professor Christopher Ricks, is British, but Americans also thought the collection a considerable achievement. A rather slick piece in *Time* magazine said: 'If Larkin is not a great poet, he is nevertheless the only British poet who still seems able to compose great poems.' And the influential American critic and poet Louise Bogan added more measured and weighty, if somewhat school report-like praise: 'this member [Larkin] of what is now becoming middle-aged British poetic generation possesses gifts that are not only perfectly controlled and strongly sustained but capable of wide and interesting variation. He is able to use such gifts as they are seldom used, to describe the tough realities of his time'" (Timms, 92) [announced in *The Times* on 6 September 1965]. Andrew Motion writes that *The Whitsun Weddings* "was the spring choice of the Poetry Book Society (the selectors were Ted Hughes and Ian Fletcher), and was awarded a prize of 250 Pounds by the Arts Council for 'the best book of original English verse by a living poet published from July 1962 to June 1965'. It did more than confirm Larkin's reputation; it turned his voice into one of the means by which his country recognized itself" (Motion, 343).

Larkin arranged the 32 poems of the collection in such a way as 'to create a variety of mood' so that if one does not enjoy a particular poem, 'at least the next one will be different': the poems show a wide range of interest, indeed. Andrew Motion writes about the major features or the wide-ranging qualities of *The Whitsun Weddings*: "Compared to *The Less Deceived*, in which traces of Larkin's Yeatsian and Symbolist inheritance rub against a simpler manner, *The Whitsun Weddings* is a more uniform book. Its gaze is steadier, and it more precisely illustrates the qualities associated with The Movement, even though it appeared nearly a decade after The Movement had been identified. It tackles the big, central issues of ordinary life in the language of ordinary speech, and makes them numinous. Its details (posters, pet-shops, parents) are the details of the everyday; the truths it wrings from them are abiding. Intensely lyrical, it is nevertheless often discursive, speculative and argumentative. Deeply personal, it diversifies its origins until they become exemplary" (*op. cit.*, 342-43). Andrew Swarbrick, at different places of his *Out of Reach: The Poetry of Philip Larkin* (Swarbrick, 1995), writes about the various subjects, moods, feelings, and elements of the poems of *The Whitsun Weddings*: "Questions of identity and its relation to love and death remain at the centre of *The Whitsun Weddings*" (p. 92); 'Elsewhere', that is the 'unfenced existence' and is beyond 'Here' is what so many poems of *The Whitsun Weddings* aspire (p. 94) (it is very significant that the collection begins with the poem 'Here' that speaks of, or aspires after, the 'unfenced existence' which is 'out of reach'); "Escaping knowledge of self is one of the most powerful longings in *The Whitsun Weddings*" (p. 100); "In poem after poem in *The Whitsun Weddings* Larkin wonders why the voice of love has failed to fall on him" (p. 111); *The Whitsun Weddings* is haunted by loneliness and death (p. 122); etc.

According to Andrew Motion, all the poems of the collection do not express level mood but show "occasional outbursts of anger" (Motion, 378), and they, of course, betray "measured arguments and elegantly contained language" (*op. cit.*, 444). Many of the themes of the poems of *The Less Deceived* have been re-worked in the poems of *The Whitsun Weddings* in more guarded, convincing and celebratory manner. As was his wont,

Larkin first published most of the poems of *The Whitsun Weddings* in magazines and only then in that collection, as he later on did also in the case of the poems of *High Windows*. The same year in which *The Whitsun Weddings* was published, i.e. in 1964, Larkin was interviewed by the young poet and literary critic Ian Hamilton for the *London Magazine*, and this speaks volumes about the acclamation of the collection. The same year, again, George Hartley recorded Larkin's reading of the poems of *The Whitsun Weddings* for his series of Listen Records. It was also for this collection that Larkin was awarded the Queen's Gold Medal for poetry in 1965. Lastly, Andrew Motion very appropriately and wittily writes about Larkin that "*The Less Deceived* made his name; *The Whitsun Weddings* made him famous; *High Windows* turned him into a national monument" (*op. cit.*, 446). We must say that he could not become a 'national monument' without previously becoming famous, and that his fame went a considerably long way in turning him into a 'national monument'. This perhaps proves beyond any shade of doubt the enormous amount of laudation *The Whitsun Weddings* received from the poetry-loving society at large.

1

Here

The original title of this poem was 'Withdrawing Room', and this original title instantaneously bespeaks the central idea or theme of the poem. But then Larkin changed the title perhaps because the alternative title is more appropriate, in the sense that in the poem Larkin not only speaks of withdrawing from, or escaping, the cacophonic and rushing out quotidian life but chooses to describe a paradisical landscape on the donnee of the fascinatingly pastoral Hull on the bank of the river Humber, in the northern part of England, that gorges into the North Sea. This is clear from an interview between Larkin and John Haffenden in 1979-80, in which when Larkin was asked if 'Here' is a 'brief for retirement, the simpler life', he retorted: "Oh no, not at all...well, it all depends what you mean by retirement. If you mean not living in London, I suppose it might be interpreted along these lines. I meant it just as a celebration of here, Hull. It's a fascinating area, not quite like anywhere else. So busy, yet so lonely" (Haffenden, 126-27). In the poem, Larkin rejoices in solitude, in things 'untalkative', in "the kind of solitude which allows him to feel that he can belong in and around 'the surprise of a large town' while remaining 'unfenced'" (Motion, 317).

'Here' is undoubtedly one of the best poems of the collection, along with the title poem 'The Whitsun Weddings'. Like 'Dockery and Son' and 'The Whitsun Weddings' of *The Whitsun Weddings* and 'I Remember, I Remember' of *The Less Deceived*, 'Here' is a poem on the occasion of a train journey—in 'Here', Larkin went to Hull by train and there accosted the surprisingly beautiful pastoral scenario beyond the city of Hull and its suburb and near the beach of the North Sea, where he found life to be unhindered and expansive (to be exact, the real train journey of Larkin ended beyond Hull, the city on the Holderness peninsula that lies between the river Humber and the North Sea in the eastern side of England). Andrew Swarbrick writes about the poem: "'Here', one of the central achievements of *The Whitsun Weddings*, take up (these) themes of identity, isolation, and community, and resolves them into images of light and silence and the ineffable disappearance of self. 'Here' manages to speak for all of us because 'here' is where we all are" (Swarbrick, 1995, 103). Nevertheless and above everything else, 'Here' is certainly 'a superlative piece of landscape poetry', 'a vista of the north-east corner of modern England'. 'Here' was dated 8 October 1961 by Larkin and was first published in *The Whitsun Weddings*. It is a poem of 32 lines divided into 4 stanzas, each stanza comprising 8 lines.

In the poem Larkin first draws a particular desired and appropriate situation, then develops a particular emotion, and ultimately arrives at a unique experience, as he also does, for instance, in 'The Whitsun Weddings' and 'Dockery and Son'. In the first verse or stanza of the poem, the speaker (Larkin) says that the train in which he was travelling turned towards east (towards the estuary or mouth of the river Humber) emerging from the highly developed industrial area with split-level buildings, having long shadows ('rich industrial shadows') (the train was supposedly running in the late afternoon; so the shadows of the buildings came to the notice of the speaker), as well as emerging from the busy commerce or movements of people of the town (of Hull), after running ('traffic') all through the night towards north. The train then turned towards, and ran through, fields which could hardly be called meadows because they were very incapacious or narrow ('thin') and full of prickly composite plants ('thistled'). The train stopped at times or intervals at different stations which had no soft names but grating or grinding ones ('harsh-named'), and on these stoppages workmen were seen in the morning as if they were being protected by the haltages or by their shades ('shields'). And after all these stoppages, the train at last arrived at a place where the sense of loneliness, privacy, remoteness, seclusion or retirement ('solitude') prevailed all around: in the corners of the sky over that place and in such objects of that place as scarecrows, haystacks, hares and pheasants. That loneliness also was noticed where the width of the river (Humber) was gradually increasing and the water of the river was running rather slowly ('the widening river's slowpresence'), where golden clouds piled up in the sky, and where bright clay with marks of the claws of gulls was seen (The place is certainly pastoral and romantically coloured).

In the second stanza, the speaker says that the solitude of the skies, the scarecrows, etc. described in the previous stanza was concentrating or accumulating so that the people of the big town (of Hull) would become astonished to notice or feel it ('Gathers to the surprise of a large town'). The speaker says that in the town (of Hull) ('Here'), hemispherical structures raised above large buildings ('domes'); sculptures ('statues') mounted over buildings; spiralling or winding and tapering high-rise structures ('spires'); and heavy machines for hauling up great weights ('cranes') were seen jumbled up, huddles, alongside streets strewn with grain from grain-storages or silos and alongside the river crowded with barges (i.e. the town is situated on the strand of a river—presumably on the strand of the river Humber). The commuters of that place were mostly from agricultural estates ('raw estates': 'raw' meaning 'natural state'), who came to the town from dull or very long distances without stopping ('dead straight miles': 'dead meaning 'dull' or 'very long') by low wheelbarrows ('flat-faced trolleys') that played or moved quietly (like wary thieves) ('stealing') [Roger Day says that here stealing means seducing or enticing: "the trolleys are enticing, seducing people to the stores" from the agricultural estates (Day, 54)]. After the people had come over to the town, they passed through 'plate-glass swing doors' (of techtonically marvellous modern towns' supermarkets of Hull) to buy their desired objects ('to their desires'), such as low-priced suits; kitchen utensils; fashionable ('sharp') shoes; iced lollipops; electric mixers; toasters; washers; machines for extracting moisters from cloth, hair ('driers'), etc.

At beginning of the third stanza, the speaker very appropriately calls or dubs those people who came from agricultural estates (to the supermarkets of Hull) to buy their desired or coveted objects a 'cut-price crowd', because they came to the town to buy cheap goods ('cut-price crowd' means crowd interested in buying 'cut-price' goods or goods sold at reduced rates). In the third stanza, the speaker further says that those people were simple though urbane or sophisticated in manners. They lived where salesman and their relatives used to visit, and they lived, or their dwelling-houses were situated, near the far-end ('terminate') of the land where there was a pasture that smelt of fishes ('fishy-smelling / Pastoral'), where streets ended at a place near which one could find ships and buy or hire labourers ('slave museum') [The term 'slave museum', Andrew Swarbrick writes, "is both a historical monument and a quietly ironic reminder that in their own way 'grim head-scarfed wives' are themselves 'slaves' to a lifestyle they never chose" (Swarbrick, 1986, 41)]. There were also shops where one could get his skin marked according to designs by pricking in colouring matters ('Tattoo-shops'), the offices of the chief magistrates ('consulates'), and sullen, serious-looking or repellent ('grim') married women wearing scarves on their heads. On the far side of the town were rows of incompletely built sturctures or buildings which were mortgaged or pledged as security for a debt ('m'rtgaged half-built edges'), and on the distant side of the rows ('out beyond') one could find heavily, deeply or extravagantly shaded (by trees or black clouds) ('Fast-shadowed') wheat-fields where the crops were as high as hedges ('Fast-shadowed wheat-fields, running as high as hedges') and scattered villages ('Isolate villages'). In that place, the lives of the people are away from ('removed lives') the hurly-burly of the town, and so are secluded, withdrawn, forlorn, desolate or lonely.

These three stanzas are conjuring up the situation or occasion in which the speaker, in the fourth or last stanza, is going to deliver his message or arriving at his projected conclusion. He says that in the seclusion or solitude ('Loneliness') of that particular place (on the outskirt of the town of Hull and the estuary of the river of Humber) reveals ('clarifies') to ourselves the true nature of our beings or our existences ('Loneliness clarifies') [Roger Day writes: "As the lines 'where removed lives / Loneliness clarifies' indicate, solitude and quiet generate a purity of existence—the construction is inverted and in prose would run 'loneliness clarifies removed lives'. The effect of the inversion is to put the stress on 'clarifies'" (Day, 54)]. In this place ('Here') calm, quiet or quiescence perpetually prevailed ('silence stands') as in townships fever of activities ('heat') eternally subsisted. In this place the leaves of trees of deep forests grow healthier ('thicken') without being seen by anybody (due to the darkness of the forests, that was caused by the thickly grown trees) ('unnoticed'); flowers of weeds, that nobody could see (again, due to the darkness of the forests, or because nobody ever did go there) ('Hidden'), blossomed; water-courses, that people did not count as necessary or valuable ('neglected waters') ran fast and lively ('quicken'); and air, in which bright or lively people breathed and moved ('Luminously-peopled'), rose upwards. [Andrew Swarbrick writes about the term 'Luminously-peopled': "Larkin seems to suggest what is almost a paradox, that it is in states of solitariness that we become most vividly aware of other almost ghostly presences of non-human life and the lives lived by generations before us" (Swarbrick, 1986, 41)]. And beyond the waste or bank of poppies, on the rind or edge of the pastoral place in the neighbourhood of Hull, one could see the indifferent or indistinct ('n'utral') distance of faded blue (the distance is neutral because it takes no part—either for or against—in human affairs, and the distance is 'bluish' because the distance merges in the junction of the blue sky and the blue water of the North Sea). The indifferent or indistinct distance terminated, ceased to accompany the stretch of land ('Ends the land'), abruptly on the other side of the strand or shore, where one could see various shapes of land or earth and of large pebbles ('shingles'). The speaker now concludes saying that at that pastoral, silent and lonely place in the neighbourhood of Hull there was uncircumscribed life or being or aseity (i.e. self-origination), or there one could feel an aseity or a life or a being that was unending, unbridled, ceaseless ('Here is unfenced existence'). The life or existence of this place was directly under the benediction of the life-nourishing and life-sustaining beams of the sun, without any adventitious interfering elements, or at this place people might straightway look up to their ideals or desired goals ('Facing the sun'). But what sort of life or existence prevails at this place none can talk out or express ('untalkative'); only this can be said that such an existence or such a life none can practically achieve, that such a being or subsistence no one can get at, reach ('out of reach').

As we have said, like 'I Remember, I Remember', 'Dockery and Son' and 'The Whitsun Weddings', in 'Here' also Larkin creates his projected situation for poetising depending on a train journey. M.L. Rosenthal writes about catenated scenarios that are evoked in the poem—scenarios that Larkin saw from the running train: "This is a poem unusual, for Larkin, in its swift movement that carries us from more industrial regions along the highway into the city of Hull, gives us close-ups of the city's inhabitants and sights, and then takes us out beyond the 'mortgaged half-built edges' past wheat fields [to be exact, poppy fields] and 'isolate villages' towards the beach and the North Sea" (Rosenthal, 242). In the poem, the speaker does not explicitly speaks of the train journey but there are a couple of key words suggestive of the train journey: the participle 'swerving', used almost neck to neck thrice in the first stanza, and 'halt', meaning a railway stoppage, also in the first stanza, reinforced by 'Gathers' at the very beginning of the second stanza and by 'terminate' in the third line of the third stanza.

The journey of the train (the whole route) and the experiences of the speaker are as follows. In the first verse or stanza, the train runs through the countryside when the speaker comes to see, one after the other, scarecrows, haystacks, hares and pheasants. The beginning of the second stanza announces the train reaching the town of Hull, and in the second and third stanzas the speaker describes the commuters of the town as well as the town itself. The last three lines of the third stanza lead us to the end of the town and the beginning of the countryside. The last stanza takes us to the end of the mainland, i.e. to the rim or edge of the beach, where there is 'unfenced existence'. Roger Day rightly says that the description of the journey is 'cinematic'; we may add, like in 'The Whitsun Weddings'. Day writes: "The method is cinematic. One scene dissolves into another, each vividly described. It is a very highly observed poem and works through its detailed account" (Day, 54). Day further writes: "Where 'Here' differs from a film is that we see everything through the eyes of the narrator who, though apparently detached, is not indifferent to what he sees" (*ibid.*). The narrator is not indifferent because he gluts the 'unfenced existence'. In fact, the poem abounds in necessary details for conjuring up some lively scenes—that of the countryside, of the town, of the beach and beyond—such as 'scarecrows' haystacks and pheasants', 'plate-glass swing doors', 'Cheap suits, red kitchen ware, sharp shoes, iced lollies, / Electric mixers, toasters, washers, driers—', etc.

'Here' very aptly expresses Larkin's intensely deep emotions about two of his major and central desires, 'the wish to be alone' and 'desire of oblivion', which two desires he earlier expressed eleven years ago in 'Wants' (1950), when, we wonder, he was only about twenty-eight years old. In 'Here', he expresses his desire to have the inexpressible joy to be had from his presence in the centre of a vast, infinite, vacant and absolutely silent space, to be had from 'unfenced existence', quite, quite away from the cacophonous commercialism of urbane space. In the poem, Larkin arrives at such a place and reaches such an existence in the morning at the end of his *long journey* through *night*. Perhaps by a quick of fancy we may compare or similise the long journey overnight with our quotidian unhappy life, and the 'unfenced existence' reached in the bright morning with our desired bliss of peaceful happiness. That happiness, Larkin seems to mean, can be got only after the end of the night, i.e., only after the end of our doleful life—only after death. In this sense, 'Here', like 'Wants' before it, is Larkin's enunciation of his desire for oblivion, for death.

The first sentence of 'Here' is quirkily extraordinary: it rolls over the beginning twenty-four plus lines of the poem, as if, mimicking the long train journey of the speaker. Andrew Swarbrick writes: "in a remarkable feat of syntactic control, Larkin makes the first sentence last twenty-four lines before suddenly pulling us up mid-way through the twenty-fifth. The contrasting brevity of 'Here silence stands / 'Like heat' mimes the sensation of a journey concluded, of arrival, silence, stillness (notice how the simile makes the silence itself tangible). That long opening sentence, uncoiling and itself 'swerving' throughout three stanzas, is a journey through a quick succession of realistic detail (as if glimpsed at speed) whilst the repeated conjunctions ('And traffic', 'And the widening river', 'And residents', 'And out beyond', 'And past') all of which come at the beginning of lines, create a surging, seemingly irresistible movement towards the sea at the poem's conclusion" (Swarbrick, 1986, 40). The final stanza of the poem, though not extraordinary, is very efficient: it tucks up all the images of the foregoing three stanzas and then builds up very abruptly the required emotion within a brief compass and thus gives the poem its final shape and meaning. Roger Day writes in this regard: "It is the final stanza that reveals the poem's subject and explains the title. Using verb in the present tense, the narrator conveys an immensely powerful awareness of his own 'unfenced existence', gloring in his solitude. It is the opposite of lifeless state—all verbs are associated with growth ('thicken', 'flower', 'quicken') and the air itself is 'Luminously-peopled' (i.e. alive with lights)" (Day, 54).

Roger Day has found in 'Here' an instance of how Larkin frequently adopts the traditional complex form of poetry (to express modern sensibilities). Day writes: "There are two rhyme schemes—stanzas 1 and 3 share one, stanzas 2 and 4 the other, thus

'ababcddc abbacdcd ababcddc abbacdcd'

My point in drawing this (to your attention) is to illustrate (again) that Larkin frequently employs what is, on examination, a surprisingly complex form of traditional methods in a poem which initially seems straightforward" (*op. cit.*, 54-55). M.L. Rosenthal is mildly critical of the prosody of the poem and writes that the poem "is hag-ridden by a rather heavily regular pattern of rhymes in each of its eight-line stanzas. Larkin varies the pattern with a number of half-rhymes and with a criss-cross arrangement in alternating stanzas: *ababcddc, effeghgh, ijijkllk, mnnmopop*. Despite the two kinds of variation, the rhyming calls too much attention to itself in the course of each long stanza, though the onward movement and the vivid, accurate details are organically so alive that they survive this dragging effect" (Rosenthal, 242). It is particularly for the 'rather heavily regular pattern of rhymes' of the poem and for Larkin's losing himself "in the excitement of sense-awareness" that Rosenthal says that the poem is "less spontaneous in feeling than it should be" (*op. cit.*, 241-42).

Nevertheless, Rosenthal has, as already said, admitted that 'the onward movement and the vivid, accurate details are organically so alive' in the poem that the bad effects of the 'heavily regular pattern of rhymes' of it are quite staved off. He further writes that "'Here' is easily the best of these newer poems (of *The Whitsun Weddings*), and the one that succeeds most in downing its own lugubriousness" (*op. cit.*, 242). We may not quite agree with Rosenthal in counting 'Here' as the best poem of the collection, but we have no reservation in admitting that 'The Whitsun Weddings' and 'Here' are the two best poems of it.

2

Mr Bleaney

This poem comes second in the order of sequence in the collection *The Whitsun Weddings*. The original title of the poem was 'Mr Gridley'. Andrew Swarbrick writes about the changing of the title and the origin of the new title: "Originally, it [the poem] was entitled 'Mr Gridley'; the change to 'Bleaney' reinforces the bleakness descried in the poem (In fact, Larkin had used the name before: Bleany is an otherwise anonymous schoolboy contempoary of John Kemp's in Larkin's first novel, *Jill.*)" (Swarbrick, 1995, 96). David Timms writes about Larkin's trick of entitling the poem: "In his work taken as a whole Larkin sees life as a bleak, sometimes horrifying business. 'Mr Bleaney' shows how mean life can be: Bleaney's very name combines the notions 'bleak' and 'mean' and ends in a diminutive '—ey'" (Timms, 97). As we have said, in 1955 Larkin left the University of Belfast, in Ireland, and joined the University of Hull, in England, as librarian. Andrew Swarbrick says that 'Mr Bleaney' was perhaps the first poem that Larkin wrote coming back to England. Larkin never forgot Belfast's 'individuality and humour and friendliness', and in the contrasting inhospitable, uncomfortable, and not agreeable environment of Hull he frequently and nostalgically recalled his salad days in Belfast. In Hull, the University provided Larkin with a low-grade incapacious and obstreperous dig on the first floor of Holtby House, a student residence. "Holtby House, he told Judy Egerton, 'is *not* suitable: small, bare floored and noisy: I feel as if I were lying in some penurious doss-house at night, with hobos snoring and quarrelling all round me. There is a negro in the next room who would benefit enormously from a pair of bedroom slippers.' ...'The inhabitants are so noisy all the time', he told his mother. 'Oh dear, the future now seems very *bleak* and difficult..." (italics mine) (Motion, 247). After 4/5 weeks, Larkin left Holtby House and put up in the house of Mrs Dowling, where the landlady was "'extremely kind and thoughtful', the food 'not bad', but 'the house too small' [the 'hired box' of the poem] and the family's *radio 'like a nightmare'* [the 'jabbering set' of the poem]. In a letter to Enright, he also fulminated against the 'blasted RADIO', complaining it 'prevents me from sitting, thinking and scribbling in the evening'" (italics mine) (*ibid.*).

'Mr Bleaney' is a dramatic monologue of the 'speaker' who has recently occupied a scantily furnished room vacated by Mr Bleaney. The speaker imagines from his perception of the room and its surrounding that the previous tenant or renter of the room and himself were mutually alter egos in many respects. P.R. King says that the poem "begins as a study of a middle-aged, lonely bachelor who was the previous tenant of the dingy lodging room the poet now occupies" (King, 18). The poem, King further says, "is a wry grimace of self-recognition built-round the notion that if the previous occupant 'warranted no better' then perhaps neither does the tenant who follows" (*op. cit.*, 19). 'Mr Bleaney' comprises seven stanzas, each stanza having four lines, invariably rhyming abab.

In the beginning stanza of the poem, we learn that Larkin (the speaker) was being shown the room, he decided to rent, by the landlady. The landlady told him that his immediately earlier renter of that particular room was one Mr Bleaney who had been occupying it during the whole period of his residence in that boarding house called 'Bodies' and that Mr Bleaney's stay in that boarding house was terminated when his (Mr Bleaney's) relatives ('They') took him away from it ("This was Mr Bleaney's room. He stayed / The whole time he was at the Bodies, till / They moved him"). 'Bodies' is a "slang for a car-assembly works" (Swarbrick, 1995, 96) and is "here perhaps functioning as a sinister joke" aimed at Mr Bleaney (*ibid.*). The cloth-blinds of the windows, which were decorated with woven designs of flowers ('flowered curtains') and which had become thin and worn off ('frayed'), were now five inches short furlong to the timber or stone at the bases of them ('Fall to within five inches of the sill'). In the second stanza we are told that through the windows of the room one could see a small area where the building of the boarding house stood ('strip of building land'), overgrown with soft ('Tussocky') grass spread over with torn pieces of things ('littered'). The landlady told Larkin that

Mr Bleaney, when he had been living in that room, took the full responsibility of looking after or taking care of her little garden ('bit of garden'). Larkin saw in the room a bed, a vertical or straight-backed chair, and a bulb with the capacity of sixty watts of electricity, but no latch behind the door to slam it strongly ('hook') and no rack or shelf to keep books or a bag on (the first line of the third stanza).

In the third stanza, Larkin says that despite the paucity of adequate facilities in the room he assured the landlady that he would take the room on rent ('I'll take it') (and, in fact, he took the possession of the room). Therefore, it is so that ('So it happens') he is lying on the same bed on which Mr Bleaney had previously been lying. Larkin now extinguished the burning ends ('fags') of his cigarettes by grubbing ('stub') on the same ash-tray which had been presented to Mr Bleaney as a memento or keepsake ('saucer-souvenir').

The fourth stanza tells us that the landlady had bought a radio that made unbearably unpleasant noise ('jabbering set') being doggedly persuaded ('egged') by Mr Bleaney ('he'). Larkin (being irritated by the unbearably unpleasant noise of the radio) attempted to stave off or suppress the noise, or prevent the noise from pestering him ('drown'), by striving to caulk or seal the passages of his ears with oakums of fleecy cotton ('cotton-wool'). Larkin says that he knew Mr Bleaney's wonts or usages, such as when he used to descend by the stairs ('came down') and his liking of sauce rather than juices from meat while being cooked ('gravy').

The fifth and sixth stanzas further elaborate upon Larkin's knowledge of Mr Bleaney's wonts and usages. In the fifth stanza, Larkin says that he knew the reason ('why': fourth stanza) of Mr Bleaney's constantly or repeatedly preferring ('kept on plugging') the number 'four' in football tournament coupons or tickets or in lotteries ('four aways'). Similarly, Larkin knew the annual programme ('yearly frame') of Mr Bleaney's relatives ('their'), who resided at Finton ('the Finton falk') of keeping or having him ('put him up') in their midst during summer holidays, and his usual staying at the house of his sister, in Stoke, during Christmastides.

In the sixth stanza, Larkin says that he also knew that if, on the other hand ('But'), standing outside his room ('stood'), Mr Bleaney would notice the beauty of cold winds ('frigid wind') disarranging or dishevelling ('tousling') clouds, he (would go inside his room and) would lie on his offensively smelling or musty-smelling ('fusty') bed and persuade himself to belief ('Telling himself') that the room (rented by him) was actually owned by himself, i.e. the room was, in fact, his sweet home ('this was home'), and so he would self-mockingly, self-deridingly and painfully laugh broadly 'setting his teeth together and drawing his lips in' ('grinned'). Mr Bleaney would then also be afraid and so would quiver ('shivered') in fear ('dread') because he could not drive away a particular fear of his ('without shaking off the dread'). In the final stanza, Larkin says that the particular fear of Mr Bleaney (for which he would tremble) was his apprehension that our characters, or dispositions, manners and habits, are commensurate with our modes of living or our life-styles, i.e. one can infer about our characters from our modes of living ('how we live measures our nature'). In his middle age ('at his age'), Mr Bleaney had nothing more to show as his own possession (i.e. he possessed nothing) other than only that incapacious rented room of his ('one hired box'), and so, perhaps ('I don't know'), he was quite certain about himself ('should make himself pretty sure') that he hardly deserved, or could hardly demand, any better life than that he had been enjoying, or that no better life was justifiable for him than that he had been enjoying ('He warranted no better'), because he lacked the capacity of achieving anything at all.

The poem has two points to make: one, the speaker strives to draw a psychological portrait of a certain Mr Bleaney, who was the immediately previous renter of the room he is now occupying, on the strength of his belief 'That how we live measures our own nature'; and two, and on the strength again of the same belief the speaker presumes that his own nature must be no different from that of Mr Bleaney. For the first point first, the speaker first gathers a few minutiae about Mr Bleaney's life style, behaviour, preference and possession. Mr Bleaney, he has come to know, was a middle aged, poor, mediocre bachelor with no social connections. Mr Bleaney lived meanly in the small rented room in the first floor of a certain landlady—the room having a 'Bed, upright chair, sixty-watt bulb, no hook / Behind the door, no room for books or bags—'. He appears to have had only one thing in his possession—a 'saucer-souvenir', understandably gifted by his once beloved. He used to spend Christmases at his sister's house at Stoke; he preferred sauce to gravy; he had a prejudicial or whimsical liking for the number four in betting; his relatives would somewhat force him to live with them during summer holidays; and if he noticed the romantic carding of clouds in the sky by vigorous winds, he would lay on his bed and smile at himself in self-degradation and pain, and tremble in fear that people may detect his psychological make-up viewing his style of life, i.e. his secret self might be exposed. This is the psychological portrait of Mr Bleaney.

The second point of the speaker in the poem is subordinate and obliquely made: he means to say that if 'how we live measures our own nature' then it can be inferred that his own nature is no different from that of Mr Bleaney's, in so far as he is living in the same room and ambience in which Mr Bleaney lived. In this regard, the poem is partially autobiographical, for, as we have already said, while in the Holtby House in Hull, Larkin lived in a living condition not very different from that in which Mr Bleaney did, and, further, Larkin's frame of mind at that time, that showed painful feeling of desolateness, despiritedness and bleakness, was also not quite different from that of Mr Bleaney. Mr Bleaney, therefore, may be conceived of as Larkin's doppel-ganger. But the similitude between Larkin and 'Mr Bleaney' is not tenable beyond a certain limit, because in the concluding stanza the speaker admits his lack of full knowledge about Mr Bleaney: 'I don't know.' Nevertheless, the key traits of 'Mr Bleaney's' character are only obvious from the look of his room: he is a drab, dull, despirited and will-less person. Andrew Swarbrick writes about 'Mr Bleaney' "The drabness of his surroundings is an extension of the drabness of himself. His life seems to have been a failure that is reflected in the physical details of the room: it is dull (a 60-watt bulb), confined ('no room for books or bags') and stale (the bed is 'fusty'). The final stanza seems to assert that Mr Bleaney, being the sort of man he was, deserved no more than this 'hired box' of a room because he was incapable of achieving anything better" (Swarbrick, 1986, 42). However, P.R. King writes that the final 'I don't know' "refers not only to Bleaney but to the poet's uncertainty as to how far he [Larkin] shares his [Mr Bleaney's] fate" (King, 18-19). King's position is attested by what Larkin in his interview with John Haffenden in 1979 (1980) said about his identity with 'Mr Bleaney': "The first two-thirds of the poem ['Mr Bleaney'], down to 'But if' are concerned with my uneasy feeling that I'm becoming Mr Bleaney, yes. The last third is reassuring myself that I'm not, because he was clearly quite content with his sauce instead of gravy, and digging the garden and so on, and yet there's doubt lingering too, perhaps he hated it as much as I did" (Haffenden, 126). And David Timms has discovered the fundamental difference between Larkin, the speaker, and Mr Bleaney: "The difference between the two men is that the speaker is an intellectual, and Bleaney was not. The speaker looks for bookshelves, but finds none: Bleaney had no need of them. Thinking too hard on his surroundings, the speaker is less equipped to cope with life than Bleaney is" (Timms, 97).

The emotional tension of the poem is not present on the surface of it but deep inside it. The poem starts "'from a poise, or a pose, to an exposure or an epiphany', presenting 'a brave deception in the strong and engaging surface, which hid a complex and sensitive disturbance within'" (Swarbrick, 1995, 96). Really, as long as the bare narrative part or component of the poem continues, i.e. till the end of the fifth stanza of it, no emotional disturbance ensues, but from the very beginning of the sixth stanza emotion sets in and rises sharply high and continues till the end of the poem. In the poem, the dull, bleak and lonely life of Mr Bleaney has been uniquely dramatised in the manner of Robert Browning. Andrew Swarbrick writes that "Beneath the surface of the poem are troubling stirrings of compassion for a comical stereotype. By the end of the poem, there are disturbing cross-currents of feeling. For Mr Bleaney, 'this was home' and there is no 'elsewhere' to underwrite his alienation from it, the 'hired box' of his life. The speaker shivers with him. The world is indifferent to them both: the 'frigid' wind tousles the clouds purposelessly. But in the end, the speaker contrives to resist a painful identification with Mr Bleaney. The final, isolated, exhausted 'I don't know' is both an admission of failure and a triumph of self-preservation" (Swarbrick, 1995, 98).

Though Larkin (or the speaker of the poem) is hesitant, shaky about quite identifying himself with Mr Bleaney, his self-degrading and self-caricaturing attitude is only obvious in the poem. The autobiographical elements in the poem certainly point to the verisimilitude between the real and the fictional persons: the 'I don't know' is just an expression of Larkin's uneasiness in accepting his own self. Larkin's raw caricaturing of his butt, Mr Bleaney, is obvious even in the name of the person, as we have already said: Bleaney means 'bleak' and 'mean'. Mr Bleaney 'was at the Bodies' and he lived in 'one hired box'. 'Bodies' is a term of 'sinister joke', as we have known, and 'hired box' "is all too coffin-like", as Andrew Swarbrick says (*op. cit.*, 96), and so 'hired box' is a term of satire hurled at Mr Bleaney. The poem is therefore built on Larkin's self-sarcasm through sardonic treatment of his fictitious alter ego, Mr Bleaney.

Larkin's habitual ventriloquising is present in the poem, beside its novelistic detailing of minutiae and sharp dramatisation. But perhaps the most striking feature of the poem is its tonal finesse that regulates and develops its purport. Andrew Swarbrick writes in this regard: "One of the most notable features of the poem is the way in which its meaning emerges by a slight change in tone. We begin with the landlady's compulsive chatter and move through the poet's weary familiarisation with the room and Mr Bleaney towards a conclusion which reveals more about the speaker than seems intended. Beneath the disdain for Mr Bleaney lies a hidden fear which, almost in spite of the speaker, surfaces at the poem's close to break the illusion of separateness between them. This irresistible pull towards a truth which the poem's speaker would rather avoid but cannot suppress is characteristic of Larkin" (Swarbrick, 1986, 43).

3

Faith Healing

'Faith Healing' may be called a companion poem of 'Church Going' in so far as in both the poems Larkin deals with what he believes to be the delusion of transcendentalism. In 'Church Going', he says that men are, in fact, deceived by their own faith in Christianity because there is no supernatural power, and because 'superstition, like belief, must die', and in 'Faith Healing' he means to say that men are deceived by their belief that a Christian preacher (or a church functionary) has the power to cure diseases, because only one thing—love—and nothing whatsoever else can cure human ailments. The Christian belief in faith-healing is spoken of in the book 'The Letter of James' of the *New testament.* In section 5, sub-sections 15 and 16, of 'The Letter of James', we read: "Is there anyone who is ill? He should send for the church elders, who will pray for him and rub olive-oil on him in the name of the Lord. This prayer made in faith will heal the sick person; the lord will restore him to health, and the sins he has committed will be forgiven" (The Bible Society of India, 288). In his interview with John Haffenden in 1979 or 1980, Larkin admitted that like 'At Grass', 'Faith Healing' also "came after seeing faith-healing in a film" (Haffenden, 126). On the authority of Andrew Motion, we learn that it was an 'Italian documentary film' (Motion, 300 and 541).

Larkin dated the poem 10 May 1960. Andrew Motion writes that Larkin began the poem on 19 March and finished it on 10 May of the same year (*ibid.*, 300). 'Faith Healing' consists of three stanzas, each stanza consisting of ten lines, rhyming a / b / c /a / b / d / a / b / c / d. It was first published in *The Whitsun Weddings*.

Larkin begins the poem drawing a graphic scene as he saw it in the celluloid tape: a queue or file of women proceeded slowly towards the priest and faith-healer of the church ('he'), who was standing erect. His hair was silver-white (due to old age) and he had worn a dark-coloured or black-coloured suit, a white collared shirt, and a rimless pair of spectacles. The attendants ('Stewards') of the church were indefatigably persuading the women who gathered in the church ('them') to move forward ('onward') and reach near the preacher-cum-faith-healer to receive his counsel or advice ('voice') and blessings ('hands', because blessings are given by touching one's head with the palm). Each woman was approaching him and staying near him for some twenty seconds and during that brief while was partaking of his sympathetic ('warm'), invigorating ('spring'), ample or inexhaustible ('rain') and affectionate ('loving') attention ('care'). The preacher was of American stock or descent (the American evangelist Billy Graham). When a woman went to him, the American preacher or missionary urgently asked her in organic or baritone voice ('the deep American voice demands') what her disease ('wrong') was ('Now, dear child, / What's wrong'). And being informed of the diseases of the women, by them, one after another, the preacher, hardly halting or waiting for a moment to think over the diseases ('scarcely pausing'), began to pray to God for drawing His attention or receiving His blessing ('Directing God') for one woman's disease of her eye ('this eye') and another's disease of knee ('that knee'), and so on. And each time after praying for a particular woman, the preacher used to suddenly take hold of her head strongly with his hands ('Their heads are clasped abruptly') in order to bless her. And then she would have been dismissed ('then, exiled').

In the second stanza, Larkin says that the woman, who would have been at last blessed by the priest, used to be dismissed by him as if they were his ephemeral stray thoughts, i.e. the priest would quite forget about them ('like losing thoughts'), and then they would silently file out. Some of the women, being now detached from the congregation, would loiter here and there like some sheep alienated from herd or flock ('Sheepishly stray') hither and thither without even yet going back home and engaging in household works ('not back into their lives / Just yet'), because not yet could they shake the hangover of the supposedly transcendental influence of the preacher off themselves. On the other hand, some other women remained anchored there quite motionlessly ('stiff'), crying with deep and rasping sound ('hoarse') loudly and spasmodically ('twitching and loud'). The behaviour of these women would make one imagine ('as if') that a sort of mute and stupid child was sleeping or existing within each one of them ('still survives') to be re-woken from sleep by kind call of someone ('To re-awake at kindness'). As if the women would be woken from sleep thinking that the kindly someone called only them, and that the kindly someone had arrived ('that hands have come') to lift them up to some transcendental sphere ('lift') and to enlighten them with spirituality ('lighten'). And then the women would be so much overjoyed ('such joy arrives') that their little-used tongues ('thick tongues') would "bellow like an animal" (Swarbrick, 1995, 99) and their eyes would be pressed by them ('squeeze') to drop tears ('grief'). [Andrew Swarbrick writes about the word 'blort', coined by Larkin: "'blort', a variation, Larkin thought, of the dialect 'blort' (meaning to bellow like an animal) and which, like 'yowl' in 'Lines on a Young Lady's Photograph Album', releases overwhelming feelings of pain and longing" (Swarbrick, 1995, 99).] The women heard a great number ('crowd') of highly consequential, great or very important, i.e. divine, responses from the transcendental sphere (in response to their prayers), which they did not hear before ('huge unheard answers'), and the barrage of divine assuring responses, as if, blocked their ears, as a result of which they rejoiced ('jam and rejoice').

In the third or concluding stanza, Larkin was puzzled, aghast at the inordinate extent of the frantic or abnormal behaviour of the women due to their (supposedly) mistaken belief (in supernatural powers) ('What's wrong!'). The women appeared to have hair on their upper lips, or appeared to be masculine, or while they were sobbing their tousled long hair fell on their lips showing them to have grown moustaches ('Moustached') and they wore frocks made of cloth with flowers printed on it ('in flowered frocks'). And the women were trembling ('shake'), understandably in joy that they were assured of being blessed so as to be cured of their diseases (of the eye and the knee). Larkin at last ('By now') says that the women were completely mistaken in their faith ('all's wrong').

He says that in each human being there is a dormant, hibernating ('sleeps') aspiration, need or demand ('sense') for the life that will be guided by love ('life lived according to love'). Some men believe that such a life ('To some it means') can be achieved by loving others and that by doing so they can change their lives for the better, i.e. they can live a higher life or a life of better quality ('the difference they could make'). But in most men the belief is prevalent or predominant ('it sweeps') that they might have achieved a better life ('might have done') if they had been loved by others ('had they been loved'). Larkin says that, in fact, the prayers of the preachers or evangelist or his compassionate blessing ('That') do not cure any disease whatsoever ('nothing cures'). The women ('when under the evangelical spell of the preacher') were experiencing great ('immense') and relaxing, refreshing ('slackening') joyful pain when they were crying ('ache'). That pain crept gingerly across their hardened whole beings ('Spreads slowly through them') like when snow melts ('thawing') the oozing water spreads throughout the hard soil tardily or sluggishly and the hard soil seems to be shedding tears ('As when, thawing, the rigid landscape weeps'). Larkin says that joyful, refreshing and relaxing pain of crying of the women ('that') and the evangelist's warmly and affectionately addressing each one of them as 'dear child' while standing taller than they—the women supposedly kneeling before him—('the voice above') and all the other such (prejudicial) things ('all') have been proved by history or experience ('time') to be incapable of curing diseases—to be false, untrue ('time has disproved').

Larkin was a non-believer; he did not believe in any supernatural powers; and so he thought that those women were simply bluntly deceived by the evangelist, that neither the relaxing pain of them nor the evangelist's compassion or his prayer could cure their diseases of the eye and the knee. Plainly, Larkin did not believe in curing of diseases by faith, in faith-healing. In 'Church Going' also, as we have seen, he was quite dubious about curing of diseases by touching special stones of a church or about treating cancer with the help of certain simple things of the church. But while in 'Church Going' he recognised at least the symbolic value of the church 'In whose blent air all our compulsions meet', in 'Faith Healing' he did not find even any symbolic value in the evangelist—whatever he found in the ritual of faith-healing was crass prejudice sustained by ignorance. In this sense, the import of 'Faith Healing' is more negative than that of 'Church Going'.

Here a cardinal question may be raised: are only those women in 'Faith Healing' and others germane to them ignorant, eluded, prejudicious and not also ourselves who may not believe in the custom of faith-healing? The answer will be: no, we all are somehow prejudiced, ignorant, eluded. And here lies the deeper layer of the import of 'Faith Healing'. We are, in fact, no different from those naïve women; we are at par with them in holding up some high ideal while remaining ignorant of the fact that ideals are always beyond reach, beyond materialisation. For instance, as the women in 'Faith Healing' held, we believe that love has 'transforming power', in converting our crass life into an ideal life. In 'Faith Healing' this supposed transforming power of love has been demonstrated through the abnormal behaviour and prejudiced faith of the simple women. We believe that ideal love can be practised and it can change our life for the better, but, in fact, in believing this we are only day-dreaming. Love is an ingredient of our being and we aspire after living a life of love: 'In everyone there sleeps / A sense of life lived according to love.' And some of us believe that they could change their lives for the better if they could love others, but most of us, on the other hand, believe that they could do that had they been loved. This is a faith, like religious faiths. But Larkin says that such a faith or ideal falls through in the context of our real life—in the context of the day-as-dust factuality. And time has proved, or our long experience has demonstrated, that this is true, that ideals only cheat us, that we are eluded by our beliefs, like we are befooled by our religious faiths ('time has disproved').

There is an obvious satiric and ironic vein in the poem, the satire and irony being aimed at the innocent and nescient women who congregated around the evangelist. The women blindly believed that benediction of the evangelist and his prayer to God for cure of their diseases would bring them physical and spiritual salvation. But, Larkin mocks at their blind and fruitless faith ('That nothing cures'). The faith of the women was anchored in the love of the evangelist for them and in the supposed love of God believed to have been received through the go-between of the evangelist. But Larkin says that the women were fecklessly depending on the illusion of their idealism of love. Here lie the satiric and ironic veins of 'Faith Healing'. Larkin's satire and irony, though, is not caustic, biting; these are leavened with sympathy, as he always allays his satire or irony with compassion in other poems as well. Andrew Swarbrick writes in this regard: "What, finally, is our reaction to these women? The poem begins by making them look foolish, willing participants in a calculated illusion, as 'Stewards tirelessly / Persuades them onwards'. We take the side of the poet, feeling superior to the women in our scepticism. But then we are shocked into sympathy. Their unrestrained, unembarassed outpouring of joy and grief moves us towards a recognition of a shared condition. *We share with these women an inherent longing for ideals* [of supernatural benefactor, of love, etc.] *which always escape us but which we cannot stop ourselves pursuing even though we are doomed to disappointment and disillusionment.* Indeed, without a momentary faith in these illusions we would be unremittingly confronted by the essential emptiness and futility of our condition. The poem charts, convincingly and movingly, a *shift of attitude from ironic detachment to compassion*" (emphases added) (Swarbrick, 1986, 47). Though in 'Faith Healing', Larkin apparently satirises only the women, the poem is self-satirical, for he does not segregate himself from them and so obliquely shares their illusion ('In everyone there sleeps / A sense of life lived according to love.... That nothing cures.'). Howbeit, in 'Faith Healing', as also in 'Here' and 'The Whitsun Weddings', Larkin is observing others' lives (the lives of the congregated women) and is comparing his lonely life with the busy lives of others, and is perhaps feeling more sad at the sharp contrast between the two sorts of lives.

Finally, a few words about the title of the poem. In the poem, the women gathered to get their diseases cured by the *evangelist* because they had the *faith* that an evangelist could do that. Evangelicalism, it may be stated here, is "a term which has been applied to the Protestant Churches because of their principles of justification through *faith* alone (i.e. personal commitment), and the supreme authority accorded to Scriptures (i.e. not to institutional figures of authority)" (emphasis added) (Goring, 166). The women went to the evangelist, as if, if not really, following the path of evangelicalism, i.e. following the path of faith alone. And so the title of the poem is quite justified.

4

Toads Revisited

'Toads' of *The Less Deceived* was written on 16 March 1954 and 'Toads Revisited' was written nearly 8 years afterwards in October 1962 (the exact date is not available). The two poems may be treated as companion poems, for, though the latter poem is not just a restatement in different verses, both the poems expresses Larkin's intention of performing his works in spite of anything. But whereas in 'Toads' Larkin is goad to do works by his conscience, in 'Toads Revisited' he expresses his wish to have the satisfaction of working till death without the involvement of his conscience. But why did Larkin lay so much stress on doing works in 'Toads Revisited', in 1962? The reason is that in October of that year he spent a week of holiday with his mother in the Lake District, and after coming back from there he felt that family life was 'boring, infuriating, hell', as he wrote on 7 August 1962 in a letter to Maeve Brennan. He was at that time being torn between two pulls from two contrary poles—Maeve and Monica. This drowned him in deep unhappiness, and at last he decided on drawing himself out of every other thing and engage himself completely in vigorous and hard works so as to drive away his unhappiness and its consequent melancholy. 'Toads Revisited' presents us with a picture of this state of Larkin's mind. 'Toads Revisited' falls into Larkin's rare category of 'animal poems'. Larkin has not written many 'animal poems' like D.H. Lawrence and Ted Hughes, and 'Toads', 'Toads Revisited' and 'At Grass' are his only three 'animal poems'. This thirtysix-line poem is divided into nine four-line stanzas. The poem is in three-stress verses and in imperfectly rhymed couplets.

Larkin begins the poem by comparing the life of busyness with the life of pleasurable laziness or sinecurism, and saying that the latter is better than the former, though in the concluding part of the poem he refutes this his own claim. He says that better than doing works are such things as walking around the park, seeing the beauty of the lake ('The lake'), bathing in the sunshine ('the sunshine'), lying on the grass (of the park), and hearing the feeble, half-audible ('Blurred') noises, coming from the playground beyond the path along which nurses, wearing black stockings or socks ('black-stockinged nurses'), walk away. If one can enjoy such things then he will feel that this world ('place') is not bad to live in ('Not a bad place to be'). But Larkin does not like such a popinjay, vacant, life of idlesse ('it doesn't suit me') (because life *sans* works or duties is detesting, abhorent, to him). He does not like to be one among the following sorts of men ('Being one of the men') whom one may come by in afternoons ('You meet of an afternoon'). Firstly, old men who are suffering from paralysis of members and who walks or take steps cautiously and slowly ('Palsied old step-takers'). Secondly, worriedly nervous clerks who fearfully look this way and that promptly and frequently like a hare ('Hare-eyed clerks') and who move along spasmodically or in confused agitation ('with jitters'). Thirdly, casualty out-patients of hospitals (i.e. those people who see doctors in the Out Patient Departments of hospitals for relatively minor ailments and do not require to get admitted) with tumefied, swollen muscles or limbs ('Waxed-fleshed') whose consciousness is yet hazy, clouded or blurred ('vague') due to accidents (from which their limbs got swollen, too). And lastly, men ('characters') who wear old-fashioned long coats and fall into profound sleep ('Deep') inside abandoned litter-baskets or things like these in which animals are provided with straw, bracken, etc. for food. Larkin says that all these people are stupid or weak-minded and so enjoy the pleasures of the park, of the beauty of the lake, of the sunshine, etc. (see the first six lines), shirking, abandoning ('dodging') their works that require of them labouring patiently sitting all the while at the same place like a toad ('toad work'). (Up to this point we have traversed eighteen verses or lines of the poem, from the beginning.)

So long, Larkin only expressed his dislike of the life of sinecure and of being one of the old, worried, wounded, worthless persons, but from the 19th line of the poem he begins to deliberately mock at them, ridicule them and asks us to watch their behaviour with an attitude of satire ('Think of being them!'). Larkin says that such people idle away their time listening to hourly chiming of the clock, i.e. the clock's indicating the passage of time by making sounds each hour ('Hearing the hours chime') or lazily watching the vendor delivering loaves of bread at the door-steps ('Watching the bread delivered') or staring at the sun when it is enveloped by clouds or seeing children returning home from the playground or the school. Larkin abhors and spurns the idea of himself (as well as of ourselves) of being like these idlers, dawdlers ('Think of being them': the 24th line). He contemptuously says that these and such other people neither muses over their failures in life over again and over again ('Turning over their failures') while sitting (in a melancholic mood) beside a certain garden or bank ('bed') of the species of flowers called lobelia ('By some bed of lobelias') (lobelia is a blue-coloured poisonous flower; the significance of lobelia here, therefore, has the tag of melancholy). He further says that, alternatively, these men, finding no place to go, are forced to remain inside their rooms ('Nowhere to go but indoors'), and finding no friends to mix with are bound to keep encircled or surrounded by vacant chairs ('No friends but empty chairs—').

Now, at the very beginning of the eighth stanza, Larkin becomes exasperated and violent at the truancy of those people ('No') and orders his female secretary, who wears her hair dressed up or arranged (at the back of her head) like a loaf of bread ('loaf-haired secretary') to hand over the tray of letters ('in-tray') to him (so that he can answer those letters). Larkin also asks the secretary, who every time receives a telephone call, asks him if she would hold the call for him ('shall-I-keep-the-call-in-Sir'), also to hand the receiver of telephone over to him so that he can answer the call. But, he asks himself, when the ultimate call—the call from Death—will come to him what will he say or how will he answer that call? That call from Death will come to him, he says, at four in the evening when offices are about to close but lights are switched on because of short days in December ('When the lights come on at four'), and that call will come to him (in the wintry December) at the close of a certain year in future ('At the end of another year'). Larkin says that he will answer that call saying nothing other ('else') than that he has done his works properly, i.e. he has answered the letters of the tray, answered telephone calls (see the eighth stanza), etc. And, therefore, he asks his duty or work (personified), which is as if sitting or squatting on him like a toad for a long time ('old toad'), to extend its helping hand so that clutching its hand he can walk along the road that will lead him to his grave or to the burying-ground, i.e. so that clutching its hand he can meet Death ('Help me down Cemetery Road').

The poem may be treated as Larkin's deliberate eulogy of labour or doing work, because here he suggests that he will take pride and feel satisfaction at the time of his death, thinking that in his life he has performed his duties properly and conscientiously. Doing his works properly and conscientiously will be his only satisfaction, and he will take it to be the meaning or value of his life. Larkin expressed similar thought in 'Toads' which he wrote about eight years ago, as we have said, and so the title of the poem—'Toads Revisited' is all the more appropriate. 'Toads' and 'Toads Revisited' follow the same trick: each of the poems begins with an argument that is elaborated through most of the body of it but the argument, at the close of it is completely overturned, subverted. In 'Toads', Larkin at first showed his envy for the free-wheeling life without the burden of works—the 'toad work'—but at the close of the poem he expressed his preference for the same burden of works, in which he discovered a sense of superiority which was absent in the other sort of life. In 'Toads Revisited', Larkin at first seems to be inclined towards the life of the sinecures, of the casualties ('Not a bad place to be'), but then he begins to lambast such life ('Think of being them!'), and ultimately resolutely decides on taking up the life of humdrum works till death, again with a sense of superiority, though he tacitly suggests that both the sorts of life ends in death. Andrew Swarbrick, comparing the imports of the two poems—the earlier 'Toads' and the latter 'Toads Revisited'—writes: "In that earlier poem, we saw how Larkin uses a speaking voice to betray itself into revealing more than it intended. The speaker began by expressing envy for a free-wheeling lifestyle shorn of all responsibility. But that envy is revealed as a pretence trying to obscure a more deep-seated sense of moral responsibility. The speaker actually prefers his own humdrum way of life.... In 'Toads Revisited', the speaker again defends his routine way of life. But this time the self-justification occurs not by the sifting and probing of attitudes, but by the speaker recognising (as in 'Faith Healing') a common predicament shared with those he despises" (Swarbrick, 1986, 48).

Like 'Toads', 'Toads Revisited' is a sort of monologue around the tension between desire and responsibility, between will and conscience, reaching a happy, poised balance between the two contraries at the concluding part of it. 'Toads Revisited' shows Larkin's lack of love for nature—he is not so much as attracted by the romantic feel of the park, lake, sunshine and the green tussocky grass, he rather hears the call of his conscience—to discharge his duties, to perform works. The poem also reveals his wakeful, ineluctable thought of death, for, at the close of it he accessorily brings in the idea of death: 'Give your arm, old toad; / Help me down Cemetery Road'. Larkin here placidly embraces the inevitable, Death, as he tacitly accepts, too, the disagreeable burden of the monotonous quotidian works.

The poem begins in a quite conversational mood and very casually in relaxed trimetric lines in half-rhyming couplets; the mood soon peters out but these features of the verses remain throughout the rest of the poem. Larkin here shows his mastery in drawing full and lively pictures with scant touches of the brush, for instance, such expressions as 'black-stockinged nurses', 'Palsied old step-takers', 'Hare-eyed clerks with the jitters', etc.

and rather more remarkably such expressions as 'My loaf-haired secretary' and 'My shall-I-keep-the-call-in-Sir'. 'Toads Revisited' is built on two extended metaphors or analogies: the leisurely sinecure life is analogised through the first seven stanzas and the life of 'toad work' ending in death is analogised through the concluding two stanzas. Larkin is generally known as a metonymic poet and two metonyms of this poem are very interesting and memorable: 'shall-I-keep-the-call-in-Sir' and 'Cemetery Road'.

5

The Whitsun Weddings

'The Whitsun Weddings', the title poem of the collection *The Whitsun Weddings*, is a "magnificent" poem of Larkin and "is justly his best-known work" (Ousby, 524). The inspiration of this poem came to Larkin about three years before the poem came out in its present form on 18 October 1958. Andrew Motion, the official biographer of Larkin, writes about the history of the composition of this romanticism-glancing poem: "The poem had first began to take shape during a journey from Hull to London on Whit [Whitsun] Saturday, 1955. On that day, Larkin said, he caught 'a very slow train that stopped at every station and I hadn't realized that, of course, this was the train that all the wedding couples would get on and go to London for their honeymoon [;] it was an eyeopener to me. Every part was different but the same somehow. They all looked different but they were all doing the same things and sort of feeling the same things. I suppose the train stopped at about four, five, six stations between Hull and London and there was a sense of gathering emotional momentum. Every time you stopped fresh emotion climbed aboard. And finally between Peterborough and London when you hurtle on, you felt the whole thing was being aimed like a bullet—at the heart of things, you know. All this fresh, open life. Incredible experience. I've never forgotten it'" (Motion, 287-88). Larkin took the image of arrow-shower of the two concluding lines of the poem ('an arrow-shower / Sent out of sight, somewhere becoming rain.') from Laurence Oliver's film of *Henry V* which "he had seen as a young man during the war [Second World War]" (*op. cit.*, 288). He wrote the poem as if he was observing interesting events and simultaneously recording his observations in a field-book somewhat indifferently. In his interview with John Haffenden in 1979 or 1980, he assured Haffenden that the poem "was just the transcription of a very happy afternoon [the happy observations in an afternoon train journey from Hull to London]. I didn't change a thing, it was just there to be written down" (Haffenden, 124). E.L. Black tells us that the incident of the train journey in which the narrator of the poem observed the behaviours and moods of some of the prospective couples occurred 'about twenty-five years ago'. Black writes about the incident enshrined in the poem: "the narrator tells of one afternoon about twenty-five years ago when many honeymoon couples were travelling by train to London, and then on to some seaside place such as Torquay (today their counterparts might fly to Spain or Majorca). The narrator is travelling to London too, and soon he becomes aware of the repeated scene on each station platform, as the wedding guests see the bridal couples on to the train and say goodbye to them by hurling confetti and smutty advice" (Black, 129).

The title of the poem was taken from the name of the Christian festival of Whitsuntide. According to *Chambers Twentieth Century Dictionary* (see entry: Whitsun), Whitsun is a particular *Sunday* on which Christians wear *white* clothes or robes (*white* plus *Sunday* makes *Whitsun*). It is the day that falls on the seventh Sunday after Easter. *A Dictionary for Believers and Non-believers* writes that Whitsun is "a Christian festival, which in the *Orthodox Church* numbers among the *Twelve Great Feasts*. It is celebrated on the fiftieth day after *Easter* (hence the ancient name, Pentecost). The significance of Whitsun is drawn from the story in the New Testament Book *The Acts of the Apostles* concerning the descent of the Holy Ghost upon the Apostles on the fiftieth day after Christ's Resurrection, as a result of which they 'began to speak with other tongues, as the Spirit gave them utterance (Acts 2: 4)" (Progress Publishers, 605). The title of the poem does not owe anything to the ritual of Whitsuntide save to the fact that Whitsun is a great holiday on which people are interested in getting marriages solemnised. It may be mentioned here that though the title is 'The Whitsun Weddings', the experiences that inspired Larkin to write this poem he got from his train journey from Hull to London on Whit Saturday, i.e. on the day before Whit Sunday or Whitsun. But Larkin saw on board the train the prospective brides and bridegrooms who were to enter the nuptial knot on the next day, on Sunday. So, the title of the poem is apt. It is apt also because Larkin in this poem deals with the theme of love and marriage or Wedding.

'The Whitsun Weddings' had had a long history of composition. It had a long gestating period as it also went through an incredible number of drafts. Anthony Thwaite writes: "'The Whitsun Weddings', begun in May 1957 with its first stanza complete, was then dropped, resumed in July 1958, reworked for twenty-three pages until 6 September, picked up again on 19 September and completed after eight further pages of drafts on 18 October" (Thwaite, 1988, xvii). Such huge labour Larkin exerted only on a few of his other poems including 'Church Going' and 'Love Songs in Age'. 'The Whitsun Weddings', chronologically, belongs to the period in which 'Love Songs in Age', 'Self's the Man' and 'Home is so Sad' were composed, and breathes the same melancholic mood as these other poems do. 'The Whitsun Weddings' is one of the few rather long poems of Larkin and comprises 80 lines that are divided into 8 stanzas, each stanza having equal number of lines invariably rhyming a / b /a / b / c / d / e / c / d / e throughout the poem. Though the poem was finished in 1958, it had to wait for around 6 years to be first published in *The Whitsun Weddings* in February 1964. As we know, Larkin usually placed two most important poems, as according to him, of a collection at the beginning and at the end of it at the time of publication, but, interestingly, neither in *High Windows* nor in *The Whitsun Weddings* has he placed the title poems of the collections either at their beginnings or at their endings. However, as Andrew Swarbrick writes, 'The Whitsun Weddings' "is one of the most widely anthologised and best-known poems written in England since 1945" (Swarbrick, 1986, 50).

In the beginning stanza of the poem, the narrator or the speaker tells us that in that Whitsuntide he was late in going to the railway station ('late getting away'). He reached the station twenty minutes past one in the evening of that sunny Saturday and boarded the train three-fourths of the seats of which were vacant, unoccupied, and then the train began to move forward (from Hull towards London). The shutters of the windows were pulled down and the seats were warm. As the train started the narrator felt that his earlier feeling ('sense') of being in a hurry to catch the train was no more with him ('all sense / Of being in a hurry gone'). The train, with its passengers, first ran on the rails ('We ran') that were laid along the back sides of a chain of houses, then it ran across a street where the narrator saw the houses whose windows were shut with opaque glass-screens meant for warding off wind ('blinding windscreens'). After this train moved along the dockyard from where fish used to be marketed and so, naturally, there narrator got the smell of fish ('smelt the fish-dock'), and then the train passed by the place from where the width ('breadth') of the waveless ('level') current ('drifting') of the river began ('The river's level drifting breadth began'), and it was that place where the sky, the city of Lincolnshire and the river ('water') seemed to merge into one another.

In the second stanza, the narrator says that during the whole afternoon of that day it was too hot ('tall heat') and the hot weather seemed to be prevailing (slept') over several miles of the interior part of the country, away from the sea ('inland'). He says that in ('through') that hot weather he along with all the other passengers ('we'), or rather the train, was proceeding towards the south gingerly ('slowly') and halting from time to time ('stopping'), and all the while a curve was being made along the path of the journey, i.e. the train was running along a curved line. As the train was moving on, large tracts of cultivated land ('Wide farms') seemed to be running towards the direction opposite to that of the train ('Wide farms went by'). Likewise, cattle having short shadows (due to the sun being near the meridian) and canals having forth or refuse from industries and factories floating on their waters also seemed to be running towards the opposite direction. A peculiar ('uniquely') house, that was always kept warm for rearing plants or for keeping dried pottery inside it before placing them in the kiln, momentarily came to notice ('flashed') ('A hothouse flashed uniquely'), and sometimes low hedges and sometimes tall hedges came to view ('hedges dipped / And rose'), as the train kept running. The narrator alternately once got the offensive smell ('reek') of the cover of a vehicle made of cloth ('carriage-cloth') which was fastened to the vehicle with buttons and the next moment got the (pleasant) odour of grass, which dispelled or subplanted ('Displaced') the earlier offensive smell, and this alterations of the smells continued for some time till the train reach the next town. (The alterations of the two sorts of smells was due to the fact that the vehicle and the train were running parallelly, but sometimes the train was faster than the vehicle and sometimes the other way round.) That next town, which was not known to the narrator ('new') and which had nothing remarkable ('non-descript'), came to his view ('Approached'), and he found in it a vast area ('acres') covered with abandoned or scrapped motor vehicles ('dismantled cars').

In the third stanza, the narrator says that at first he was not aware of the noises that the wedding parties (which boarded the train at each railway station and added to the number of the already existing parties on board the train) made. He rather could not take notice of the noises because he was all in discomfort due to the heat of the scorching sun and so was not interested in what was going on in the shades of the succeeding railway stations wherefrom the noises were coming ('sun destroys / The interest of what's happening in the shade'). (In the shades, the wedding parties were seeing off the newly married couples who boarded the train with wild elations and bursting joys, hence the noises at every station.) However, along the extended shades of the railway platforms that were at a distance ('down') there prevailed a cool atmosphere, from where 'whoop' 'whoop' sounds and sounds of shrieks or shrill singings ('skirls') were coming to the narrator ('And down the long cool platforms whoops and skirls'). But he mistook these sounds (not to have been made by the marriage parties but) to have been made by the coolies ('porters'), mischievously frolicking ('larking') with postal bags ('mails') (while draughting), and so he went on reading (a book or a newspaper). However ('though'), when the train began to move on (from each station) the narrator and his co-passengers ('We') left those people, i.e. the members of the wedding parties ('We passed them'). The members of the wedding parties included girls who used hair-cream ('pomaded') and were smiling broadly ('grinning')—girls (who perhaps belonged to the working class) who wore clothes ludicrously imitating the fashion of the rich people ('parodies of fashion'). There were also women who wore shoes or sandals, having high heels, and veils that were unmistakably noticeable ('heels and veils'). All the members of the wedding parties were standing with relaxed attitude ('posed irresolute') and were watching the train move away ('watching us go').

The narrator or the speaker, we understand at the very beginning of the fourth stanza, has for the first time been able to recognise that those girls and women formed wedding parties. He says it seemed to him ('As if') that the girls and women, after the event of marriage had been over ('on the end of an event'), were waving their hands meaning to wish good ('Waving goodbye') to the newly married couples who now boarded the train ('something') after coming out of the event of marriage ('survived it'). Being impressed by the scene or spectacle of waving hands meaning wishing good for the departing brides and bridegrooms bound for making honeymoons ('Struck'), the speaker or narrator, as the train reached successive stations, very swiftly ('More promptly') and with increased curiosity peeped out of the window ('leant') to watch other wedding parties ('it') there. And thus he observed the behaviours of other wedding parties again and again, and saw that they showed different modes of behaviour ('And saw it all again in different terms'). He saw fathers, who wore 'broad belts under their coats and who had furrowed ('seamy') foreheads, mothers with bulky bodies shrieking loudly, and also an uncle who was loudly uttering dirty, obscene words ('smuts') (with reference to the wedding night of the couple and intended for their hearing). And then he saw the girls having artificially created permanent waves in their hair as a style, and having worn gloves made of nylon, imitation jewellery ('jewellery-substitutes'), a special kind of slippers or sandals ('lemons'), and having coloured their faces with purple aniline dyes ('mauves') and mixes of olive and yellow (ochre) colours ('olive-ochres').

In the fifth stanza, the narrator says that with such decorations the girls seemed fantastic ('unreally') and quite different from ('Marked off') the other women ('the rest'). He now understood ('Yes') that most of the functions related to the marriages of the couples, who boarded the train from successive platforms, were by then over. He enlists these functions: the functions of the cafetarias ('cafes') to start with ('from cafes'), then the functions of the banquet-halls which stood near the front space of the houses ('yards'), and then entertainments of guests who had arrived by coaches ('Coach-party') in the extensions of the houses ('annexes') that were richly decorated with flags and cloth ('bunting-dressed'). After all these, all the functions of the marriages were nearly going to be over ('the wedding-days / Were coming to an end'). However, as the train stopped at successive stations, newly married brides and bride-grooms ('Fresh couples') boarded the train walking in files ('All down the line') and climbing up the steps of the carriages. The people who accompanied them and came over there kept back and stood in a circle on the platform ('the rest stood round'). Some of them handed over to the couples their remaining sweetmeats and advised them so hurriedly (the train was then slowly moving on) that it seemed that they were hurling the sweetmeats and advices at the couples ('The last confetti and advice were thrown'). As the train began to move slowly forward, the narrator, as if, could read in the face of each one of the persons of the marriage parties, who were standing on the successive platforms, what each person exactly ('Just') thinking about the newly married couples who were going away ('departing'), i.e. each face was like a definition or a printed page ('define') which could be read so as to know what each one was thinking about the couples ('each face seemed to define / Just what it saw departing'). The children, who also were on the platforms, expressed their dissatisfaction ('frowned') at the whole affair of saying goodbye to the couples, which seemed boring, uninspiring to them ('At something dull'). But the fathers of the brides and bridegrooms who were present on the platforms felt otherwise.

The fathers thought, the narrator tells us in the sixth stanza, that they never knew so great success as they got from getting their wards married through the wedding events ('fathers had never known / Success so huge'), but they also thought all at the same time that everything of the wedding ceremonies were in fact quite ludicrous ('wholly farcical'). The women were whispering among themselves about some secret matters of the weddings ('women shared / The secret') in so low voice that it appeared that they were talking about the funeral of a person for which they were inwardly happy ('like a happy funeral'). The girls, on the other hand, were strongly squeezing their handbags ('gripping their handbags tighter') and looking hard ('stared') at the brides who were going away by the train to express their envious and highly unhappy sentiment at the brides' loss of virginity in solemnised wedlock by getting their hymens ruptured ('a religious wounding'). Now the train was gathering momentum to run for London without stopping ('We hurried towards London'), every now and again puffing out ('shuffling') swelling amounts ('gouts') of steam, and so the narrator could as if disentangle himself from those framed spectacles ('Free at last'), but he was nevertheless stuffed with ('loaded with') the aggregate of the different thoughts that were passing across the minds of the various persons of the wedding parties now left behind on the successive platforms ('the sum of all they saw'). As the train advanced further, the narrator could see fields presently being converted into plots for buildings, and then (as the sun declined in the west) he saw elongated shadows of poplar trees cast across wide roads or high-roads ('New fields were building-plots and poplars cast / Long shadows over major roads'). However, the narrator says that for about fifty minutes the train ran on till then.

In the seventh stanza, the narrator further says that within that fifty minutes—the space of time in which the passengers could well adjust their hats and express their boredom saying such expletives as '*I nearly died*'—he saw as many as a dozen wedding parties to have boarded the train ('got under way'). The brides and bridegrooms ('They') viewed the landscape from the train sitting next to each other. They saw the cinema house named Odeon and a 'cooling tower' running to the opposite direction and past the train, and also a certain cricket player running forward to bowl in a pitch ('someone running up to bowl'). No one of the passengers ('none') was thinking about others whom he / she would never meet again ('and none / Thought of the others they would never meet'), but only of himself / herself or about his / her companion (the bride or the bridegroom). And alternatively ('Or'), no one of the passengers was musing or pondering over the possible means of keeping ('contain') in his / her memory or mind ('lives') the impressions he / she received during the hour of the train journey ('this hour'). The narrator says that at that time (before reaching London) he was visualising the city of London ('thought of London') as displayed or laid out in the bright sun ('spread out in the sun') and he visualised the postal divisions of London so much jammed with human beings that they looked like square sacks of wheat ('Its postal districts packed like squares of wheat').

The narrator, in the concluding stanza, says that he and all the other passengers of the train ('we') were destined to, or bound for ('aimed') London ('There'). As the train now was running fast through junctions of rail-lines focused with strong sunlight ('Bright knots of rail') after leaving the railway coaches, made by the Pullmans company, that remained stationary ('standing'), walls of houses overlaid or coated with black colour (that came from the smoke of railway engines), that seemed to be black-coloured boggy mud ('walls of blackened moss'), came to near view or sight ('Came close'). [This suggests that the train now entered the thickly populated area of London.] The train's journey was now almost completed and so the ineffectual or inconsequential ('frail') meeting or co-existence of the narrator with the wedding parties, while journeying so long, having no causal link between them ('coincidence'), also almost ended ('and it was nearly done, this frail / Travelling coincidence'). [The meeting or co-existence was ineffectual or inconsequential because the narrator had no conversation or interaction with the wedding parties; he only thought about them and observed their behaviours.] And the only thing ('what') that was there in that chance meeting or co-existence ('it held') was prone ('Stood ready') to be shaken off, or forgotten by, the narrator ('to be loosed') under the impact or influence ('power') of the new and changed state which he would enter into when, coming out of his solitary existence or loneliness he would get down from the train and commerce or interact with the society at large, i.e. he would exist in a different state or condition ('That being changed can give'). However, the train ('We') once again reduced its speed and then came to a halt due to its brakes being pulled hard ('as the tightened brakes took hold'). And as soon as the train stopped, there came over the narrator a great feeling ('there swelled / A sense') that the passengers of the train (particularly the newly wedded couples) were, as if, a shoal or swarm of arrows released from a hard pulled bow-string. Throughout the train-journey they were as though flying across the space unseen by the person who released the arrows ('Sent out of sight') and now, when the train halted, they were descending to the ground ('falling') in a shower ('an arrow-shower') at some place or other ('somewhere'), meanwhile being converted from their aseity, actuality, essence, existence, reality or being as a swarm of arrows to the aseity, actuality, existence, etc. of a shower of rain ('becoming rain').

The immediate charm of 'The Whitsun Weddings' is its catenated scenarios viewed through the window of a moving railway carriage, that appear to be a kaleidoscopic slot. The slot may be divided into three parts. In the first part of it, that sprawls through the two beginning verses of the poem, we move down from the city of Hull to the countryside and a sequence of flashing sights appear before us: 'blinding windscreens', 'fish-dock', 'river's level drifting breath', 'short-shadowed cattle', 'Canals with floatings of industrial froath', 'hothouse', hedges that dipped and rose, 'buttoned carriage-cloth' and acres of nondescript 'dismantled cars'. In the second part of the slot, we watch minute descriptions of the motley gang of low-class relatives of the newly married couples who boarded the train at different stations: 'porters larking with the mails', 'grinning and pomaded, girls / In parodies of fashion, heels and veils, / All posed resolutely, watching us go', 'fathers with broad belts under their suits / And seamy foreheads; mothers loud and fat', an 'uncle shouting smut', girls with 'perms' / The nylon gloves, and olive-ochres', 'last confetti and advice' thrown, children frowning at something, women sharing a secret 'like a happy funeral', girls, gripping their handbags tighter' and staring at a 'religious wounding', etc. All these extend over the third, the fourth, the fifth and the first part of the sixth verses. The third or the last part of the footage spreads over the latter part of the sixth and the seventh verses. In it we see the countryside, outside the city of London, now undergoing fast radical urbanisation but yet retaining its residual green: 'Now fields were building-plots, and poplar cast / Long shadows over major roads' and 'An Odeon went past, a cooling tower, / And someone running up to bowl'.

Larkin, or the narrator, was all through an indifferent observer of the landscapes and the manners of the people on the platforms and also of the vibrant newly married couples who sat 'side by side' of each other. The difference between the elaborate descriptions of the landscapes and the farewell parties, on one hand, and the bare reference to the newly wedded couples travelling along with him, on the other, is strikingly noticeable. This is due to the fact that, though Larkin in 1955 actually saw some wedding parties travelling with him and though he was then a thirty-three-years-old bachelor, he was always inordinately insoucient about marriage. However, Larkin's observation and his verisimilar staccato word-painting are praise-worthy. Consider, for instance, 'short-shadowed cattle', 'porters larking with the mails', 'girls / In parodies of fashion', 'perms' / ... / Marked off the girls unreally from the rest, etc. The kinaesthetic description of the train and a truck, one once overtaking the other and then lagging behind, is very gleg: 'now and then a smell of grass / Displaced the reek of buttoned carriage-cloth'. The evocative description of some passing objects beautifully conjures up a photographic image of Larkin's contemporary London: 'Canals with floatings of industrial froth', 'hothouse', 'next town, new and nondescript', 'acres of dismantled cars' (second stanza); 'long cool platforms', 'porters larking with the mails', 'parodies of fashion, heels and veils' (third stanza); 'uncle shouting smut', 'the perms, / The nylon gloves and jewellery-substitutes, / The lemons, mauves, and olive-ochres' (fourth stanza); 'confetti' (fifth stanza); 'Now fields were building-plots, and poplars cast / Long shadows over major roads' (sixth stanza); and 'someone running up to bowl' and 'postal districts packed like squares of wheat' (seventh stanza).

Tony Curtis, himself a poet of some standing with *Selected Poems: 1970-1985* (1986) and *The Last Candles* (1989) to his credit, has, in his book *How to Study Modern Poetry*, done an in-depth analysis of 'The Whitsun Weddings' and made an evaluation of the poem. Due especially to its longishness, Curtis says that the poem is 'quite a taxing poem'. He writes about it: "The overriding impression is that *The Whitsun Weddings* is a narrative that traces the writer's train journey from somewhere in the north of England down to London. The poem opens with a sense of rush, of discomfort and the unattractive inner city landscape that characterises the beginnings of many British train journeys. The mood becomes more relaxed and rural between the various towns encountered on the journey. At its ending the poem mixes feelings of urban order and closure with what at first seems to be a strangely inappropriate image of movement and escape" (Curtis, 95). Curtis thinks that in the poem Larkin 'sees himself to be outside the events, dispassionate, wry, a voyeur even'. He says that there is 'certainly a sense of caricature' in the way Larkin draws the portraits of the groups of people on the platforms. But the most important discernment of Curtis in the poem is the point that Larkin in it has brought in a connection between the event of marriage and procreation on one hand and the progression of civilisation on the other. Curtis refers us to the poem's somewhat unconnected and 'rather strange sentence, an apparent *non sequitur*—

I thought of London spread out in the sun,
Its postal districts packed with squares of wheat:
There we were aimed.'

He says that those 'postal districts' are a symbol of civilisation. He writes: "People settle and grow in those areas; the buildings and communities there are the fruits of our civilisation. And all of that life is founded on the procreation of human beings, the focus of which in our society is the institution of marriage."

This position of Curtis is reinforced by the concluding part of the poem:

there swelled
A sense of falling, like an arrow-shower
Sent out of sight, somewhere becoming rain.

Curtis says that the shower of arrows becoming rain means movement, progression, change, procreation and growth, all at once. He writes: "How can a shower of arrows become rain? Well, Larkin is turning the original metaphor back on itself: might not a shower of arrows—weapons of death after all—become positive, refreshing rain out of sight of their archer and beyond his original intention? The lives of the passengers are like a sheaf of arrows directed from their various stations and backgrounds, but flying with the possibility of quite different targets and an unlimited power to affect change in themselves and the society which has produced them" (Curtis, 100). There may also be a hidden suggestion of sexuality and procreation in the metaphor of 'an arrow-shower...becoming rain' in so far as the god Cupid is a master archer and with shower of the seeds or the 'juice' of his arrow he refreshes and procreates. Roger Day calls the last two and a half lines mysterious and says that they are symbolic. Day explains these lines thus: "Each couple, the 'arrow-shower' image suggests, will set off their own direction, and the ending of the journey is really a beginning for those on board. The ritual over, there is a movement towards a new growth, subtly suggested by the notion of 'swelling' and rain falling. The idea of fertility has been introduced in the previous stanza in the description of

London's postal districts 'packed like squares of wheat' where, Larkin says, he was aiming at conveying both 'overcrowdedness ...but also fruitfulness' (In the first draft, he had written 'fields of wheat'.)" (Day, 52). The contention of Roger Day is attested by what David Timms writes about 'The Whitsun Weddings': Anthony Thwaite once produced a radio programme that introduced a reading of the poem, and he wrote to Larkin for advice on how it should be performed. Larkin explained that it should hold a carefully sustained note until the very end, when it should 'lift off the ground'. The young couples will bring life to London: there are rain falling on the 'squares of wheat' that are the postal districts of the city" (Timms, 120). It is because of this enlivening, invigorating, life-enhancing element of the poem that Tony Curtis has found in it a reference to T.S. Eliot's *The Wasteland*.

The most of 'The Whitsun Weddings' is narrative, to be precise, the whole of it barring only the concluding two and a half lines, as we have said. But Larkin certainly did not intend to make it absolutely a narrative piece and, as Tony Curtis says, he "as obviously invested a lot of effort in his desire to counterpoint the narrative power of his poem with its run-on lines, by his weaving of rhymes which are, in the main, masculine, as, for example, 'ran' and 'began'. In each verse, too, the *a b a b* rhymes are undercut by the more distanced and less obvious *cde cde* rhymes which have the effect of propelling the verse to its conclusion, or into the next verse-paragraph" (Curtis, 96). Andrew Swarbrick has more praise in store for the poem's language than for its content. Swarbrick writes: "The poem's real triumph is the mastery of language by which the shape and feel of experience are precisely rendered. The regularity and rhyme helps to create a sense of inevitability, a pattern of movement. The landscapes of contemporary England are observed with delicate precision. Notice the vivid compactness which makes a hot-house flash 'uniquely' where that surprisingly abstract word seems inevitable and just in suggesting the momentary alignment of sun, glass and observer.... The pause in the run-on line between 'swelled' and 'A sense of falling' itself imitates that sense of falling. This ability to capture physical sensation can also be seen in 'the tall heat that slept / For miles inland', conveying the claustrophobic stillness and numbing drowsiness of a hot summer's day.... If the poet commands little else in life, he can command language" (Swarbrick, 1986, 52-53).

6

Talking in Bed

Two poems of *The Whitsun Weddings* are particularly concerned with failure of ideal and very close human relationship, failure of love and intimacy: 'Broadcast' and 'Talking in Bed'. In 'Broadcast', Larkin wanted to imaginatively capture a feel of the close presence of his beloved but he found him, on the contrary, engrossed in the concert on the radio wave-band. Likewise, in 'Talking in Bed' he says that the unspecified and unlocalised bed-partners are passing days, physically contiguous to each other but psychologically distant from one another, in unbroken silence—without mouthing even a single true and kind word for each other. Thus in both of these two gloomy poems Larkin has demonstrated that ideal human relationship is simply unrealisable. Each human being is living in the cocoon of his own self, absolutely insulated from the not-self, throughout his life. We may here recall Coleridge's 'Alone, alone, all, all alone, / Alone on a wide, wide sea, / And not a saint took pity on / My soul in agony.' And Matthew Arnold's 'Yea, in the sea of life enisled.... We mortal millions live alone.' 'The Whitsun Weddings', 'Afternoons' and 'Talking in Bed'—all the three poems deal with the "people who seem to exist at a 'unique distance from isolation' (young couples, young mother and two people in bed)" (Motion, 290). Such people are not in a sense isolated because they live near some others, but as they are not in happy interaction with them they live away from them, in reality, i.e., they live away from isolation in a peculiar way. In 'Talking in Bed' we encounter such a life in which an individual exists in a 'unique distance from isolation'.

Andrew Motion writes that Larkin's 'Talking in Bed' is "one of the few poems he wrote about himself and Monica [Jones]" (*loc. cit.*). But the poem perhaps also betrays a shadow of Larkin's intimate relationship with Maeve Brennan. For a time, Larkin's affection plied like a shuttlecock between Monica and Maeve: he was being as much drawn by Monica's physical charm as by Maeve's sweet kindness. 'Talking in Bed' may reflect Larkin's oscillation between those two magnetic pulls during around 1960, the year in which this poem was written. Andrew Motion further writes: "Occasionally the modesty of Larkin's letters to Maeve makes them seem—in their well-meaning way—deceitful.... As the correspondence unfolds, it shows Larkin associating Maeve not just with romance but with kindness. In 1961 he refers to 'Dear, kind Maeve' as a 'kindhearted companion', and in a copy of the New English Bible that he once gave her for a birthday he wrote, '"Love is patient, love is kind and envies no one" because, he said, that summed me up'. 'Kind' was a word which, in 'Talking in Bed', he had recently (in August 1960) struggled to reconcile with the truth of his feelings about Monica, reaching for 'Words at once true and kind, / Or not untrue and not unkind'" (*op. cit.*, 307).

However, this short poem of only twelve lines was dated 10 August 1960 by Larkin. The poem is divided into four stanzas of three lines each, the rhyme-scheme of it being a / b /a, c / a / c, d / c / d, e / e / e.

In the first verse of the poem, Larkin says that a conversation between two persons (a lover and the beloved), while they are lying in bed side by side, is expected to be flowing, natural, uninhibited ('Talking in bed ought to be easiest'). While the two persons are thus together lying (notice here the possibility of a pun on the word 'lying': 'lying' is staying prostrate or at length; but 'lying' is also uttering falsehood or deceiving) on the bed and are engaged in flowing, natural and uninhibited conversation between them, they pose as an ideal ('emblem') of two faithful ('honest') persons (in love with each other). In the second stanza, Larkin says that in fact or actually such ideal relationship between two love-partners, or rather flowing, uninhibited and faithful parley between two love-partners, lying on bed, gradually grow rarer and still rarer so that longer and yet longer periods of silence or mutism prevail between them ('Yet more and more time passes silently.'). Outside the room in which the lovers lie on the bed silently, the wind blows gradually more and more restlessly, agitatedly to grow absolutely restless and agitated at some time ('the wind's incomplete unrest / Builds') and the wind drives and scatters the cloud randomly in the sky. (The silently lying lovers on the bed then implicitly become attentive rather to the raging wind instead of to one another.)

In the third stanza, Larkin says that as the two lovers are mutely lying side by side on the bed, the edged (horizon) of the towns become enveloped by the gathering thick pall of darkness ('dark towns heap up on the horizon') (The two lovers, understandably, are also aware of the horizons being covered by the imperviable darkness, as they were conscious of the up-raging wind, but not of the contiguous existence of each other: 'None of this cares for us.'). The raging wind and the towns getting darker and darker—no one of these two phenomena, Larkin assures us, are taking note of, or is concerned about, the fact that the two mute lovers (who are like all of ourselves) are not honestly (and kindly or sympathetically) parleying with each other ('None of this cares for us.'). Two individuals, in happy interaction with one another, do not feel that they are isolated, desolate, forlorn, or completely insulated from the world—neither of them. They feel that they are away from 'isolation', loneliness, solitariness. But if the two individuals are mutual lovers, says Larkin, and they are in the same bed, they should feel that they are far, far away from 'isolation', loneliness, solitariness, that they are superlatively keeping themselves distanced from 'isolation'. This is what Larkin means to mean by the expression 'unique distance from isolation'. In the fourth or last stanza, Larkin says that there is nothing that can explain the reason ('Nothing shows why': the third stanza) of the fact that in this 'unique distance from isolation' the love-partners are finding it even more hard ('It becomes still more difficult') to come by or get words for conversation between themselves—words that are all at the sametime both honest or faithful ('true') and loving or sympathetic ('kind'), or, contrarily, words that are at the least not dishonest or unfaithful ('not untrue') and not hateful or unsympathetic ('not unkind') ('to find / Words at once true and kind, / Or not untrue and not unkind.').

Andrew Swarbrick in his *Out of Reach: The Poetry of Philip Larkin* (1995) has given an elaborative and sufficing explanation of the poem, and we cannot do better than quoting him here at some length. Swarbrick writes about the poem: "The dominant attitude to love in *The Whitsun Weddings* is of baffled and resigned disappointment, often turning to rancour. 'Talking in Bed' looks to put it at its bleakest. It is a poem of declarative statement within which there is working a more lyrical mode of feeling and expression. We begin with the couple 'Lying together' (the pun on 'lying' is all too obvious), 'An emblem of two people being honest'. But contrary to the poem's title, there is no talking in bed. The poem hurries to its gloomy conclusion: 'At this unique distance from isolation / It becomes still more difficult to find / Words at once true and kind, / Or not untrue and not unkind', where the characteristic double negatives of the final line serves to twist the knife a little more. But contrasting with these prosaic statements is the more elaborately metaphorical centre of the poem which takes us outside the silent couple's bedroom and challenges the logic of the poem's surface. As 'more and more time passes silently', what is heard is the wind's 'incomplete unrest'. As we have seen, from his earliest work the wind is contemplated in Larkin's poems as a disruptive and distracting force ('Wedding-Wind', 'Absences', 'Mr Bleaney'). Here it is as if the lovers' ears are attuned 'Outside', listening to the wind which mirrors their own condition of unsettled incompleteness. The wind is ceaselessly roaming, changing, sifting, reflecting the unfinished ebb and flow of the lovers' feelings for one another. The strangely insubstantial 'dark towns heap up on the horizon' suggests random purposelessness, as if the world is governed by accidental and capricious forces, forces which brought these lovers together quite arbitrarily. And this world outside is indifferent and impersonal. The motion of the wind and clouds, the sprawling mass of the towns, all seem incalculable and inexplicable: 'None of this cares for us'. But this central moment in the poem is oddly consoling. That 'Nothing shows why' the couple cannot be both 'true and kind' is not quite true: the wind expresses a universal condition of purposeless change in which relationships are inevitably fragile. But by introducing the wind, the poem withdraws from the couple and insists on a presence (as so often in Larkin, an elemental force) which, though it is indifferent to them, nevertheless couples them. The wind functions rather as the onlooker in 'The Whitsun Weddings' who draws into unity otherwise separate experience, and as the glass of water in 'Water' where 'any-angled light / Would congregate endlessly'. It is by talking that the couple hurt one another; in silence there is a shared isolation. Contrary to first impressions, 'Talking in Bed' is another poem which wants to integrate what lies separated" (Swarbrick, 1995, 109-10).

And yet Swarbrick says elsewhere—in his *The Whitsun Weddings and The Less Deceived by Philip Larkin*—that 'Talking in Bed' "is another poem in which Larkin explores the difficulty and the ultimate futility inherent in human relations. A couple lying together in bed, as they have done for years, seems to represent an intimacy and honesty that is complete. Yet the poem goes on to suggest that even in the physical closeness of lovers, true unity and understanding remain beyond us" (Swarbrick, 1986, 54-55). As in all Larkin poems, here in this poem also the argument crystalises in the ending part of it, in the last three lines where the gathering pessimism as if solidifies. Swarbrick writes about the poem's concluding lines where the lovers, each in one's own psychological integument, irreversibly suffers from absolute solitariness in frustrated bafflement: "In bed together, they should be at the farthest point from loneliness, 'this unique distance from isolation, and yet 'It becomes still more difficult to find / Words at one true and kind'. This rhyming couplet disconcertingly asserts that what might be 'true' is very different from what would be 'kind', that 'truth' and 'kindness' are mutually exclusive [in such specific cases, of course]. The final line is even bleaker: 'Or not untrue and not unkind.' The problem has suddenly become not one of expressing both truth and kindness, but of positively avoiding deception and cruelty. The lovers in their bed not only fail to be honest and gentle with each other; they fail to avoid the opposite, mutual deception and bitterness. And with this final line we become aware of a grim pun at the end of the poem's opening, for 'Lying together' is what those lovers have inevitably done. "The repeated double negative of the final line is bleakly pessimistic; in a poem expressing the absence of our capacity for mutual involvement, those double negatives are cruelly appropriate (in a way which recalls the repeated negatives and 'unspent' childhood of 'I Remember I Remember'). The lovers of this poem are unspecified and unlocalised; lying in bed, their imaginations are occupied only by the awareness of 'Outside', not each other. They remain apart, individual, solitary, sharing only their essential human condition of lonely isolation" (*op. cit.*, 55).

David Timms praises the strikingly memorable ending of 'Talking in Bed'. He writes: "'Talking in Bed' illustrates Larkin's great talent for ending his poems memorably. His endings are memorable not necessarily because they are resounding and aphoristic—though Larkin can end resoundingly (as in 'Church Going') or with an aphorism ('Nothing, like something, happens anywhere')—but because they catch the mood of the poem as a whole in a few words:

> Never such innocence again.
> ('MCMXIV')
>
> Truss advertisement, truth.
> ('Send No Money')
>
> And age, and then the only end of age.
> ('Dockery and Son')

The list could be multiplied" (Timms, 107). Timms is quite right because the ending of 'Talking in Bed' ('Words at once true and kind, / Or not untrue and not unkind') is at once witty and pregnant. Witty, because the latter line is but simply the negation of the contrary of the former; and pregnant because, as regards its deeper meaning, the latter line is not simply the negation of the contrary of the former but contains a sense of failure on the part of the lovers to contain deception and bitterness—the lovers 'fail to avoid...mutual deception and bitterness' (see in the just now cited quote from Swarbrick).

'Talking in Bed' is a most deceptive title because there is actually no talking in the bed and also perhaps no hope of it in future. The poem is very economic as regards use of words and highly concentrated regarding thought. As to its prosodic skill David Timms writes: "The poem (also shows Larkin's technical mastery of the iambic pentameter. The lines in 'Talking in Bed' are all recognisably iambic pentameters, with the exception of the last and next last, an iambic tetrameter and an iambic trimeter respectively. Almost all the lines have the standard ten syllables, but there is no one line that is completely regular. The impression of someone speaking, or rather thinking, is achieved through subtle modifications in rhyme, and maintained throughout. It is not that Larkin has written in an irregular metre, but that he has taken full advantage of the almost infinite variations possible to the English iambic line in terms of substitution and reversal of feet (*loc. cit.*).

7

Ambulances

This is the 21st poem of the collection *The Whitsun Weddings* and was dated 10 January 1961 by Larkin. Andrew Swarbrick says that it is "One of Larkin's most assured poems" (Swarbrick, 1986, 56). In 'Ambulances', Larkin probes into our general response to the incident of other person's death. Curiously enough, after about 52 days of the composition of this poem Larkin himself (when he was around only 39 years of age) nearly accosted his own death: "On 5 March [1961], without any warning, Larkin collapsed during a Library Committee meeting and was carried 'unconscious and incontinent'—by ambulance—to Kingston General Hospital" (Motion, 311). On 7 April 1961, Larkin said to Monica Jones: "'Funnily enough,'...'the last poem I wrote (in January) was about *ambulances*.... Little did I think how soon I should be in one myself. One of life's little ironies, as my favourite poet [Hardy?] puts it'" (*op. cit.*, 316). In 1964, Patrick Garland was filming Larkin, when, in one shot, John Betjeman was placed beside Larkin. After the shot, Betjeman was requested to recite from Larkin whom he much respected. Betjeman obliged by reciting from 'Ambulances'—of course misquoting 'so permanent and blank and true' for 'so permanent and black and true' of the poem (the misquotation is negligible and can certainly be overlooked) (*op. cit.*, 347). However, the importance of 'Ambulances' can perhaps be much gauged from this fact.

Like 'Aubade' and 'Next, Please', 'Ambulances' is concerned with death, but in unlike the former two poems, 'Ambulances' is involved with man's essential condition of solitariness—man's inherent individuality or separateness. 'Ambulances' underlines the fact that however much men may feel to belong to their loved ones or to their families, they are but separate existences, each one of them, and their individual or separate deaths confirms this beyond any doubt. In short, the poem emphasises the nullity of human existence or the meaninglessness of life: 'the solving [i.e. dissolving] emptiness / That lies just under all we do'. However, the poem comprises five stanzas or verses, each verse having six lines of iambic tetrameter. The rhyme-scheme of the poem is a / b / c / b / c / a.

Larkin, in the first verse of the poem, compares an ambulance with the confessional or 'the seat or enclosed recess where a priest hears confessions', confession being 'acknowledgement of sin to a priest' (*Chambers Twentieth Century Dictionary*, 1981, entry: confess). (The identity or similarity between the two is justified on the score that just as the confessional is secretive so the look of the ambulance is also occult or privy or guarded against discovery—the body of the ambulance being fully covered and its windows having gray screens.) Larkin says that ambulances ('they'), having their bodies completely covered and guarded against observation ('Closed'), commute, or ply over, ('thread') the routes of cities even during middays ('noons') when the cities happen to be highly busy and boisterous ('Loud'). He says that one may glance at the ambulance (or enquiry about why it is moving inside the city) but none of the ambulance will look at him in return (or answer his enquiry) ('giving back / None of the glances'). The men inside the ambulance will only take notice of the inquisitive person's glance or look at the ambulance or hear of the person's anxious enquiry ('they absorb'), because their extreme hurry. The body of the ambulances are painted with moderately shining grey colour ('Light glossy grey') and plates or tablets that are hung on their bodies show pictures of arms, perhaps one clutching another, that are symbols of help, succour or friendship ('arms on a plaque'). The ambulances stop at all places by the pavement edges ('rest at any kerb') of any street (to take in critical patients), and in the course of time they move through all the streets of the city or town.

In the second verse, Larkin describes a scene in which a patient is whisked away in an ambulance. When sometimes an ambulance arrives to take a critical patient, children are seen playing on the doorsteps or on the road scatteredly, helter-skelter ('strewn on steps or road'), or women are noticed to have come out of shops and walking past eateries from where savoury smells of food items happen to be spreading, radiating. Those women see a moribund patient, covered with red blankets and lying on a stretcher, with his anaemic and violent-looking distressed face ('wild white face') out of that blanket ('overtops'). The women, though, see the ambulance but for a very short while when that face ('it') or the patient is drawn into the ambulance and then whisked away. In the next verse, Larkin describes about the reactions of those women at their sighting of the ambulance that swiftly took away the patient in critical condition. When the women see the ambulance thus hasten away with the moribund patient, they realise the vacuity or nullity behind whatever we do, or behind our quotidian life—the vacuity or nullity or ontological nothingness ('emptiness') in which everything that we are and everything that we do are dissolved, are converted into nothingness ('solving emptiness'). And then the women fully ('whole') realise the truth, apodicticity or reality of death ('it') for just a fraction of a while ('for a second get it whole'). They also realise that death is essentially eternal ('permanent'), and that death is nullity or emptiness ('blank'), and, moreover, that death is real or ontological ('true'). However, after the critical patient is taken inside the ambulance and its doors are closed tight ('fastened doors') and it goes back ('recede'), the women (unawares, perhaps) pronounce the words '*Poor Soul*' inaudibly or covertly, musing on their particular ('own') inevitable and fated pain ('distress') of mortality ('*Poor Soul* / They whisper at their own distress').

In the fourth verse, Larkin says that the ambulance, that critical patient within it, is driven away ('borne away') in deathly, fatal or utterly debilitating atmosphere ('deadened air'), and soon after the departure of the ambulance the awareness of the women as concerns the patient's death ('loss') may abruptly cease ('May go the sudden shut of loss'), i.e. as soon as the ambulance goes out of sight, the women stop thinking over the deprivation of everything attached to the patient who is very near his extinction ('Round something nearly at an end'). For years together ('across the years') many events happened in the life of the patient, or were somehow attached to the life of the patient ('what cohered in it'), to wit, many families were connected ('blend') with the life of the patient peculiarly ('unique') and stochastically ('random'), and the patient adopted or internalised verious modes of thought and behaviour of his time peculiarly and stochastically. But, Larkin says in the fifth or final verse, that with the patient being critically ill and so being near extinction, all his connections with different families and all his connections with his adopted or internalised modes of thought and behaviour start to slacken ('begin to loosen') at the end of his life ('At last'). The patient then lie in a ward of hospital ('room') which is beyond the reach of the public, and there he exists far away from those whom he loves and who love him in return ('exchange of love'). That ward is also away from the noisy commercial area of the city or town ('The traffic parts to let go by'). In the last two lines, Larkin does not simply neutrally narrate but expresses his own thought and feeling generated out of the perception of the pathetic spectacle. He says that when we observe such a moribund patient shied away in a sombre ambulance we are momentarily brought nearer to what has yet not come to us—to death, to our extinction ('Brings closer what is left to come'). And such a horrid spectacle shoves ourselves, who are vibrant, hunky-dory, off to a far away space where we become ghostly pale in spite of all our identities and acquirements ('dulls to distance all we are'). Andrew Swarbrick explains the last two lines thus: "Watching the ambulance, we are brought closer to the nothingness of our own death. It 'dulls to distance all we are' in confronting us with the essential, inescapable reality of death. The living identity we feel ourselves to have and which is given substance by our daily habits and behaviour suddenly perishes in the face of death's continuous presence. Ambulances confront us with 'what is left to come': our own death" (Swarbrick, 1986, 57).

The ambulances, which lend the title of the poem, are a symbol—the symbol of death, or of extinction of our beings. The phenomenon of death is the central theme of the poem and so the poem at once reminds us of Shakespeare's sonnet no. 65: 'Since brass, nor stone, nor earth, nor boundless sea, / But sad mortality o'ersways their power'. Both David Timms and Andrew Swarbrick have noticed that Larkin's ambulances are fearfully secretive and mysterious as well as suggestive of emergency, extinction or voidance, and dissolution of everything—of 'solving emptiness'. Timms writes about the secrecy and mysteriousness of the ambulances: "Larkin's ambulances are grey and neutral and mysterious: like a man wearing dark glasses, they disconcertingly return 'none of the glances they absorb'" (Timms, 99). And Swarbrick writes: "Larkin's ambulances, suggestive of disaster and emergency, are secretive and mysterious" (Swarbrick, 1986, 57). According to Swarbrick, in 'Ambulances' Larkin's objective is to reveal our general reaction to the grim experience of a man who is soon going to die. The poem may be divided into three parts. The two beginning stanzas, which make the first part, describe the urgent arrival of an ambulance and swiftly transporting away a moribund patient for hospitalisation; and in the third stanza, which is the second part, Larkin tells of the reaction of the women to their experience of that patient, with 'wild white face that overtops / Red stretcher-blankets', being whisked away in an ambulance. This experience immediately brings in their mind the awareness of the certainty of their deaths in the not-very-far-away future: '*Poor Soul* / They whisper at their own distress.' The rest of the poem is the third part, where we are told of the consequence of death—nothing of us will endure after our deaths; nay, just since the enunciation of the arrival of death all our moorings in this world 'begin to loosen' and we begin to be reduced into nothingness, horribly frightened. Swarbrick says that according to Larkin we are actually not frightened by the death of someone else but by the thought, consequent upon the observation of someone else's death, that we too are mortal. Swarbrick writes: "We are distressed not by someone else's accident, but because we have been sharply reminded that our own lives might at any moment be so finally unravelled. Suddenly, everything we are, everything we have done, is threatened by the final nullity of death" (*op. cit.*, 58).

'Ambulances' shows its great concern about death, and thus far the poem's theme is existential in nature; but more than nakedly exposing the nature of death the poem rather obliquely but more effectively betrays the sadder condition of our life—the bald uniqueness and individuality that constitute the care of life itself. So the poem deals with a twin theme: the theme of death and that of uniqueness and individuality of our lives. Andrew Swarbrick explains the two overlapping themes of the poem: "'Ambulances', (however,) whilst it insists on final things [death, etc.], succeeds in rising above a sense of futility and manages a tender regard for individual life. "The first stanza presents ambulances as impersonal, frightening reminders of unpredictable fate. Onlookers find themselves randomly caught up in someone else's tragedy, accidental spectators of 'A wild white face' which interrupts their mundane routine. For a moment, normal life stands still and the onlookers apprehend with a shock the tenuousness of their own lives. For a second, they are vividly conscious of their own mortality. As the ambulance drives off in 'deadened air', its shut doors signifies the close of a *unique, individual life*" (italics mine) (Swarbrick, 1995, 120). Swarbrick is quite perceptive here. Ordinarily, we perceive, think and feel ourselves as in conjunction with others, enmeshed with society, and not as quite unique, unitary and isolated beings. It is only the apprehension of death, of our severally merging into nothingness that gives us the sense of our uniqueness, unitariness, isolatedness—when we think of death we do not fear that *we* must die but each of us is afraid that *he* is doomed to die. In support of his position, Swarbrick justly notices that in the poem "The narrative perspective silently shifts from third to first person plural as individuality merges in the shared isolation of 'we'" (*loc. cit.*).

Three things of the poem may particularly be brought under focus. Firstly, the only italicised expression of the poem, '*Poor Soul*', has raised a controversy as concerns its meaning. David Timms says that the soul is 'poor' in the sense that ontologically it is non-existent. '*Poor Soul*' is therefore ironic in meaning—the soul is supposed to be a *being* but in actuality it is just *nothing*. Timms writes: "the cliché '*Poor Soul*' is charged with ironic meaning. If death is 'permanent and blank', 'emptiness', the very idea of soul is out of place. It is a '*Poor Soul*' because it doesn't exist" (Timms, 99). But Andrew Swarbrick does not see any ironic content in the expression '*Poor Soul*'. He writes about the horrified women's private ejaculation '*Poor Soul*': "when they whisper '*Poor Soul*' they are in fact pitying themselves, suddenly made aware of the unpredictable inevitability of their own deaths" (Swarbrick, 1986, 57). Irony and pity cannot exist at the same place and time, and if the soul does not exist, how can the women pity themselves—pity their own souls, to wit? And in that grave existential crisis of theirs how could they use ironic language? Secondly, Swarbrick writes that "As the patient's particular identity dissolves, the poem accumulates noun phrases ('the sudden shut of loss', 'something nearly at an end', 'the unique random blend') in a studied contemplation of substance becoming insubstantial" (Swarbrick, 1995, 121). And thirdly, though the persistent mood of the poem is assuredly pessimistic, the poem ends not with a negative but with a positive note. Swarbrick again writes: "The final, convoluted sentence [of the poem], even in confronting extinction, ends affairmatively with the exposed present indicative: 'we are'" (*loc. cit.*).

In the year 1961, Larkin wrote, all told, eight poems: 'Ambulances', 'Naturally the Foundation will Bear Your Expenses', 'The Large Cool Store', 'Here', 'Nothing To Be Said', 'And Now the Leaves Suddenly Lose Strength', 'Broadcast' and 'Breadfruit'. Of these, perhaps, the first, the fourth and the seventh stand out as excellent ones. Andrew Motion finds autobiographical elements in 'Ambulances'. In the period of time when Larkin composed this poem he was in Hull and was jactitating between the pulls of Maeve and Monica, and to keep him out of the painful situation he was holding 'his life in suspension'. Perhaps in this state of mind he was also thinking of death, of nullity of life. Motion writes about 'Ambulances': "every imaginable pain in life, it says, is as nothing compared to the 'permanent and blank and true' fact of death. Elaborating its argument, the poem becomes a celebration of the values of consciousness. In Belfast,..., he [Larkin] had admitted to a 'desire for oblivion' [see 'Wants']; in Hull, facing the greatest drama of his life, he clung to 'the unique random blend / Of families and fashions', which he realized he could not possess easily or for ever. 'All streets in time are visited' by ambulances, and all people are eventually:

> Carried in and stowed,
> And sense the solving emptiness
> That lies just under all we do...."
>
> (Motion, 311)

The structure of the poem is simple and regular and based on, as we have said, iambic tetrameter. Andrew Swarbrick writes about the prosodic appropriateness of 'Ambulances': "The poem is structurally regular and close-knit. The five stanzas follow a simple a / b / c / b / c / a rhyme-scheme, so that the central four lines have the interlinked firmness of the traditional alternately-rhymed quatrain. This, together with the regular iambic tetrameter, gives the poem a solidity which challenges the dissolution of death" (Swarbrick, 1986, 58). And David Timms writes about the rhetorical and linguistic qualities and excellence of the poem: "'Ambulances' employs almost no similies or metaphors. The vehicles are 'closed like confessionals', and death is described as a 'solving emptiness'; but these are the only examples of figurative language in the poem. The statement is lucid and unencumbered: death seems to defy figurative expressions to come to terms with it, as if no manipulation of language can have more impact than the fact itself" (Timms, 100).

Andrew Swarbrick does not credit Larkin for any originality of conception in the poem, but all at the same time he does not fail to understand that the objective of Larkin is not to describe the tragedy of death but to 'clarify our common response' to someone's death. However, Swarbrick praises Larkin's skilful employment of language in the poem. Swarbrick writes: "The meaning of the poem may be disconcerting but hardly original. That is not Larkin's intention: he uses familiar incident—an ambulance in an emergency dash through the traffic—to articulate and clarify our common response. But if the poem is not original in proffering the thought that ambulances frighten us, we can nevertheless admire Larkin's skilful and economical use of language" (Swarbrick, 1986, 57). And Andrew Motion writes: "'Ambulances', like all Larkin's best poems, modestly and devoutly collects evidence of ordinary life to create a truth which can be universally acknowledged" (Motion, 311).

8

Sunny Prestatyn

'Sunny Prestatyn' is one of the three poems in *The Whitsun Weddings* that are written on the subject of advertisement, the other two being 'Essential Beauty' and 'Send No Money'. Curiously, all the three poems were written in the same year, 1962. Again, 'Sunny Prestatyn' is one of the three poems of the same collection that deal with our 'longing for what must remain unattainable', the two other poems being 'Essential Beauty' and 'Wild Oat'—all the three having been written, once more, in the same year, 1962. 'Sunny Prestatyn' is the twenty-third among the 32 poems of *The Whitsun Weddings* and is distinguished for its curious blend of scornful bitter laugh and grave seriousness. The poem was written within days of finishing 'Toads Revisited', Andrew Motion tells us (Motion, 327), and according to Anthony Thwaite it was written sometime in October 1962 (Thwaite, 1988, 149). 'Sunny Prestatyn' was first published in *The Whitsun Weddings*.

The painful tension of Larkin between the contrary pulls of Monica and Maeve that, as we have said, distally contributed to the origination of 'Ambulances' also worked behind the birth of 'Sunny Prestatyn' as well as that of 'Love'—the poem that he wrote about two months after 'Sunny Prestatyn'. Andrew

Motion writes: "Within days of finishing 'Toads Revisited' Larkin wrote 'Sunny Prestatyn' and then, in early December, 'Love'. In the first, a girl on a poster is defaced and judged 'too good for this life'. In the second, the rival claims of self-interest and self-effacement in love are resolved into the claim 'My life is for me'. Whichever way people turn, the poems say, love lets them down: all images of perfection are unreal, all compromises are disappointments. Torn between his requirements for himself, his need for Monica, and his attractions to Maeve's romantic innocence, Larkin ensured that he possessed nothing entirely" (Motion, 327). From this, a faint autobiographical reference may be available in 'Sunny Prestatyn'.

The title of the poem seems uncommon and curious, but it is none of these. The title was taken from the logo of an advertising poster near the sea beach of Prestatyn. Prestatyn is an urban district in Flint in Wales and a Welsh coastal resort. The expression 'Sunny Prestatyn' refers to the cloudless fine sandy beach of the Irish Sea in Prestatyn. The logo of the advertisement read: 'Come To Sunny Prestatyn' (which has been utilised by Larkin as the beginning line of the poem: *Come To Sunny Prestatyn*). The advertisement, mounted on a hoarding, showed a beautiful and sexually attractive girl slyly flaunting her amorous parts and was laughing and, as if, whispering 'Come To Sunny Prestatyn'. P.R. King tells us that the advertisement was mounted in the railway station near the beach of Prestatyn and that in it there was "the alluring image of a girl in a swimsuit" (King, 20).

'Sunny Prestatyn' is one of the best satirical poems of Larkin. Larkin has at least three poems which were inspired by pictures of women: 'Lines on a Young Lady's Photograph Album' (*The Less Deceived*), 'Wild Oats' and 'Sunny Prestatyn' (*The Whitsun Weddings*). Andrew Motion says that in all the three poems, "working unseen, Larkin transforms a masturbatory impulse and an addiction to solitude into poems of great beauty and sociable truthfulness" (Motion, 234). However, 'Sunny Prestatyn' comprises three stanzas, each staza having eight lines, rhyming a / b / c / a / b / d / c / d.

The beginning italicised line of the poem was exactly the logo of the previous advertisement on the hoarding at the coastal resort of Prestatyn: '*Come to Sunny Prestatyn*' (it is for this reason that all the words begin with a capital letter). The logo invited people to come to Prestatyn and enjoy its coastal beauty. The beautiful and sexually inviting girl of the advertising poster was laughing while she, in her tightly sewn ('tautened') (suggestive of amorousness) white (symbol of virginity) silk cloths ('satin') was sitting down on her knees in the sandy beach ('Kneeling up on the sand / In tautened white satin'). In the background ('Behind her') one could see the lump or hunch ('hunk') of the coastal line and a hotel with palm trees. The coastline and the hotel were overshadowed by the girl's picture; so much so that they seemed to originate ('expand') from her thighs. Her arms were spread out upwards so fully that along with the arms her breasts were hauled up, too ('Spread breast-lifting arms').

In the second verse Larkin tells us that the picture of the (amorously postured) girl was later on one day in March violently humiliated, as if with blows of the hand ('slapped up'). As a consequence, within two weeks her face was roughly combed and scratched ('snaggle-toothed') and one of her eyes was torn off while the other was in tact ('boss-eyed'). Her abnormally big nipples or teats ('tits') and the sulcuses chasm, groves, clefts or bifurcation points in the lower part of her body where the two legs originate ('crotch') were done or pointed quite well in the poster of the advertisement ('Were scored well in'). Further, in the gap or distance between her two legs some scribblings or hasty and bad writings ('scrawls') were done, so that it seemed that she was cosily sitting, or sitting at ease, on a fleshy or swelled out external male genital organ or penis ('tuberous cock') and testicles ('balls'), keeping her two legs on the two sides ('astride') of those male pudenda.

In the third or the last verse, Larkin says that the scribbling or hastily done bad writings were an autograph that read 'Titch Thomas' (which was a sort of defilement of the picture of the girl as was the partial destruction of it by combing and scratching). [Andrew Swarbrick writes that "The autographed name 'Titch Thomas' suggests, however jokily, a male anxiety about sexual deficiency and the defacement of the poster might express 'every man in every penetration, a hatred, an assertion of ownership, a desecration of a false ideal'" (Swarbrick, 1995, 117). The first assumption of Swarbrick seems to be weak in foundation as there appears no dependable behind it.] In addition to all these defilements or vandalisms of the picture of the girl, someone stabbed with a knife right through the lips of the girl—the lips on which small hairs had grown and through which she was smiling ('moustached lips of her smile'). (The persons who vandalised the picture of the girl did so because she represented unrealisable, unattainable, illusory but romantic appeal, and because they thought it justified to wipe off, to efface such an appeal that only gives us pain.) Larkin says that the girl was an absolutely ideal, gracious, excellent and the most appealing and desirable object but not at all realisable or materialisable in this our real world or life ('She was too good for this life'). (And, we repeat, this was the reason why she or her picture was mutilated.) After the first act of mutilation or vandalism of the picture a second such act was committed not long afterwards, for within a short time after the first bouts of vandalism, another long ('great') tearing or rending or rupture of the remaining part of the picture of the girl was rendered, and this time the tearing was done cross-wise or obliquely ('a great traverse tear'). As a result of the cross-wise tearing of the poster only a hand of the girl and some portion of the poster, that was of blue colour, remained in the hoarding ('Left only a hand and some blue'). And after all these incidents at present ('Now') it is seen that another advertising poster is pasted over the previous and mutilated one, and this poster's logo is '*Fight Cancer*' (an appeal to the public to help eradicate the disease of carcinoma) ('Now *Fight Cancer* is there.'). (The second advertisement persuaded the people to eradicate cancer with a view to enjoy immortality, which is our another romantic ideal like the ideal or desire of sexual bliss. And as the ideal sexual bliss is beyond reach, so is the ideal of immortality, and therefore both the ideals are fraudulent, illusory.)

The core theme of the poem is rejection of the out-of-reach ideal romantic world that is illusory but most potentially attractive. In the poem that world is symbolically conceived of as the bawdy look of the beautiful girl in the advertising poster whose magnetic attraction irresistibly arouses male sexual fantasy. The picture of the girl was mutilated, vandalised by those who, like Larkin, suffered the tension between the tantalising attraction of the ideal and the frustrating tenter-hooks of the insensate reality. The supposedly male vandalisers mutilated the picture of the girl because they realised that they could not partake of the ideal world of the girl while they were only suffering from the painful attraction of the girl or of the ideal world. They, that is, deliberately rejected the ideal world, their dream-world, the invitation of the out-of-reach illusory world. The vandalisers mutilated the picture of the girl—i.e. they rejected the ideal world—because they *refused to be deceived any more* by the girl in the poster, or, which means the same thing, by the ideal world. But the irony here is this that the vandalisers' ideal world was of course created by themselves and that by rejecting the ideal world they simply revealed their own impotency, defeatism and self-deprecation.

In his books *The Whitsun Weddings* and *The Less Deceived*, Andrew Swarbrick explains the meaning of 'Sunny Prestatyn' thus: "The knife that has cruelly stabbed 'right through / The moustached lips of her smile' punctures an inflated dream-world by which the advertiser's image [of the 'hot' girl would attempt to deceive us. Both Larkin and 'Titch Thomas' respond to the romantic appeal of the poster before recognising it as a dangerous, unattainable illusion which only creates unfulfillable expectations of life" (Swarbrick, 1986, 59). In the poem advertiser is the deceiver, the girl is the deceiving object, and Larkin or 'Titch Thomas' and all male persons were supposed to be deceived ones. The advertiser devised to deceive all male persons by presenting before them an out-of-reach romantically ideal object as something real, as something reachable. But the cozenage of the advertiser was seen through by Larkin or 'Titch Thomas' and the other vandalisers, and so none of them were sufficiently or damagingly deceived. They were, of course, initially deceived, for they were for a while unhinged by their own fantasying about the girl, but before they lost their reason they escaped from their fantasy world, and so, Swarbrick says that they were but less deceived by the advertiser's ploy of tantalising sexual appeal from the girl. Swarbrick writes: "'Titch Thomas' and the poet are the less deceived and the less deceiving [they certainly deceived themselves initially by their own sexual fantasying]; the real obscenity lies with the creators of such images who knowingly exploit our fantasies in a callous pretence that they can be turned into reality. The new poster ('*Fight Cancer*') returns us more honestly to our bleaker, grimmer reality" (*loc. cit.*).

Roger Day has raised a very pertinent question about 'Sunny Prestatyn': is the poem humorous, funny? Day says that the poem contains two things: one, the 'grim consciousness of human suffering' which grows out of the frustrating incapability of materialising the ideals; and two, the resulting self-deprecating humour that gives rise to the urge to laugh at oneself. The fact of the despoliation of the image of the girl in the poster at first seems funny, but at the close of the poem when we learn of the replacement of that image by a new poster calling out of fight cancer we are mortally shocked and pained by the reminder of death. Therefore, Roger says that the dominating and sustained humour that is evoked in us by the poem is a 'wry' humour—the humour that is at once sardonic and painful (Day, 57-58). Andrew Swarbrick, on the other hand, says that the poem is a congeries of irony, playfulness and mockery. Swarbrick writes: "The language used by Larkin to describe the poster is tinged with irony and a comic playfulness which makes fun of the advertiser's cliches: the girl's 'white satin', her expansive thighs and breasts. This mockery, though, is intensified by the crude slang of the second stanza which robs the advertiser's image of its beguiling, deceptive appeal, and bludgeons it into conformity with reality" (Swarbrick, 1986, 59).

The tension in 'Sunny Prestatyn' arises out of our everlasting longing for fantasy-laden ideal and our recognition of it as unreachable and so illusive. Though the ideal—instantiated in the poem as the most sexually exciting female figure—is unattainable, its pull can hardly be averted, ignored. And when we cannot reach the ideal an enervating and self-deprecating dissatisfaction engulfs us, which more frequently than not ultimately leads us to avenging reaction. Nevertheless, in course of time the beacon of the ideal returns to tantalise us once again, and to exploit. Andrew Swarbrick writes about the progression of the argument of 'Sunny Prestatyn' from our intense romantic desire for the ideal to our ferocious negation of that desire—the desire behind which lurks the original desire: "The process of composition [of 'Sunny Prestatyn'] is towards ferocity: 'the glimpse of beauty, paradise, escape, is (also) pretentious mockery of "this life", our life, and therefore deserving of assault'. The pristine girl as one image of desire is translated by her violation into another: an expression of vengeance on everything that is tantalisingly unattainable. It is not that the image is 'unreal', but that its representation of sexual longing is all too urgently real. The poem's satirisation of the female fantasy figure gives way to the gleeful destruction of erotic icon; behind that destruction there lies an attitude of sexual self-disgust. The poem's conclusion pastes over the desecration with what at first appears a chestening reminder of mortality: 'Now *Fight Cancer* is there'. But this poster holds out a promise as fradulent as the first, for we can satisfy neither our desires for erotic bliss nor for immortality. 'The cancer advert is the last twist of Larkin's ironic knife. Our girl then takes a sordid journey into oblivion and the male participants in the drama queue up to follow her: Titch Thomas, the knifer, the ripper, the poet—and you and me, hypocrites lecteurs'" (Swarbrick, 1995, 117-18).

In 'Sunny Prestatyn', we come across a couple of pornographic, unsavoury words and terms: 'thighs', breast-lifting arms', 'tits', 'fissured crotch', 'tuberous cock' and 'balls'. But Larkin had no pornographic interest in employing these words and terms in this poem. He perhaps did not believe in any words or terms being treated as outcasts in the domain of literature. Modern literature also is not squamish about purity of words. Further, Larkin wrote this poem well after the case under the Obscene Publication Act against D.H. Lawrence's

Lady Chatterley's Lover (Penguin Books), in its unexpurgated form, was dismissed as untenable in 1960, reinforcing the view that for literary purposes no words or terms or phrases are anathema, and as such this poem should not be rejected as unchaste. Roger Day writes that those words of the poem, mentioned above, "themselves are not especially 'bad' (there are worse) but they are precisely pointed up by exact adjectives like 'fissured', the language of an educated observer, and this acts as a foil, one setting off the other. And could Larkin have achieved his aim *without* being so direct [i.e. without using those words which "have no place in a serious work of literary art"]? Probably not, and the contrasting language both sets off and offsets the vulgar" (Day, 59). We think that the sexy girl in the poster works as a symbol of unrealisable, unreachable and extremely attractive pull of the ideal, and to make her all the more sexy those words are very apt. However, Martin Booth, a poet of some stature and a perceptive critic, has unqualified praise for this 'famous poem' of Larkin. Booth thinks that 'Sunny Prestatyn' "indicates superbly his [Larkin's] skill" (Booth, 219). Booth writes about the poem: "Eventually, the girl is covered with a poster advertising the fight against cancer. And this is what poetry should do: it should take life at all its levels and make it into what it is but is not seen to be. This is the poet's task and Larkin meets it, not always so flippantly" (*op. cit.*, 220).

9

Dockery and Son

Though this is the twenty-fifth poem of this collection, it is not only one of the most important poems of this collection but one of the most important poems that Larkin ever wrote. This poem may be said to be the emotional hinge or centre of this collection of poems. Andrew Swarbrick writes about the position of this poem among all the poems of this collection: "Although Larkin chose 'The Whitsun Weddings' as the title poem [of *The Whitsun Weddings*] to foreground its note of celebration, the collection's [*The Whitsun Weddings*'s] emotional centre is 'Dockery and Son', an extended self-scrutiny which weighs bachelorhood and marriage, isolation and community"

(Swarbrick, 1995, 111). 'Dockery and Son' is a dramatised description of the bachelorhood of Larkin and his defence of evading wedlock. In the poem, writes Swarbrick, "cast as a dramatic monologue, the speaker's [i.e. Larkin's] return to his Oxford college and the news that his junior contemporary, Dockery, now has a son there prompt a series of reflections in which the speaker tries self-justifyingly to deny the difference between Dockery's life and his own" (*loc. cit.*). The poem refers to Larkin's revisiting Oxford where he had been a student in 1943 when he was around 21. In the poem, Larkin is speaking in the first person, in his own detached voice, of a bleak life, as he does in 'Mr Bleaney' and 'Ambulances'. Andrew Swarbrick justly says that 'Dockery and Son' "meditates on the futility of the choices we make in life and asserts that life composes a pattern beyond our control or will" (Swarbrick, 1986, 61).

Like 'Lines on a Young Lady's Photograph Album' and 'I Remember, I Remember' of *The Less Deceived* and 'Mr Bleaney' and 'The Whitsun Weddings' of *The Whitsun Weddings*, 'Dockery and Son' is an autobiographical poem. Andrew Motion writes: "Bitterly funny and grievously melancholic, 'Dockery and Son' is a compressed autobiography. It encapsulates Larkin's views about the effect of his parents on his personality, it reports spiritedly on his undergraduate career, it grimly sketches the attitudes which dominated his adult life" (Motion, 334). Roger Day also suggests that the poem tends to be autobiographical, in so far as it contains a few biographical elements. Day writes: "The poem recounts a return visit to the speaker's old college and his thoughts about his contemporaries" (Day, 55). And Andrew Motion writes that 'Dockery and Son' "describes a visit Larkin had made to his old college at Oxford, St John's, on the way back from the funeral of Agnes Cuming, his predecessor as librarian at Hull, almost exactly a year earlier (than the date of composition of the poem, for Agnes Cuming had died on 8 March 1962)" (Motion, 333). 'Dockery and Son' may also be clubbed with 'I Remember, I Remember' of *The Less Deceived* and 'Here' and 'The Whitsun Weddings' of *The Whitsun Weddings* because all these poems were occasioned by train journeys that Larkin actually undertook. The bleak, gloomy view life that Larkin paints at the end of 'Dockery and Son' ('And age, and then the only end of age') is also very personal. In his interview with John Haffenden in 1979 or 1980, Larkin told Haffenden about the bleak view of life that the poem suggests: "It's a bit simplified, I suppose, but I think it's all perfectly true. I can't see how anyone could possibly deny it, any of it" (Haffenden, 120).

One specially remarkable thing about 'Dockery and Son' is that the poem demanded much linguistic exercise from Larkin. It is well known that Larkin used to devote much labour in giving finishing touches to his poems—much time and labour in making multiple drafts in order to arrive at the most refined version of his final manuscript—and 'Dockery and Son' is one of the few poems of Larkin that was drafted over and over again. Larkin began the poem on 14 February 1963 and after making fifteen pages of drafts completed it on 28 March of that year. It was chosen by him after much consideration in June of the same year for inclusion in *The Whitsun Weddings* (which was published in February 1964). Larkin wanted to make 'Dockery and Son' an epigrammatic poem, and so at the last moment drastically changed an earlier version of the concluding stanza of the poem to what it is now, the earlier version being the following:

> And how we got it; when we turn, they rear
> Like sand clouds, blocking the way back, bodying
> For Dockery a son, for me nothing,
> Nothing with all a son's harsh here-and-now.
> Life is first a boredom, then fear.
> Whether we use it or not it goes,
> Twisting us to the element we chose,
> And we are dead before we quite see how.

'Dockery and Son' is a poem of six verses, each verse containing eight five-stress iambic lines, rhyming a / b / b / c / a / d / d / c.

In March 1962, Larkin, as we have said, visited his old college, St John's, Oxford, where in 1943 he had been a student, and there he met the Dean or the President of the academic faculty. When Larkin had been in that Oxford college, a certain student, a few years' junior to him and Dockery by name, also had been reading there. Larkin, in the beginning verse of the poem, says that when he met the Dean, the latter asked him if Dockery was junior to him ("'Dockery was junior to you, / Wasn't he?' said the Dean.").

The Dean then informed Larkin that Dockery's son was then reading at that college ('His son's here now.'). Larkin went to St John's after attending, as we have said, the funeral of Agnes Cuming, and so the thought of his own death was then fresh in his mind and he felt himself somewhat like a ghost, not a living being. In the third line of the beginning verse, therefore, Larkin says that at that time he preferred death, rather than life, i.e. *death then suited him*—was welcome to him—('Death-suited') and that he then felt himself a *ghost that had returned to earth* ('visitant'). In this state of mind, Larkin acknowledged the information that Dockery's son was then reading at the college supplied by the Dean by swinging his head ('I nod'). [The phrase 'Death-suited, visitant' does not offer single meaning but three, and, following Roger Day, we have adopted the most appropriate meaning above just now. Day writes: "The phrase suggests three different meanings: 1. that he [Larkin] is wearing a dark suit as for a funeral occasion; 2. that he is a ghost returning ('visitant' = *revenant*); 3. that 'death suits him'. The appropriateness of the last suggestion becomes apparent when the poem reaches its conclusion. Unlike 'The Whitsun Weddings' with its final, positive image, this conclusion declares unambiguously that life is frustrating, determined, hard, meaningless and leads only to death" (Day, 55).] However, the Dean further asked Larkin if he till then maintained connection or correspondences with a certain person ('And do/ You keep in touch with—'). Alternatively ('Or'), Larkin asked himself if he remembered that during the time of his stay in the college he would, on a few occasions, be summoned by the Dean. The Dean would enquire about some incidents that had occurred in the previous night. Larkin and some of his friends or/and associates would then meet the Dean wearing dark-coloured gown, eating no breakfast, and till then being under the hangover of the previous night's drinking bouts ('still half-tight'). They would assemble along the Dean's chest of drawers or table ('stand before that desk') and tell the Dean about their observation, testimony or evidence ('Our version') as concerned the happenings of the previous night ("of 'these incidents last night'"). After meeting the Dean, Larkin went to the room of the hall or hostel where he had stayed, while a student at Oxford, and endeavoured to open the door of the room ('I try the door of where I used to live').

In the second verse of the poem, Larkin says that when he tried to open the door he found that it was shut from inside (which meant that the old room of Larkin was now occupied by someone else, and consequently he felt *excluded*) ('Locked'). Larkin then went to see the lawn which was vast in size and which was then sparkling in the sunlight ('dazzlingly wide'). At that moment, he heard the sound of a bell (either of the college or of a nearly church, which indicated that it was time for him to leave the place, and to catch the train) which was familiar ('known') to him ('A known bell chimes'). Larkin then took a train (bound for Hull from where he went to Oxford). During his visit to his old college nobody, except the Dean, took notice of him, regarded him at all—he was neglected by everyone, except the Dean ('ignored'). While he was returning by train, the canal and the colleges (or the college buildings) along the train-line and the clouds in the sky tardily or laggardly passed away out of his view ('subside / Slowly from view'). Larkin was wonderfully ('good Lord') thinking that if Dockery's son was then in the Oxford college then the son must have been born in 1943, like any other boy who went up to the Oxford university ('Anyone up today') and that in 1943 he (Larkin) was twenty-one years of age ('when I was twenty-one'). Larkin doubtfully or wonderingly calculated that if Dockery was younger than he, as Dockery really was, then Dockery must have got his son (through marriage) when he (Dockery) had been nineteen years of age, or, at the most, twenty years of age ('If he was younger, did he get his son / At nineteen, twenty?'). Larkin reflected or wonderingly asked himself if that Dockery ('he') was that reserved, remote, secluded, shy ('withdrawn') person that he knew of at the college in the past.

He further reflected, or asked himself, if that Dockery was that rich ('High-collared') boy who graduated from a public school ('public-schoolboy') and then went up to Oxford and lived in the rooms (of hostel) with another student, Cartwright by name, on sharing basis ('sharing rooms / With Cartwright') that Cartwright who was later on killed. Thus Larkin continued to ruminate on how much or how little the things (connected with the life in Oxford) changed ('How much... How little...'). While he was so ruminating, reflecting, Larkin took a deep and involuntary breath ('Yawning') and then he thought that he perhaps fell asleep ('I suppose / I fell asleep'). When the train reached the industrial town of Sheffield, Larkin woke up from sleep and saw smokes ('fumes') rising up from chimneys and radiations of fires coming out of vast ovens ('furnace-glares'), and there in Sheffield he got down from the train in which he was travelling and boarded another train ('where I changed'). Also in Sheffield, he ate an uncommonly big cake ('ate an awful pie') and walked along the platform up to its furthest limit, from where he saw the vast or wide area ('ranged') where railway tracks or lines once joined with each other and then parted from each other ('joining and parting lines'). And those (polished lines reflected the very bright ('strong') light or glow of the moon which was not fenced or shielded or encumbered by clouds ('reflect a strong / Unhindered moon').

(In that romantic and ponderous situation, Larkin began to reflect on his life.) In the fourth verse, he says that even at that rather advanced stage of his life ('still') it seemed to him quite normal ('natural') not to have a son or a wife, and not to possess a house or some landed property. Nevertheless, he was inescapeably ('Only') stupefied or driven out of his senses ('numbness') due to his receiving the jolt or blow ('registered the shock') of knowing ('Of finding out') that the greater part of his life by then had already passed away ('how much had gone of life') and that he became very much different from other people (for not marrying, not having a son, not possessing property, etc.) ('How widely from the others').

Dockery now had everything that Larkin did not have ('Dockery, now'), and this was so because at the age of only nineteen Dockery had made an inventory of whatever he had desired to get in life and succeeded in getting them (wife, son, property, etc.). ('Only nineteen, he must have taken stock / Of what he wanted, and been capable / Of...'). (On the other hand, Larkin had not made any inventory and had not succeeded in achieving those objects that Dockery had possessed, and anyone might say that this was the difference between Dockery and Larkin.) Larkin denied that the real difference between Dockery's life and his life was not Dockery's having wife, son, etc. and his not having those things ('No, that's not the difference').

Rather astonishingly, says Larkin in the fifth verse, he thought that what actually constituted the difference between Dockery's life and his life was Dockery's having the conviction ('Convinced') that it was proper ('should') for him to have advanced or prospered by having a wife and children ('added to') and his not having such a conviction ('rather, how // Convinced he was he should be added to!). Larkin could not understand (or he questioned) why Dockery thought that by having (or adding to him) a wife and children he could advance or prosper, or increase, the value of his life ('Why did he think adding meant increase?'). (Larkin did not subscribe to, or agree with, Dockery's conviction.) He thought that getting a wife and children ('it') rather meant decrease ('dilution') in the value of one's life ('To me it was dilution'). Larkin asks from where all these a priori, inborn, non-empirical beliefs or suppositions ('assumptions') come, i.e. he does not believe that these suppositions are based on empirical facts or observations. He says that these suppositions do not originate in, or come out of, fundamental or apodictic truths ('what / We think truest') or our most urgent or basic instincts ('most want to do'). He asks us to strongly ward off, or to strongly keep out of consideration, like tightly closed doors ('tight-shut, like doors'), those distortions, perversions or misinterpretations of truths ('Those warp'). (This means that according to Larkin the suppositions that having a wife and children contributes towards prosperity or to enhancement of life's value are distortions of truths, and so these suppositions must be strongly warded off, like very tightly shut doors.) Larkin says that these things are, i.e., having a wife and children are ('They're'), in greater number of cases ('more'), customs ('styles') that are entailed with our lives ('Our lives bring with them'). These things for some time remain with us as our habits, i.e. for some time wife and children remain the objects of our affection and we cannot do without them ('habit for a while'). But after that abruptly, unexpectedly these things (wife or marriage and children) become converted (from being objects of affection) into properties, i.e., we begin to treat them as merely concrete, material objects ('Suddenly they harden into all we've got').

In the final stanza, Larkin says that these things (marriage, wife, children) not only become material objects to us in course of time but these things, as if, become part of our customs, or better, hereditary possessions ('And how we got it'). Larkin says that when he thinks about the things and events rise up or lift up or build up like clouds of sand (i.e. sand blown up by potential wind) ('they rear / Like sand-clouds'), and then thicken and concentrate or crystalise ('thick and close'), and thus form a mass or body ('embodying'). For Dockery that mass or body is his son ('For Dockery a son'), but for him (for Larkin) that mass or body was just a sort of nothingness or vacuity. That nothingness or vacuity has brought in along with it and for Larkin a reproving or censuring or negative support or privilege ('Nothing with all a son's harsh patronage'). [Having sons is not all desirable because sons, in front of their parents, pose as if they are great assets and great sources of pleasure. So Dockery did not benefit from having a son, for he would have to bear his 'son's harsh patronage'—for he can boast only of his son's barbed Palladium or censorious support. On the other hand, Larkin has no son, and so he is free from 'a son's harsh patronage'. Therefore Dockery's life, says Larkin, is no better than his: 'No, that's not the difference'.] Larkin now concludes that in the beginning life is uninteresting, flat, wearisome, and in the end part of it, it is frightful, terrific, horrendous ('Life is first boredom, then fear.'). He says that life (not someone's life or any one's) never stands still; we may or may not utilise it, but it, unconcerned, must run its course ('Whether or not we use it, it goes'). And as life runs its course, it abandons behind for each man or bequeaths to each man ('leaves') a particular sort of fate, lot, fortune or destination ('something') which life selects ('chose') for him but keeps it secret from him ('hidden from us'). In the end, each one of us must become old ('And age'), and then each one of us must meet the ultimate event or the end-point of his growing old—death ('and then the only end of age').

The six-stanza poem that 'Dockery and Son' is may be divided into two equal halves as concerns its content: the first three stanzas or verses are quite narrative, where Larkin describes his memory of the past and his surprisingly contrasting perception of the present; and the remaining three stanzas are reflective, where he first tries to see the difference between Dockery's life and his, but then forthwith negates the superficial difference and jumps to the universal conclusion that life is fated to prove itself but a vacuity extended through a limited time-frame. The first half is nostalgic but not fancifully so, for Larkin never loses his moorings with the reality—he tries to open the door of his old room, hears the bell, notices the canal and clouds and colleges sliding past his moving train and observes the 'fumes' and 'furnace-glares' of Sheffield. The second half, especially the epigrammatic concluding quatrain of it is prognostic, augural, prophetic, and therefore weightier, graver. The first half innocuously surprises us, the second shocks and knocks us off our insoucience and existential comfort or mental stability: 'And age, and then the only end of age.' The first distinguishes itself from the second by its stochastic novelistic details in drawing the tete-a-tete between the Dean and Larkin and Larkin's travelling back by train; the second, on the other hand, is distinctive against the first for its philosophic glum. And while in the first half we are interested in the particulars, in the second we are made wiser by the reminder of the universal and inescapable human attrition.

The title of the poem, 'Dockery and Son' may remind one of Charles Dicken's novel *Dombey and Son* (1848), and one may discern at least one common point between the poem and the novel. The poem says that man's life is determined and controlled not by himself but by adventitious forces, and in the novel Dombey's life is an illustration of this proposition. Dombey wanted a son as the heir to his sprawling firm, but his wife first bore him a daughter whom he resented and then a son who early died. A second marriage proved fruitless. Broken in old age, Dombey was comforted, ironically, by his loving daughter, and this led him to self-scrutiny. Self-scrutiny is also a subject of the poem 'Dockery and Son', in so far as in the second half of it Larkin compares his bachelorhood with Dockery's family life. Larkin of course does not suffer from self-scrutiny like Dombey, for it does not reveal his loss against Dockery's gain, rather it clarifies the truth that man's life is a series of habits enforced by tradition and perpetuated under illusion, and also the truth that life must end in death. In this regard, in the end, Larkin becomes wiser than both Dombey and Dockery. However, Roger Day says that the title lays emphasis on fatherhood as a component of the theme of the poem and that it bears a sense of mockery. Day writes about the title of the poem: "The title, besides being a reflection on the implications of fatherhood, suggests the image that Dockery has of himself—that his identity is formed by his role. And there is an odd sort of joke: 'Dockery and Son' sounds like a business, not to mention the hint of the nursery rhyme 'Hickory Dickory Dock', with the suggestion of time recorded mechanically by a clock" (Day, 56).

In the three poems 'Here', 'Faith Healing' and 'The Whitsun Weddings', all of *The Whitsun Weddings*, Larkin merely closely observes the lives of other persons quite detachedly, but in 'Mr Bleaney' and 'Dockery and Son', again of *The Whitsun Weddings*, he not only observes others' lives but compares his own with theirs. In 'Mr Bleaney', he observes Mr Bleaney's life with almost a prying instinct and arrives at the universal psychological proposition that 'how we live measure our own nature' without getting his mood clouded by melancholy. On the other hand, in 'Dockery and Son', particularly in the concluding part of it, his mood is morbidly grave and his vision bleak and frightful. Again, in 'Mr Bleaney' Larkin finds identity between Mr Bleaney's life and his, but in 'Dockery and Son' he initially discerns a divergence between Dockery's life and his, though in the end he quashes that divergence.

The central argument of 'Dockery and Son' is that man's life is not determined by himself but by forces external to him, and that from the beginning of his life to its end man is subject to various illusions and habits and mores. Man thinks that he freely chooses the course of his life, and this is his most fundamental illusion or self-delusion. P.R. King writes that "The price that the individual may have to pay for his refusal to be under any illusions about life is the theme of 'Dockery and Son'" (King, 12). Larkin says that it might have occurred to Dockery that Dockery himself had chosen the life of parenthood for self, but in fact Dockery's life was shaped by forces external to him. When a man thinks that his particular sort of life is the result of his voluntary selection, he suffers illusion or delusion. Larkin says that Dockery's particular life was shaped by the fashions ('style') or the customs of the society that are concomitant with our lives, i.e. the fashions or customs that our lives inescapably entails: 'They're more a style / Our lives bring with them'. In 'Dockery and Son', Larkin presents and clarifies this point very superbly and interestingly with just the single image of joining and parting of railway tracks in the frawningly bright moonlight: 'and walked along / The platform to its end to see the ranged / Joining and parting lines reflect a strong // Unhindered moon.' Andrew Swarbrick writes about these three lines of the poem: "The speaker, in looking at an image of his own life. The tracks take him away from his past at college to a destination which remains always beyond sight. As he stands by the tracks, he is momentarily standing by the side of his own life and trying to assess its direction and the 'joining and parting lines' act as a reminder of how his own path has diverged from that of Dockery. Moreover, *the direction of his own life, of any life, is as predetermined, as devoid of choice, as the trains which run along these tracks*" (emphasis added) (Swarbrick, 1986, 63).

Roger Day says that in the poem, Larkin has portrayed the Dean as a funny figure, but whether the Dean is a funny figure or no, it is undeniable that his words immediately sets the conversational and dramatic tone of the entire poem. Day also identifies the concluding quartet as a 'coda' or the finishing piece of the poem, that acts as an epilogue. Swarbrick says that "the conclusion is one the poem takes care to portray, even parade" (Swarbrick, 1995, 113), but, nevertheless, Roger Day is not happy with it, and, we believe, justifiably so. Day writes: "Is the lapidary statement of the conclusion integral to the poem, or has it been tacked on as the answer to a question which has not really been raised? It does not seem as integral to me as, say, the conclusion of 'The Whitsun Weddings' where the final image relates directly to all that has been described" (Day, 57). Barring the last four lines of it, in the poem Larkin was first hinting at the difference between Dockery's life and his, and then summarily dismissed the difference producing a potential argument. So long, the poem was especially concerned with only two particular lives—the life of Dockery and that of Larkin. But then without any justifiable premises Larkin jumps to the universal conclusion about life in general in the concluding four lines. This is untenable; the gap is fallacious, it has to be bridged, Roger Day would like to demand. P.R. King also rejects the blanket and blunt comment on life in general that Larkin makes in the concluding lines of the poem: "that final stanza remains an assertion. It may result from the poet's being honest to his own experience, but it cannot be generalized except as a dogmatism" (King, 14). Roger Day rightly says that "the concluding statement might be justified simply by the fact that it *is* what the poet's reflections lead him to" (*loc. cit.*). In that case, of course, 'Dockery and Son' will have to be treated as a '*personal* poem', as Day tells us (*loc. cit.*).

'Dockery and Son' is Wordsworthian as regards its colloquial language. In the second Preface to his *Lyrical Ballads*, Wordsworth argued that the language of poetry should be the language of the common man in the natural setting, and the language of 'Dockery and Son', like that of most poems of Larkin, is like that. Andrew Swarbrick writes: "In its idiomatic language and conversational address, the poem keeps faith with Wordsworth's real language of real men" (Swarbrick, 1995, 113).

The beginning four lines of the poem, which reproduces the Dean's speaking voice in his own words, perfectly ventriloquise and "are delivered in a squeaky, mimicking voice" (Day, 56). 'Dockery and Son' is distinguished for its heavily condensed language that is very appropriate for the poem's highly compressed ideas. Examples are: 'strong / Unhindered moon', 'adding meant increase', 'Those warp tight-shut', 'they rear / Like sand-clouds', 'what something hidden from us choose', etc. P.R. King, however, is appreciative of both the linguistic register and the prosodic arrangement as well as the imagery of the poem: he says that the "bleak conclusion and the preceding meditations have been bound together in regular eight-line stanzas rhyming abbcaddc and moving forward on a steady iambic rhythm. This solid frame is upheld by a colloquial diction and imagery drawn from everyday experiences. These combine to set the keynote of ordinariness which convinces the reader of the authenticity of the experience" (King, 14).

'Dockery and Son' is a representative poem of Larkin for, among other things, its mix of mimicry and melancholy. The poem, for instance, begins with poking a fun with the Dean and ends with a gloomy philosophy. Roger Day writes: "...'Dockery and Son' is not unrelieved gloom: As well as the initial lines there are other humourous flashes—the vignette of hung-over undergraduates explaining their misdeeds, the joke about railway catering ('an awful pie'). This combination of pessimism and humour is an interesting feature of Larkin's work" (Day, 57). P.R. King writes, "The success of the poem lies in its precise rendering of the changing tones of voice and the tension between the idea of divergent paths in people's lives and the poet's personal conviction that our lives are determined by powers outside our control" (King, 14). Finally, it should be noted that when he was selecting poems to be included in *The Whitsun Weddings*, Larkin's last choice was 'Dockery and Son', and Andrew Motion says that "it was a good last choice" (Motion, 334).

10

Essential Beauty

This is one of the three poems—the other two being 'Send No Money' and 'Sunny Prestatyn'—that Larkin wrote under the impression of expansive commercial advertisements ('Sunny Prestatyn' we have already discussed and 'Send No Money' we shall treat next). The three poems were produced on the heels of one another in the same year: 'Esential Beauty' on 26 June, 'Send No Money' on 24 August, and 'Sunny Prestatyn' most probably in October. Both Andrew Swarbrick and Roger Day have in the word 'essential', which occurs in the title of the poem, a reference to Platonism. Swarbrick writes: "In 'Essential Beauty', Plato's ideal forms have been ironically diminished to images on advertising hoardings" (Swarbrick, 1995, 115). And Day writes: "I think the title fairly clearly refers to the Platonic notion of essences, which is applied to the impossible perfection of life as pictured in advertisements" (Day, 59). The word 'essence' derives from the Latin root *esse*, meaning 'to be', and so essence means the perpetual possibility of being. Philosophers since antiquity have been distinguishing between essence or form or idea and substance. The former is a summation of all the common properties of a class of particular objects. Thus the two common properties of the class of man (past, present and future), animality and rationality, constitute the essence, form or idea of the class of man. Plato believed that the essence of man, or for that matter of any other thing, belongs to the transcendental and rational and non-sensual world while particular men (Jack, Harry, Dick), or for the matter of that any kind of sensible objects, exist or inhabit this immanent world of senses. According to Plato, beauty is an essence or form or idea, and so it exists in the transcendental world, and for that reason, beauty cannot be physically possessed; it can only be rationally, intuitively or imaginatively comprehended. This explains what Swarbrick and Day mean when they say that Larkin's essence, as concerns in this poem, is a Platonic form or notion.

In the poem, Larkin says that the beauty of women or the beauty of life in general is transcendendal, i.e. beyond the contour or perigeal reach of this our immanent world of senses, and so beauty is an *essence*, or beauty is *essential*, and, for the reason of that, beauty of women cannot be physically possessed—it can only be imaginatively comprehended. The title of the poem, though it at first sounds queer, is witty, finical and smart. Roger Day, however, has discovered another meaning of the title. He says that the title means that "'beauty is essential'" (Day, 59). The poem is distinguished for, among some other things, its two long stanzas, each having sixteen five-stress lines.

Larkin opens the poem by referring us to the large advertisements, on hoarding frames, that are as 'large as rooms'. The advertisements are positioned towards all the directions of the different streets and roads ('that face all ways'). Some of them are obstructing 'the ends of streets' with advertisement of loaves of bread of huge size ('giant loaves'); some are blocking the view of the graveyard with advertisement of a composition of milk, eggs, etc. sweetened and flavoured ('Screen graves with custard'); some are obstructing the view of the slums with advertisement of motor-oil along with a logo in praise of that substance ('cover slums with praise / Of motor-oil'); and some are obstructing the view of the slums with advertisement of slices of the genre of fish called salmon ('cuts of salmon'). The images or portraits of the advertisements are acutely or finely drawn, and these look sylvan because of their profusely or liberally drafted trees ('these sharply-pictured groves') are glowing as if timelessly or unendingly ('shine perpetually'). Moreover, the images of the advertisements, it seems, are holding before us or before the commuters of those streets and roads the image, visage or idea of the ideal life ('Of how life should be'). In the image of yet another advertisement, that stands high above a sewer ('gutter') by the street, a man 'in a meadow' is seen cutting a block or chunk of golden coloured or exorbitantly priced butter ('golden butter') with a knife made of silver ('A silver knife sinks into golden butter'), while a glass of milk is waiting to be consumed. The man is not alone but with several families from the creamy layer of the society that gathered in the meadow in the pleasant weather of midsummer ('Well-balanced families, in fine / Midsummer weather'). The members of the families went there by cars, and they are now smiling and also enjoying the vitality of their young ages, and all these are due to ('owe') their plan of gathering at that idyllic pastoral spot and sharing a repast there of little solid squares (or solid bodies, each having six equal square faces) ('cube') of food article to which each one of the family members who assembled there is now seemingly reaching out a hand to receive one of those solid squares ('owe their smiles, their cars, / Even their youth, to that small cube each hand / Stretches towards'). There are also some other things in the picture or image of the advertisement: there are 'deep armchairs' near ('Aligned to') a number of cups of bedtime drinks (on a table); there are luminescent bars fed by gas or electricity; and (an image that shows only) quarter parts of a few cats ('a quarter-profile cats') who are on 'warm mats' (because it is summer) beside 'slippers' or loose shoes. Nothing of all these scenes of the advertisements does mirror or show ('Reflect') the 'streets and squares' of that place which are away from the houses of those families ('outdoors')—the 'streets and squares' over which those advertisements ('They') are prevailing or holding some sort of command or sway ('dominate') and on which rain is pouring continually ('rained-on') ('Reflect none of the rained on streets and squares // They dominate outdoors').

In the second stanza of the poem, Larkin says that the painted scenes of the advertisements ('they'), on the contrary ('Rather') so to say stand up ('rise') gravely or seriously ('Serenely') to announce the desirableness of quality bread and quality liquor and absoluteness of atmosphere in air-conditioned rooms ('pure crust, pure foam, / Pure coolness'). Those painted scenes announce or hawk those inviting, attractive things (quality bread, quality liquor and cool air) to our ordinary or low-grade ('imperfect') lives, or to us who are living ('live') ordinarily and seeing only paltry things ('imperfect eyes'). With our low-grade life we are not content and so we very eagerly desire or look up to ('stare') the imaginary ideal life (such as displayed in those advertisements) which is far away from this world (quotidian sordid life of ours). In this our drab, insipid, poor, level, flat world or life everything is old, jaded, stale ('where nothing's made / As new'), and nothing is quite unalloyed, unsoiled, uncontaminated, or dazzling, or sparkling ('where nothing's...washed quite clean'). All of us, who live in this our low-grade world or lead such low-grade life, desire, or aspire after, such homes as such families as are there in the advertisements live in, or all of us who live in this our low-grade world or lead such low-grade life, desire, or aspire after, such a life as the people in the advertisements do lead ('seeking the home / All such inhabit'). In that desired, or aspired after, world—the idealised world of the advertisements—('There'), there are dimly or poorly illuminated public houses of entertainments ('pubs'), whose roofs are trussed or supported by beams ('raftered'). People of the creamy layer of the society, who are members of tennis clubs and who wear white shorts for playing tennis, go to those public houses of entertainments, after playing tennis, and fill them ('pubs / Are filled with white-clothed ones from tennis clubs'). And the attending boy of a certain such club is (perhaps) vomiting out ('puking') his heart, i.e. exhausting all his energy serving his gentlemen-masters ('Gents'), i.e. those tennis players or the attending boy is exhausting all his energy running after the gentlemen-masters for receiving lips from them ('And the boy puking his heart out in the Gents'). But the boy narrowly falls short of catching them ('Just missed them'), because he is engaged in receiving an additional tip ('more') of 'halfpenny' from an old and retired ('pensioner') gentleman who condescend to give the boy an extra tip for bringing for him 'Granny Graveclothes' Tea' (a certain brand of tea) which the old gentleman desired to sip in order to enjoy that particular moment of his old age ('Just missed them, as the pensioner paid / A halfpenny more for Granny Graveclothes' Tea / To taste old age').

And at this moment, some smokers, who are going to die of tobacco-smoking, feel or imagine ('dying smokers sense') (understandably, being in their intoxicated state and under their belief that smoking whets libido) that a dimly visible beautiful damsel ('unfocused she') is coming near them across a certain various-coloured (because of there being flowers of different hues) park or garden which seems to float on water ('through some dappled park / As if on water'). The damsel or girl is dim, penumbral because no light has focused her, i.e., there is no light to illuminate her ('No match lit up'), and there is no force to pull her closer to them ('no drag ever brought near'). (Larkin, the poet, thinks that the smokers perhaps are desiring physical intimacy or contact with the damsel, being driven by the tobacco-intoxication and falsely feeling that smoking sharpened their libidinal urge, but as she is actually just the creation of their hot, exotic imagination, she cannot be hugged, drawn towards them.) However, now, at this moment, the umbrageous girl is standing in the clear view of the smokers, and she is smiling at them after identifying them and perhaps also being identified by them ('Who now stands newly clear, / Smiling, and recognising'), but soon she is gradually being enveloped by darkness ('going dark').

The title of the poem is a little uncommon and ambiguous in meaning. For one thing, beauty cannot be of two sorts: essential and inessential or non-essential. Nevertheless, the two interpretations of the title put forward by Roger Day, which we have already discussed, may help us getting around the sense of the title. Beauty—ideal or absolute beauty—is of course Platonic, and so out of our reach; but then the ideal beauty is essential, for it ever inspires us, soothes us in this our detestable dry-as-dust world and thus saves us, though only momentarily. The beautiful damsel, the 'unfocused she' of the imagination of the 'dying smokers' existed in the out-of-reach transcendental world, no doubt, but she certainly inspired the morbid smokers all the same like the Abissinian damsel of Coleridge inspired Kubla Khan. In this sense, as Roger Day has said, beauty or rather ideal or absolute beauty is essential. As in another advertisement poem, 'Sunny Prestatyn', so here in 'Essential Beauty' Larkin highlights the divide between the ideal world and this sordid world of practicality, and says that the world of unreachable ideality incessantly entices us—the 'hot tamale' in 'Sunny Prestatyn' and the 'unfocused she' in 'Essential Beauty'—and thus cause us suffer disillusionment. In 'Essential Beauty', the group of advertisements in the hoardings also allure us with the wished-for glamorous life in which, say, we may enjoy 'golden butter' with quality bread and liquor and cool atmosphere in midsummer in the plush meadow. Such a life is essentially beautiful, i.e. such a life encompasses ideal pulchritude or essential beauty.

The last five and a half lines of the poem may at first seem unconnected with the rest of it, for here Larkin brings in sexual desire and its deceptivity quite all on a sudden. But a little close attention will reveal that as the deceptivity of the ideality of the hoardings are self-imposed (we are deceived because we knowingly and voluntarily look up to that ideality) so is also the deceptivity of sexual desire imposed on us by our own selves. The argument of the last five and a half lines reinforces and elaborates that of the rest of the poem. Andrew Swarbrick, in his *Out of Reach: The Poetry of Philip Larkin* writes: "The poem's final image intensifies (these) painful feelings of desire and exclusion. Advertising's association of smoking with sexual secession, crudely trading on masculine fears and desires, yokes together for Larkin two powerful forces: sex and death. The 'dying smokers' momentarily sense the object of their desires 'Walking... As if on water', miraculous and other-worldly, an 'unfocused she / No match lit up, nor drag ever brought near', a vision of female attractiveness which floats out of reach.... There's no irony by the poem's end, only the pathos of unsatisfiable desire. She stands 'newly clear' at the same time as 'going dark', glamorised fantasy-object who complicitly recognises her adorers but fades beyond their grasp, 'a decadent, beautiful harbinger of death'" (Swarbrick, 1995, 115-16).

The images of the group of advertisements collectively present a beautiful pastoral scenario—green, soft, open, dreamy, innocent and unadulterated—far away, though perhaps not spatially but of course imaginatively, from the decaying urbanity. This pastoral scenario Andrew Swarbrick calls 'pastoral metaphor' and a dream, and very rightly, for, the images of the advertisements stand for the ideal life or world and that life or world is only to be wished for, imaginary, unrealisable, ever and ever. Further, such a life or world titillatingly always allures us, coaxes us unstopably, and as it is unrealisable we, consequently, at the end of all our efforts, succumb to deception and lose the peace of our mind. Roger Day, on the other hand, says that 'Essential Beauty' evokes in us not one single emotion but more than one. He writes: "The emotions present in the poem seem to me of several different kinds—there is astonishment at the outrageous unreality of advertising (reflected in the 'butter / gutter' rhyme), and in the second part of the poem a sadness and compassion for those falling so far short of 'essential beauty'. There is also, perhaps, a tinge of amusement in the way the hoardings are described. But behind these one senses a repressed anger that life does not measure up and is made worse by the promises of duplicit, 'essential' images, and this anger is, as it were, kept at bay by the making of the poem" (Day, 60).

However, about the prosodic finesse of the poem, Andrew Swarbrick writes: "The poem shows Larkin's command of elaborate and large-scale structures. The sixteen-line stanzas (their bulkiness resembling large advertising frames) are mirror-images, following the same rhyme-scheme (a / b / a / c / b / d / d / e / c / f / e / g / f / h / h / g) with a penultimate three-stress line varying the pentameter. Within this framework, five syntactically complex sentences uncoil. For example, notice how the main verb of the first sentence ('shine') is given its emphasis. First, its position in the sentence is delayed. Secondly, it comes at a point when we expect a rhyme with 'loaves', an expectation which it does not fulfil. Furthermore, the line-ending cuts off the verb from its qualifying adverb ('Perpetually') so that both words are given extra weight. Thus, the verb is given enough force to stand as an ironic contrast to the grim 'streets', 'graves', 'slums' and 'rained-on streets and squares' which actually surround the advertisements. The poem's final line is dramatically effective because of its heavy pauses and rhythmical departure from the prevailing iambic pentameter. It comes as the conclusion to a long final sentence whose rhythm slows and fades with the vision of unreachable beauty" (Swarbrick, 1986, 68). So much of prosodic and rhetorical subtlety is there in the poem, but all this is noticeable only to the very discerning eye. In fact, 'Essential Beauty' is an exemplar of Larkin's superior mastery over prosodic and rhetorical technicalities as well.

11

Send No Money

In *The Whitsun Weddings*, Larkin's third advertisement poem, 'Send No Money', immediately follows the second, 'Essential Beauty' (the first was 'Sunny Prestatyn'). 'Send No Money' distinguishes itself from most other Larkin poems by having no description or drawing of a situation or occasion appropriate for the message it has to deliver. It moves straight to the point of the message, its marrow, like a released arrow aimed at the bull's eye. It strikes us a sockdologer, for which we were not prepared. The title of the poem at first seems a whit queer and unexplicative of the substance of the poem, but our somewhat puzzlement may fizzle out once we try to understand that the benign request, 'Send No Money', of advertisers is but a shrewdly calculated fob, a dupe, an innocent-looking trick to gain the confidence of customers in their displayed honesty. Some sellers advertise their goods, but, as a ploy to purchase the confidence of customers, insistently ask them *not to send money in advance* for those goods, but instead receive, on request, free specimens of those goods, consume or test or verify them, and only then decide on buying those goods. In 'Send No Money', Larkin says that our ideals or the truths of life are like the images of free specimen goods seem to be genuine, unadulterated, but are in reality full of deceit and are illusory. Now, if we once understand this, the import of the title of the poem will appear clear and its appropriateness will be revealed. Roger Day writes about the title of the poem: "The title relates to the controlling metaphor of the poem, that 'the truth' turns out to be a 'truss-advertisement', and is the instruction usually attached to small advertisements which offer a 'free trial' before purchase" (Day, 60). This is a common experience of the commercial world, but Larkin has utilised it very fittingly and aptly in the field of literature.

Curious it is that all the three advertisement poems mentioned above were written in the same year, 1962, one after a gap of about two months after the other: 'Essential Beauty' on 26 January, 'Send No Money' on 21 August, and 'Sunny Prestatyn' in October. Why was Larkin so very attentive to advertisements during just this time? Perhaps we do not know the answer, but one thing which may have relevance to the poem deserves to be kept in mind. On August 1962 fell Larkin's 40th birthday and about that date his congenital moroseness might have led him to pensively mull over his past about half life: 'Half life is over now'—which is the beginning line of the third stanza of the poem. At that time, Larkin must have had enough realisation of the incongruity and variance between the paradisical ideal life of desire and imagination and the loveless crude and dishevelled life of the reality. We cannot avert our eyes from the hint of the ideal life but then we cannot embrace the crudity of this real life, and hence our unending sufference. Larkin says in the poem that the advertisements of the profit-and-loss commercial world are like the insinuation of the unachievable and deceptive ideal world that perpetually annoys us with its titillating and coruscating allurement. Another thing also may have been entwined with the origin or source of the poem. 1962 was also the year in which occurred Monica's 40th birthday. We have said that Larkin had had sexual relationship with Monica, when he definitely realised that sexual pleasure was a sort of cheating, deception or disillusion so far as it is immediately followed by the realisation that absolute or ideal enjoyment is impossible, and so far as it is immediately followed by depression and a sense of loss. This realisation of Larkin may have been a contributing factor in the generation of the poem. But more probably 'Send No Money' grew out of Larkin's looking back to his past life, on reaching the age of forty, when he wrote: "Looking back on my first forty years, I think what strikes me most is that hardly any of the things that are supposed to happen or be so do in fact happen or are so. What little happens or is so is't at all expected or agreeable" (Motion, 325). An echo of this comment of Larkin on his own bygone life is to be found in the last stanza of 'Send No Money': 'bent in / By the blows of what happened to happen.'

'Send No Money' is a poem of 24 three-stressed short lines that are divided into 3 stanzas, each stanza having 8 lines, rhyming a / b / c / d / e / f / e / f.

The poem begins with Larkin (or the speaker), the supposedly naïve boy or young man, asking a certain knowledgeable person to tell him what was really the truth or what was the actual reality (here Larkin is interested in knowing not what we suppose to be the truth but what is the absolute truth) ('*Tell me the truth*, I said'). Larkin asked the question while he was under the deceptive ('fobbed') and uncontrollable ('independent') power or governance ('belly') of Time ('belly' meaning 'interior' or 'inside') or under the deceptive and uncontrollable tow of the course of life ('Standing under the fobbed / Independent belly of Time'). Larkin also requested that knowledgeable (avuncularly or headmasterly) person to instruct or edify him about why and how everything is happening in the world, or about the course of life ('*Teach me the way things go*'). The other boys or young persons, who were at that moment around Larkin, were not interested in knowing the truth (or mystery) of life, but they were feeling recurrent urges ('itching') to have a confrontation or a pugnacious encounter with life, or 'to have a try' with life or to go on the spree with life, or to have sex ('bash'). But Larkin lacked in ('wanting') such a motive which, he thought or believed, was not agreeable, desirable or well-meaning ('unfair'). He, therefore, rather meditated ('thought') about the nature of the truth or mystery of life ('It') and saw or observed the incompatability or incongruence or jarring ('finding out clash') between the absolute metaphysical truth of life or the radical pattern of life ('*the way things go*'), on the one hand, and the quotidian truth or the relative truth of life or the way we actually live in this world.

The seemingly or affectedly knowledgeable person then affectionately and gently tapped ('patted') Larkin's head and in a forced baritone voice or commandingly loud voice ('booming') told Larkin that he (Larkin) had no sign of jealousy or envy in his eyes ('*There's no green in your eye*'). That person then asked Larkin to sit there and notice the catena or sequence of events or happenings of life (or of the world) that was occurring in time—i.e. the kaleidoscopically passing events of life in incessant series—('*the hail / Of occurrence*'). The person pointed it out to Larkin that this (glittering) catena, cascade, chute or rapid of events of the (illusory) life camouflage, overpaint or hide the (unsavoury) true nature or truth of the real life ('*clobber life out*'). He said that this concatenation of the events of life metamorphose or disfigure life itself beyond recognition ('*To a shape no one sees*'). And after imparting to Larkin so much of metaphysical instructions about life, that knowledgeable person asked Larkin if he did see through the point right away without fear, or courageously ('*Dare you look at that straight?*'). Larkin then thanked him (understandably for his wise instructions) ('*Oh thank you*') and submissively said that he (Larkin) did understand his teaching or edification ('*Oh yes please*'). Larkin then stayed there for a long period to see the concatenation of the (illusory) events or happenings of life that camouflaged the truth of life ('And sat down to wait').

In the third or last stanza, Larkin recalled that he had expended or passed half of his longevity (recall in 1962 he stepped into his 40th year of age). Now, in the depressing mornings ('dark mornings')—to him all mornings are now gloomy and despondent—when he looks straight up to his own countenance he perceives it not as his own face but as that of a beast ('I meet full face on dark mornings / The bestial visor'), i.e. his own being now appears to him as sub-human. He sees that his (formerly-kept-high-up) face is now pressed downwards (like the faces of beasts) ('bent in') by the buffets of the worldly events or happenings that occurred without any rhyme or reason, or arbitrarily, or stochastically ('By the blows of what happened to happen'). Larkin now raises a question: what do all these happenings that he has so far had lead us to conclude ('What does it prove')? And he himself answers: all these only prove that life is worth, or all these happenings of life collectively are worth, just a rectangular-shaped tuft of grass, or sword, (or, if we agree to an abusive or a pejorative meaning, all these happenings are an act of sodomy or depravity), i.e. all these are just meaningless incidents ('Sod all'). Larkin laments that he passed his youth thus observing with a searching eye ('Tracing') the worn, faded, hackneyed, uninspiring ('trite') truth of life—that it is quite meaningless—in these aleatory and stochastically occurring happenings of life. This truth or fundamental knowledge of life no one can impart to another because each one of us has to individually acquire it ('untransferable'). And this truth may be compared to a commercial advertisement that is mounted on a framed structure ('Truss-advertisement, truth'), because, like a commercial advertisement, the insidious truth of life outwardly holds up glittering promises of profit or enjoyment but inwardly contains a deep deception, a hideous illusion, a shattering trap.

Roger Day calls 'Send No Money' 'a parable or an apologue', because like the parable, or the apologue or beast fable—both of which entails a moral tag or edification—this poem imparts to us a moral teaching through a tale. Day writes: "The most appropriate way of describing the poem is, surely, to call it a parable, or an apologue? The moral of the tale [of the poem] turns as follows: the poet as a nanaïveoung man seeks to find 'the truth' by waiting for the course of events to reveal a pattern and, meanwhile, refrain from active interference in them, from having 'a bash' (i.e. at 'life' or even, perhaps, sex). Helped in this by lack of envy ('no green in your eye') he resolves simply to watch life even though Time is teaching him that there is no recognisable pattern. Eventually, his half life over, he recognises that life in a physical world ('the bestial visor', i.e. his own face) is altered by completely arbitrary events ('what happened to happen') which reveal its complete meaninglessness" (Day, 60-61).

In the poem, Larkin has employed Time as an animate, or rather, as a conscious and sensible being. The illusions of life are the designs and factures of Time: it is Time that deceivingly assures us that it will show us the truth of life, but even at the fag end of our lives we fail to see the truth of life—we ever remain illuded. Roger Day says that, according to Larkin, Time, like the commercial advertisements which give us only hollow promises, is all deceptive. Day writes about the nature of Time as in the poem: "The truth promised by Time is like a 'truss-advertisement' because it promises a support and comfort for an injury which in reality it cannot give. There is also the possible hint that Time itself, with an independent belly, is in need of a truss" (Day, 61).

David Timms has found in 'Send No Money' Thomas Hardy's pessimistic attitude of life. Hardy had a tendency to see the darker side of life; he had a 'bias in life towards unhappiness'—life's unhappiness was to him a sort of dulcamara. In this regard, Larkin was almost commensal with Hardy, for Larkin too saw the darker side of life sooner than its brighter side. Pessimism and suffering led Larkin to the shrines of the Muses or to sit on the wings of Pegasus, and this poem may be seen as an illustration of how. Timms writes: "In 'Send No Money' (in particular,) the suffering attendant upon learning truth through experience turns a naïve young man into a poet" (Timms, 110). Andrew Swarbrick also says that 'Send No Money' presents Larkin's congenital or native pessimism, but he adds that the poem further shows Larkin's bias towards fatalism and resignation—his tendency to passively accept whatever life provides him with, without grudging. This passive acceptance of fate's offerings is also present in 'A Study of Reading Habits'. Swarbrick writes: "...'Send No Money' presents the familiarly rueful, resigned Larkin" (Swarbrick, 1995, 102).

As we know, ventriloquism is a very common feature of Larkin's poetry, and this peculiar feature of his occupies a major portion of 'Send No Money': more than eight lines out of a total of 24 lines of the poem are ventriloquistic. In the poem, Larkin speaks in the registers of two persons: one of the naïve young man and the other of the knowledgeable older person. Andrew Swarbrick says that the poem also contains veins of pantomime caricature: "It ['Send No Money'] makes a caricature (Time as a 'fobbed / Independent belly', a loud avuncular or headmasterly figure, 'booming' worldly wisdom) out of deep feeling, pantomime out of philosophy: '*watch the hail / Of occurrence clobber life out / To a shape no one sees*'" (*op. cit.*, 103). Swarbrick says that the dramatic monologue of the poem has been used by Larkin to camouflage his identity and to be oblivious of his own self, like he did in 'Naturally the Foundation will Bear Your Expenses' and 'A Study of Reading Habit'. Swarbrick writes that these three poems "illustrate how by using dramatic monologue Larkin's poems might actually distort the portrait of his own identity and so escape, in [Andrew] Motion's phrase, 'knowledge of self'" (*loc. cit.*).

M.L. Rosenthal is critical of 'Send No Money' principally because its mood is not attached with any justifiable subject, though, of course, he praises its language extraordinarily, saying that the language simply 'admirable'. Rosenthal says that "the poem suffers from the obvious fact that its mood is anchored in no justifying referent. The poem is a voice without a body; there is no dive into the specifics of observation and experience that would give it a body, however fantastic or removed from ordinary life the images chosen" (Rosenthal, 235).

12

An Arundel Tomb

The inspiration of the poem Larkin got from a visit of his, along with Monica Jones, to the Cathedral at Chichester at the end of 1955. Though the poem is entitled 'An Arundel Tomb', the referred to is actually not at Arundel but at Chichester. David Timms writes: "The tomb in question ('incidentally') is not at Arundel: it is a tomb belonging to the Howard family, once Earl and Countess of Norfolk, in Chichester Cathedral. This tomb is differentiated from most monumental sculpture of a similar kind because the stone figures are holding hands, and this affects the poet" (Timms, 107-08). And Andrew Swarbrick writes about the statues and how they might have impacted Larkin: "Larkin visited the tomb of the Earl of Arundel and his wife in Chichester Cathedral, at the end of 1955.... The style of the carving is plain and unadorned and there seems little to interest us until we notice 'with a sharp tender shock' the earl's left-hand gauntlet held empty in his right hand, thus leaving his left hand free to hold his wife's hand" (Swarbrick, 1995, 113). Initially, the sculpture did not show joined hands; the joined hands were a subsequent elaboration. Andrew Motion writes: "Larkin subsequently discovered that the joined hands were a later addition—in fact the work of Edward Richardson (1812-68) who reworked the sculpture in the 1840s to repair damage it had suffered during the Reformation and the Civil War" (Motion, 274). In that Cathedral, the Earl of Arundel and his wife, the Countess, were buried, and there two pre-baroque statues were installed over their graves. Larkin went to the south coast on a short holiday-making, along with Monica, particularly to visit the Cathedral. He was greatly touched by the pose of the statue of the Earl holding the hand of the statue of the Countess. The statues were about 600 years old, and were in supine and not standing position. To Larkin, the statues of the Earl and his wife appeared as a symbol of the overwhelming endurance of human tenderness against the ravages of Time, for the statued couple succeeded in continuing to exist in their ceaseless mutual warm affection through six hundred years' vagaries and batterings of time. This most impressive symbol of the superlative power of human love momentarily took hold of Larkin and inspired him poetically, though in the poem, as Andrew Swarbrick says, Larkin concludes that 'our human capacity for love cannot triumph over time's destructive force' and we can at best nobly dream of, or aspire after, only our 'almost perpetual love'.

'An Arundel Tomb' is a dramatic monologue and is one of the very few poems in the Larkin canon in conjuring up a melancholic atmosphere in the most of the body of the poem, as is generally expected in any Larkin poem, but ending up 'almost' affirmatively. The fact that this poem concludes the collection, *The Whitsun Weddings* shows how much importance Larkin did attach to it, for, as we know, he did invariably place one of the best poems of a collection at the head of it and such another at its end. Not only this, the poem is also one of the best-known poems of Larkin. This 42-line poem is divided into seven stanzas, each stanza containing six four-stress lines, rhyming a / b / b / c / a / c. It was dated 20 February 1956 and it appeared for the first time in *The Whitsun Weddings*.

Larkin begins the first stanza of the poem saying that the faces of the stone effigies or statues of the Earl of Arundel and his wife, the Countess of Arundel, situated side by side, i.e., engraved on the same slab of stone close to each other, have become hazy for being smeared, blotted or blemished with and by the elements (continually for over 600 years: the statues belonged to the medieval age) ('Side by side, their faces blurred'). The Earl and the Countess are not alive now but are dead: their lying effigies were carved out in a stone slab or slate.

Their decorous, becoming or fit ('proper') effigies were engraved not in high relief but in bas-relief or low relief so that their accoutrements or dresses can be perceived only obscurely or ambiguously ('vaguely'). Their accoutrements comprise defensive or protective coverings or heraldic insignia that are closely fitted to their bodies ('jointed armour') and have hardened or metal foldings ('stiffened pleats'). The statues are bearing a slight ('faint') suggestion of something that is unbelievable, unrealistic, bizarre ('absurd'). (What that unbelievable thing is Larkin does not divulge; perhaps it is the over-weaning attitude of both the Earl and the Countess that defied the erasing, nullifying, destructive power or energy of Time that has always been bent upon blotting out their honoured memory.) There were also stone statues of some small dogs or doglings below the feet of their excellencies ('little dogs under their feet').

In the second stanza, Larkin says that the statues were engraved following the simple pre-baroque style of sculpting. (The baroque style prevailed during the reign of Louis XIV and distinguished itself by its extravagant ornamentation or embellishment. The pre-baroque style of art or engraving, therefore, refers to the art or engraving that shuns extravagant ornamentation or embellishment, i.e. it refers to the style of art or engraving that is simple in design and execution.) Larkin says that the statues were so simply done in the pre-baroque style that there is hardly anything in them that can draw the attention of anyone ('Hardly involves the eye'). There is of course one thing in the statues that draws the attention ('It') of a person, and so long as one does not see this ('until') there is nothing special in the statues. This special thing is that the gauntlet of the Earl's left hand was even then not filled with his palm and fingers ('empty') and was in the tight grip of his right hand ('Clasped empty in the other'). Further, one can see the Earl's left hand—that is not covered with gauntlet and is not engaged in any works, i.e. is retracted from all worldly or pragmatic busyness ('withdrawn')—is clasping the hand of the Countess ('His hand withdrawn, holding her hand'). And one cannot see this (romantic spectacle) without being highly touched by emotion or without being highly affected ('shock') by the cute or dainty ('sharp') and softly pleasing ('tender') love going between the Earl and the Countess, as suggested by the Earl's clasping the hand of the Countess ('One sees, with a sharp tender shock, / His hand, withdrawn, holding her hand').

The statues, Larkin says in the third stanza, are remaining in that posture for a long time, but the Earl and the Countess in their real lives, certainly could not or would not expect ('think') to remain in that state, posture or attitude for so long (in that romantic spectacle) ('They would not think to lie so long'). Such mutual honesty or marital moral probity ('faithfulness'), as apparent from the Earl's clasping the hand of the Countess, was engraved elaborately or in detail in the stone statues ('in effigy') only for those people who loved them ('Was just a detail friends would see'). The sculptor who had been ordered or authorised ('commissioned') to execute the statues had left in the elaboration of the carving or in the ornamentation or minute execution of the statues, i.e. in showing the Earl as clasping the hand of the Countess, his lovable magnanimity or benignity ('grace') ('A sculptor's sweet commissioned grace'). And that sculptor had left ('Thrown off') that attractive benignity of his onto the statues with a view to helping the names of the Earl and the Countess, carved out in Latin alphabets or characters on the pedestal or foundation of the statues, live longer ('in helping to prolong / The Latin names around the base').

In the fourth stanza, Larkin says that the Earl and the Countess ('They') perhaps did not or could not think or understand ('guess') that in a very short time ('how early') their statues, in that posture of lying on back ('supine') and motionlessly or inertly going along the perpetual onward course of Time ('stationary voyage'), would be disfigured ('change') and silently ruined ('soundless damage') by the elements, i.e. by the heat of the sun, rain and wind ('air'). And perhaps they could not believe that thus the traditional Feudal system of tenancy (in which the Earl and the Countess and their family prevailed and succeeded) would have been erased or thrown off ('Turn the old tenantry away'). They (the Earl and the Countess) could not think or imagine that the elements would very soon ('How soon') so much deface or obfuscate their names (engraved at the base of the statues) by battering on them that generation after generation ('succeeding eyes') would not be able to decipher ('not read') those names and would only curiously stare at them to try to decipher them ('to look').

The statues ('they': last line of the fourth stanza), of course, says Larkin in the fifth stanza, are very strenuously braving all the difficulties ('Rigidly': last line of the fourth stanza) to continue to exist ('Persisted') hand in hand ('linked') through the course of Time till now ('through lengths and breadths / Of time'). For a long time, on innumerable days ('undated'), snow fell upon the statues, and each summer invading sun-rays tried to destroy the almost glass-like (compared to the ruining power of the elements, the stone statues are as if glass) fragile stone statues ('Light / Each summer thronged the glass'). And also for a long time, a good number ('Litter') of bird-catcher's instruments for imitating birds' notes ('birdcalls') were laid here and there ('strewed') around the Arundel tomb which is surrounded by many graves, such that the place appears to be enveloped by some conundrum or puzzle ('Bone-ridded ground'). Innumerable visitors of succeeding generations, who continually changed or modified themselves as regards their thoughts and manners during those generations ('endless altered people'), have come to the Arundel Cathedral or Arundel tomb walking along those paths that lead up to the cathedral or the tomb ('up the paths / The endless altered people came').

In the sixth stanza, Larkin says that those innumerable visitors have come to the Arundel Cathedral or the Arundel tomb after erasing, obliterating, or wiping off ('Washing') their sense of being proud or their awareness of their own falsely-prided selves, i.e. after reducing themselves to the commonality, to the level of the common man (thinking of the ephemerality of human life) ('Washing at their identity'). Larkin says that the present age is not an age of wars or battles like the age of the Earl and the Countess in which age armours were required ('An unarmorial age'), and, in this sense, this present age is eventless or vacant ('hollow'). In this vacant age, the Earl and the Countess are wearing coats-of-arms quite meaninglessly and they are now existing with all their show of chivalry in desolation, solitariness ('helpless'). This is an industrial age, in which coils of slowly rising up smoke from factories always seen to be hanging in the air like shreds or strands of ropes ('skeins'). So much smoke is emitted from the factories or industries (in this age) that this age seems to be a vassel ('trough') of smoke. The time of the Earl and the Countess is now archaic; their time has now become like wastage of metal ('scrap of history'). And the strand-like coils of smoke from the factories of this age are, as if, hanging over the wastage-of-metal of the age of the Earl and the Countess ('a trough / Of smoke in slow suspended skeins / Above their scrap of history'). Nothing of that age of chivalry is now existing in the statues of the couple but only the physical expression of the thought and feeling, or the philosophy ('attitude') of that age ('Only an attitude remains').

The long passage of time has changed, metamorphosed ('transfigured') the statues of the couple to such an extent that they now do not appear to be the real Earl of Arundel and the Countess of Arundel ('Untruth'). The natural faithfulness between them that has been given expression in the engraving of the stone statues ('stone fidelity') the Earl and the Countess did not believe in or did not want to be expressed ('They hardly meant'). And yet this apparent mutual faithfulness has now ultimately ('final') become their real or actual coats-of-arms or 'heraldic bearings' or their public displays ('blazon') (and not their coats-of-arms that are carved in stone which are now on the verge of complete or near complete ruination). And this mutual faithfulness of theirs, as given expression to in the engraving of the statues, is now present for us to substantiate ('to prove') our nearly inborn, congenital or inherent ('almost instinct') and nearly accurate, authentic or legitimate ('almost true') belief that nothing of us will perpetually remain in this world after our deaths but only our love for each other ('What will survive of us is love').

Larkin is repeatedly—and very legitimately—censored for his nagging hang-over of melancholic strain in almost all his poems save in a very rare few, and 'An Arundel Tomb' belongs to that microscopic minority that hold up some hope of optimism. In the majority of his poems, death and exclusion predominate, or time daily dwindles our very existence, but 'An Arundel Tomb' distinctly stands out with the chalice of trust and expectancy. Love here is no chameleon; here it provides at least a semblance of assurance. The poem, as expected of Larkin, does not land us, when we finish it, in a dark quagmire of pathos or pessimism but shows us a dawn of bird-songs, hazy though it is. True, but for its concluding line the whole poem of forty-two lines is suffused with melancholy, but the last line is enough reassuring so as to whiff away the screen of gloom, so that we can almost believe that 'What will survive of us is love'.

To David Timms, the poem is Larkin's "greatest success" (Timms, 107). Timms compares the poem with Andrew Marvell's 'To His Coy Mistress', but, in fact, there are more difference between 'An Arundel Tomb' and 'To His Coy Mistress' than similitude. For one thing, the former is about two statues of lovers while the latter is about two live lovers. Secondly. Marvell is more carnal in this poem than Larkin in his. But, most importantly, the difference lies in Marvell's being more cynically resigned to fatality than Larkin. Marvell despairs:

> Thy beauty shall no more be found,
> Nor, in thy marble vault, shall sound
> My echoing song; then worms shall try
> That long-preserved virginity,
> And your quaint honour turn to dust,
> And into ashes all my lust:
> The grave's a fine and private place,
> But none, I think, do there embrace.

Bur Larkin is cautiously and critically comforted:

> Our almost-instinct almost true:
> What will survive of us is love.

And, therefore, we cannot agree with Timms when he says that "'An Arundel Tomb' might be an ironic rejoinder to Marvell's *carpe diem*, 'To His Coy Mistress'" (*op. cit.*, 108). For Timms himself writes: "Though Marvell says, 'The grave's a fine and private place, / Though none, I think, do there embrace', Larkin's Earl and Countess *do* embrace in the tomb, or so the sculpture would have us believe" (*loc. cit.*).

Andrew Swarbrick also understands this poem as "One of Larkin's best-known poems" (Swarbrick, 1986, 69). According to him, the poem develops two of Larkin's 'abiding themes': "how our individual lives seem rendered virtually redundant by the passage of time and how our human capacity for love cannot triumph over time's destructive force" (*loc. cit.*). Thematically, the poem poses to be quite pessimistic, but Swarbrick agrees with us, over against David Timms, in believing that it has a streak of brightness around its rim. He writes about the terminal message of the poem: "The conclusion, though unsentimental, is yet far from bleak. In the context of the poem's development, it is consolatory and compassionate. The final line stands as an assertion to which the poet cannot give complete assent. But it represents an ideal which, even if we fall short of it, ennobles us. In a structure of reality that refuses to accommodate our dreams and desires, that is flawed, painful and disillusioning, 'almost' may be the best for which we can hope" (*op. cit.*, 71). Swarbrick wrote this in 1986 in *The Whitsun Weddings and The Less Deceived by Philip Larkin* but in his 1995 work, *Out of Reach: the Poetry of Philip Larkin*, he changed his position a whit saying: "Supporting the prominence given to the volume's title poem, 'An Arundel Tomb' wants to end the collection on a note of positive optimism by celebrating the triumph of love over time. In fact, the poem cannot offer such comfort, and it is that thwarted desire which gives the poem its own 'sharp tender shock'" (Swarbrick, 1995, 113). All the same, we cannot deny that in the last line of the poem there is at least a hint of optimism, uncertain though it is: that love will survive us may not be 'true' but, of course, must be 'almost true'. What then will be our final conclusion about the predominant mood of the poem? Andrew Motion has a solution. He writes: "At the end of the manuscript draft of 'An Arundel Tomb' Larkin wrote, 'Love isn't stronger than death just because statues hold hands for 600 years.' It's a remark which reinforced, privately, the sense of futility that hovers around the poem's conclusion in words like 'helpless', 'scrap', 'attitude', 'Untruth' and 'almost' (and it typifies his habit of writing cynical graffiti on his own most monumental lines). *Publicly, the rhetoric of the final line takes charge and establishes it as a separate truth: an Augustan wisdom arising from a part-medieval, part nineteenth-century monument*" (emphasis added) (Motion, 274).

Pessimistic or no, our next question about the poem is: is it romantic or does it show any romantic vision? To answer this question, we should first recall that the collection *The Whitsun Weddings* begins with 'The Whitsun Weddings' that was built on a romantic experience of Larkin—his accompanying several marriage parties. When asked if there was at the end of 'The Whitsun Weddings' 'hopefulness' and 'a romantic visionary quality', Larkin boldly said, 'Yes' (Haffenden, 124-25). And so we can only expect that characteristically Larkin ended the collection with a consonantal poem—with 'An Arundel Tomb'. Further, about 'An Arundel Tomb' Larkin directly said: "Well, that is rather a romantic poem; there's even less reservation in that" (*op. cit.*, 125).

Andrew Swarbrick highly appreciates Larkin's language in the poem. He writes: "The poem reveals the masterliness of Larkin's poetic gifts in his ability to control language so as to say things in a way that seems inevitable, moving, true" (Swarbrick, 1986, 69). The language of the poem is appropriate, precise, plain and unadorned, colloquial and conversational, familiar, and superbly and highly economic, as in the other best poems of Larkin. But, curious it is that in spite of the poem's many virtuosities, poetic and technical, Larkin himself was not impressed much by it. To his interviewer John Haffenden, Larkin once confessed: "I don't like it much, partly because of this; technically it's a bit muddy in the middle—the fourth and fifth stanzas seem trudging, somehow, with awful rhymes like voyage / damage. Everything went wrong with that poem: I got the hands wrong—it's right-hand gauntlet really—and anyway the hands were a nineteenth-century addition, not pre-Baroque at all. A friend of mine who visited the tomb in Chichester Cathedral told me that the guide said, 'A poem was written about this tomb by Philip Spender.' Muddle to the end" (Haffenden, 125). Artists sometimes cannot well appreciate their own works!